Canary
HEALTH

by **Dr. Rob Marshall**

Copyright© 2005 by Dr. Rob Marshall, B.V.Sc., M.A.C.V.Sc. (Bird Health)

Published and Distributed by:
ebirds inc.
5405 Alton Parkway, Suite 357
Irvine, CA 92604
United States of America

Joanne McGinnis
Publisher/Owner
www.ebirdsinc.com
Joanne@ladygouldianfinch.com
800.579.7974 Fax: 949.733.2403

**Author: Dr. Rob Marshall,
B.V.Sc., M.A.C.V.Sc. (Bird Health)**
Carlingford Animal Hospital
772 Pennant Hills Road
Carlingford NSW 2118
Australia

www.birdhealth.com.au
robmarshall@birdhealth.com.au
Phone: Sydney Australia 9871 7113
Fax: Sidney Australia9873 2156

ISBN Number 0-9768919-052995

Designed by: Susan Johnson
Edited by: Casey Rowe and Gene Jacobson
Cover Photography: Laraine McGinnis

Printed in the United States of America

Disclaimer

Very few medicines are registered for canary use. Their use and dosage has usually been extrapolated from poultry or mammalian models. The onus of the responsibility therefore lies with the canary enthusiast to follow the instructions given by the prescribing veterinarian and to cease treatment immediately if untoward side effects occur. The dose rates and available information for the various medicines for canaries are based on scientific references, practical experience and therapeutic trials. However, all medicines have potential side effects and many of these side effects have not been recorded. The author and publisher takes no responsibility for the safety of the medicines mentioned in this book.

This book does not promote the sale of prescription medicines without a consultation with a veterinarian.

Wise legislation restricts the sale of prescription medicines by veterinarians to their bone fide clients. Dr. Marshall must be consulted before prescription medicines can be made available. In Australia, this book is only available to existing and prospective clients of Dr. Marshall. Here and abroad, it is in no way intended to advertise prescription medicines or to promote their use without veterinary consultation.

Acknowledgements

This book explores novel health programmes designed to improve the breeding performance of canaries and in so doing should help to make this challenging hobby more enjoyable. Dr. Marshall acknowledges with gratitude the help he received from the eminent canary breeders, Mr. Sam Cavallero, Mr. Mal Coulston, Mr. Roy Dowling, Mr. Michael Fogarty, Mr. Maurice Hunt, Mr. Bob Moore, Mr. Stan Nichol, Mr. Paul Sant and Mr. Don Swavely.

Table of Contents

Chapter 7
First Aid and Choosing a Medicine

Chapter 8
Canary Diseases, Medicines & Problem Solving

Chapter 9
Troubleshooting

Chapter 10
Health Products

Appendix

Index

introduction
Introduction

Breeding canaries for competitive exhibition has always been an extremely difficult challenge for seasoned fanciers, let alone newcomers to the hobby.

Some varieties are more difficult to breed than others. Yorkshires and Norwich Canaries are considered difficult varieties to breed in numbers. I have noticed a sensitivity of Yorkshires to many diseases that have little effect on other varieties. The Border Fancy, although a most popular canary in Australia and throughout the world, has also experienced poor breeding outcomes associated with infertility.

The smaller types and varieties of canaries appear to breed more readily and are good parents. The Gloster Fancy is a beautiful crested miniature breed that comes in two distinct types — the Corona and the Consort. Glosters breed very well and now rival the Border in popularity. The Lizard Canary is bred for the pattern of its plumage and is regarded, evolutionarily, as the oldest canary in the world. It is a relatively easy bird to breed.

The desire to select birds that are good show specimens instead of for their ability to reproduce effectively appears to have initiated the poor breeding results experienced by some varieties. Some varieties of canaries have a limited gene pool, and that, coupled with inbreeding, the preferred breeding system, further deteriorates breeding ability. The notion that inbreeding is an important cause of impaired breeding ability gains further support when it is noted that mongrel varieties are remarkably easy to breed in large numbers.

The physical size of a variety appears also to have an impact on the ability of canaries to breed. Smaller varieties such as Glosters readily breed, are good parents and produce high numbers of offspring with few problems.

Inherent weakness against some diseases is also recognized as the cause of infertility and poor breeding outcomes in some canary varieties. Border Fancy and Yorkshire canaries are especially susceptible to infections with Ornithosis (now known as Chlamydophila infection). Circovirus (Black spot Disease), Megabacteria (AGY infection), Trichomonas and Mycoplasma infections may also result in poor breeding outcomes for some canary families. Colour canaries are especially prone to Trichomoniasis, whereas some Border Fancy lines are easily infected with Megabacteria and Mycoplasma infection at an early age.

There appears to be a strong negative correlation between the best show-quality birds, inbreeding, disease and breeding ability. It is the diminishing ability of the best quality exhibition birds to breed that creates the difficulties experienced by canary breeders because this heritable characteristic is passed onto future generations. Exhibition budgerigar and show pigeon fanciers also share these breeding problems. The breeding performance of exhibition budgerigars and pigeons has been improved over the past years as breeders have embraced the principles encouraged by my health programmes. The use of these programmes promotes a "stronger" breeding bird. The best breeding results have appeared from the second generation of birds bred under these Programmes.

First and foremost, fanciers must rely upon the "laws of nature" in order to improve breeding performance and produce more canaries to "show standard." An understanding of the concept of "breeding condition" as well as knowledge concerning the nutritional needs of the more delicate "top quality" birds must be developed before improved breeding results can be enjoyed. This book addresses these important issues and provides the canary fancier with new knowledge and practical solutions to help improve breeding outcomes.

Canary breeders should anticipate improved breeding results, especially from second generation progeny when they adopt or incorporate the programmes outlined in this book into their own systems. These programmes incorporate the latest knowledge of canary biology, nutrition and disease into tried and true systems used by successful fanciers, past and present. The systems used to breed canaries have been passed down from generation to generation and have remained basically unchanged for the past 50 years. These tried and true methods must be retained but improvements in breeding outcomes are made more possible when they are incorporated with new knowledge about nutrition and disease.

The fragile and delicate nature of some canary varieties necessitates a planned approach to the breeding season. Difficult to breed varieties, such as Yorkshires, will be the first to show breeding problems, mainly infertility, during the first round of breeding. This is especially so when climatic and environmental conditions become adverse for breeding. This book attempts to provide canary breeders with a successful and practical plan.

Background Information

There are many different varieties of canaries, some of which have been developed over hundreds of years. Varieties have been bred for body shape (type), colour, feather pattern or song.

Songbird Canaries

In Australia there are two songbird canaries. The Common Canary uses its natural singing ability and the Roller Canary is selectively bred for its singing ability. Overseas, the Harzer, Mechelse and Timbrado are bred solely for their ability to sing. Special training techniques are required to teach songbird canaries known song patterns.

Type Canaries

Type canaries are bred for their body shape, stance and appearance. Exhibitors must carefully select pairs and breed to the official standard of each variety. The reason many canary enthusiasts take to the hobby so passionately is because of the difficulty and skill required in breeding a canary to the fixed standard. It is a rare event for a bird to be judged as near perfect. There are many varieties of type canaries around the world.

Type Canary varieties include:

- With Frills
- Parisian Frill, Frisé du Nord, Frisé du Sud, Frisé Suisse, Gibber Italicus, Giboso Espagnol, Padovano, Fiorino.

Purely for Type

Belgian Bult, Scotch Fancy, Munchener, Japan Hoso, Lancashire, Yorkshire, Berner, Reinländer.

For Shape

Border, Fife Fancy, Norwich, Raza Espagnol, Irish Fancy.

With Crests

Gloster Consort, Gloster Corona, German Crest.

Colour Canaries

Colour canaries originated as colour mutations during the sixteenth century. After World War II

Parisian Frill

Yorkshire

Fife Fancy

Gloster Corona

Red Factor
Apricot Cock

The above photos are examples of Canary Varieties. Frills (Parisian Frill), purely for type (Yorkshire), for shape (Fife Fancy), crests (Gloster corona) and colour (Apricot red factor cock).

the Siskin was crossed with canaries to create red coloured feathers and plumage markings with regular patterns. Pet shops adopted the term Red Factor to these Red Canaries although there is no red factor that will produce a red canary. The yellow colour of the feathers in Yellow Canaries comes from a genetic ability to convert a yellow pigment called xanthophyll in egg yolk and yellow, orange and green coloured vegetables and fruits into a yellow pigment that is deposited inside the cells of growing feathers. The yellow colour is conversely pale when eggs and greens are not provided to yellow canaries during their moult. Yellow Canaries have a limited ability to convert red coloured carotenes whereas Red Canaries have the reverse ability. They are able to convert carotenes but not xanthophylls into their feathers. Special substances containing red coloured carotenes (canthaxanthin) must be added to the food or water during the moult in order to produce the red colour found in Red Factors. The intensity of the red feather colour can be enhanced by selectively breeding those birds with a genetic ability to accept more carotene and less xanthophyll into their feather cells during the moult. There are many different colour possibilities that are combined with patterned canary varieties.

Nowadays there exist many colour and patterned canaries that have been divided into the melanin (black, brown, agate, isabel), lipchrome (red, rose, yellow (gold and gold ivory) and white (silver and silver ivory) groups. The coloured birds are further divided into colour-fed birds (using xanthoids) and naturally coloured birds.

Feather Types

Canaries have two types of feather known as Buff Feather and Yellow Feather.

Buff feathers are the naturally occurring feather-type of the original canary. They are coarser and broader than Yellow Feathers.

Yellow Feathers retain colour to the very edge of the feather, are silky, lie flat against the body and produce a "tight" feather cover. Yellow feathers are an evolutionary mutation.

In exhibition canaries buff feathers are used to give substance to the plumage and to maintain the size and shape of the breed. Buff-feathered birds are usually paired to yellow-feathered birds to produce the desired show quality plumage. It is therefore necessary for breeders to understand the difference in structure and appearance of Buff versus Yellow feathers. A description of these two feather types is expertly described in the Australian Canary Handbook written by Mr. J. Leaney and Mr. F. Williams (1993).

Buff feathered bird.

chapter 1
Canary **Health** & **Happiness**

It takes some time to understand the needs of canaries.

Some mistakes may be made when caring for hybrid canaries without ill-effect because they are hardy and adaptable creatures. The consequences of some mistakes in the care of these mongrel canaries often go unnoticed.

There is however little room for error when keeping and breeding canaries bred for exhibition. Knowledge of what makes canaries happy should help improve breeding outcomes in these more fragile varieties.

Contented canaries become the best breeders and the aim of all fanciers must be to achieve conditions that make their birds happy. This chapter explores the best ways to keep canaries happy and healthy.

Essentials of Happiness

- Clean Food
- Clean Water
- Good Nutrition
- Fitness
- Sunlight, Warmth & Dryness
- Regular Baths
- Avoid Overcrowding

Clean Food

Clean seed is vitally important for the continuing health of canaries. They are primarily seed-eating birds and consume 30% of their body weight in food daily (compared with 10% for the larger parrots). Their basal metabolic rate is approximately 65% higher than that of non-passerines. Contaminated food, therefore, has a more marked and rapid effect on the health of canaries compared to many other birds.

Fresh, clean food is the starting point for a healthy and successful breeding season. The protection of the food from contamination during storage is equally important.

Seed, seeding grasses and sprouted food fed to canaries must be perfectly clean and fresh. Some fanciers store freshly harvested seeding grasses in the freezer to guarantee a continual supply throughout the breeding season.

Seeding grasses must be free of insecticides and perfectly clean.

Plain canary seed is the favoured food of canaries. Canaries prefer a seed mix that includes a high proportion of plain canary seed. Maw is also a favourite of canaries. Canaries are not as fond of millets as are other birds. The oil seeds (niger, linseed, rape, maw) should be fed in moderation to help avoid obesity and bowel irritation. The seed combination that is chosen should aim to provide a good nutritional balance and at the same time reduce the opportunity for excessive weight gain (obesity). A typical seed combination includes at least 50% plain canary, 30% millets, up to 12% rape and about 2% each of lettuce, niger, maw and hulled oats.

Canaries prefer the taste of tonic seeds above all else. Tonic seeds are specialized seeds that are softer in texture and easier to break open than the hard seeds (eg plain canary, millets). Lettuce, niger, maw and hulled oats are examples of tonic seeds. Young birds accept tonic seeds readily and this provides the perfect base to add E-Powder and F-Vite. Tonic seeds should not be fed continuously because of their high energy and oil content and tendency to result in overweight canaries.

Traditionally, canary breeders have preferred canary grass seed (Phalaris canariensis), commonly known as plain canary seed, over millet (Setaria italica) because of its relatively high protein content (16.6%). Most of the top breeders recommend levels from 45% to 75% of this seed mix. Canary seed contributes high levels of Glutamate to the amino acid profile but is very low in the more important breeding amino acids, methionine and lysine. Canary seed is used more for its high energy content than as a contributor of quality protein.

Millet seeding heads create interest for canaries as they spend time pulling the seeds from the sprays. Increasing the millet content of the seed mix helps to prevent obesity because the birds do not over eat millet. Millet is, however, a very important seed for breeding because of its high levels of methionine.

The amino acids, lysine and methionine, are the most important parts of the protein equation during the breeding season. Canary seed is low in both of these amino acids. Millet has very high levels of methionine but is lacking in lysine.

Lysine is essential to breeding success because deficiencies limit the availability of useable protein for breeding birds.

Rape and groats must be included in the seed mix of canaries as they offer the richest source of lysine. Groats is a most important grain for the breeding canary. It provides a potent source of energy for feeding parents and is also very high in the amino acid, lysine. A level of 5% in the seed mix is recommended because when provided in higher ratios its high fibre content may cause large soft droppings and a predisposition to "sweating disease." Rape is an energy and lysine rich seed.

Sunflower seeds are particularly useful during breeding. Soaking and sprouting makes it possible for canaries to eat this nutritious oil and protein (Methionine & Lysine) rich seed. Sunflower is, however, susceptible to contamination with mould and bacteria during the soaking process.

Soft wheat is recommended for breeding canaries. Wheat provides the most balanced ratios of amino acids, especially lysine for breeding birds. It is soaked for energy and is a tasty source of lysine.

Some fanciers separate the seeds into individual feed containers in the aviary or flight in order to avoid waste as canaries like to flick through the seed to find their favourite seed type. The seeds are placed into dishes of a size that corresponds to the ratio of seed type being fed. This allows the fancier to monitor and ensure the birds are eating a balanced ration.

Mr Sant's tonic seed mix, containing niger, rape, plain canary and hulled oats.

The beaks of young canaries up to five weeks old are not strong enough to crack any hard seed. They must instead receive broken hard seed from their parents or receive soft food or sprouted seed. Tonic seed mixes usually contain a variety of small seeds that young canaries relish, including niger, rape and maw (poppy). These are fed in order to attract and help wean young canaries.

Many different seed combinations may be used. The following is an example of a proven Australian Canary seed mix.

50%	Plain canary
30%	Millet seeds (French white, Panicum, Red and Japanese varieties)
5%	Hulled oats
5%	Wheat
3%	Rape
2%	Linseed/Niger

Belgium fanciers prefer to feed a richer mix:

62%	Plain canary
22%	Rape
8%	Hulled oats
3%	Linseed
2%	Niger

This mixture has a high oil content that may help breeding canaries but may lead to obesity for birds housed in an aviary or flight.

Spoiled seed is a common cause of poor breeding performance and recurrent illness in canaries. Infertility and nestling deaths between 3-10 days of age are typical signs of a possible food cleanliness problem. Unclean or "bad" food should also be suspected when there is unexplained or recurrent illness.

Clean seed is needed in order to enjoy a successful breeding season. Leaney and Williams (1993) describes a useful method for checking the cleanliness of seed in "The Australian Canary Handbook." They write "To check the quality of plain canary seed, place your hand in the seed. It should sink in easily and come up free of dust and clean. If the seed is crushed on a clean sheet of paper, its oil content should be evident. Old seed loses its oil content and goes to powder when crushed. Fresh seeds sprout within three

Culture testing is a reliable method for testing seed cleanliness. The seed above is contaminated with a harmful mould. Canaries fail to thrive and experience poor breeding outcomes when fed contaminated seed.

days." Culture testing performed by a veterinarian is a reliable method for checking the quality of seed.

Canary fanciers may also sprout their own seed in order to test for cleanliness. Healthy seed gives a 90% sprout rate and has a sweet, fresh smell after 72 hours. Contaminated seed emits a foul odour (a sign of bacterial contamination) and may develop mould growth between 72 and 96 hours.

Soaked or spouted seed is commonly used to feed canaries during and outside the breeding season. The use of mould contaminated seed for sprouting is a most common cause of disease in canaries.

Mr Sant's example of sprouted seed contains a mix of sunflower, hulled oats and rape.

Seed contaminated with mould has a lower nutritional value compared to perfectly clean feed. It is also capable of producing poisonous toxins that kill nestlings between 1-10 days of age. Many of these toxins also harm the immune system, causing disease in weaker individuals and varieties.

Mould will not grow on "dry" grain and it is important to select food that is low in moisture content. As a guide, grains with a moisture content between 10% and 12% at the time of harvest are unlikely to be contaminated with mould.

Some varieties of canaries are quite resistant to mould-affected food while others are sensitive to it. Many breeding failures experienced by Yorkshire breeders may be directly attributed to contaminated feed.

Canaries housed indoors are more susceptible to the effects of contaminated feed because they are often without the benefits of direct sunlight and fresh air. Direct sunlight, fresh air and free flight appear to instill "happiness" in canaries that cannot be duplicated by artificial lighting, air conditioning or small cages. Delicate varieties housed indoors are particularly difficult to keep healthy because of their weak constitution and fragility. It is not surprising, therefore, that they are the first to be affected by mould contaminated food while strong healthy varieties in the same aviary often remain healthy.

Symptoms of "going light" or "wasting disease" combined with breathing difficulties or tail bob are signs suggestive of mould affected food. Bacterial and yeast contaminated food may also produce poor breeding outcomes and illness in canaries.

Clean Water

Canaries are free of naturally occurring bowel bacteria and are more susceptible to environmental germs than, for example, parrot or poultry species. The drinking water of canaries must, therefore, remain perfectly clean.

Canaries, belonging to the finch family of birds, have no caeca and therefore do not require intestinal bacteria (flora) for microbial digestion. Instead, the high-energy food intake required by these small birds is digested by an increased activity of the enzymes lipase and amylase.

Other bird species rely on the "friendly" bacteria that inhabit their bowel to repel potentially harmful environmental bacteria that may be ingested in the process of their daily foraging activities. Canaries and finches do not share this physiological adaptation and must rely upon perfect cleanliness to remain healthy. Refer to page 163 for a detailed explanation of my Sterile Bowel Theory.

The best water containers are made from glass and are placed on the outside of the cage. The water may then be accessed through a feeder tube or through two small holes in the wire through which the canary can put its head. The latter system is the best system as the water is not able to drip into the cage and cause moisture within the cage that predisposes the birds to bacterial and fungal illnesses. This type of container also allows the fancier to easily monitor the condition and availability of water and help maintain a very high water quality. The fancier must be diligent and ensure the water containers, caps and the water itself, are kept clean and free of harmful germs that affect the health of canaries. The containers are easily removed for cleaning and disinfection. Many fanciers use a rotation system of cleaning the water containers where KD is used overnight to soak the caps and containers once a week.

This type of water container is placed on the outside of the cage and is easily removed for cleaning and disinfection.

Dirty water is a common cause of illness in canaries. Good water hygiene and the regular addition of water cleansers (Megamix, KD) to the drinking water help achieve protection from these potentially harmful bacteria.

Water cleansers stimulate health in a purely natural way. Water cleansers are recommended for canaries of all ages, but are most beneficial in protecting and nurturing the health of juveniles. Water cleansers protect the natural immunity of the strongest birds and strengthen the natural resistance of weaker ones by keeping the germs in the water as low as possible.

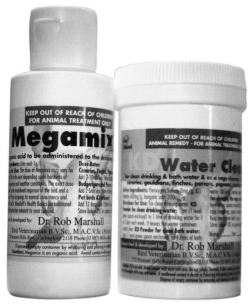

KD and Megamix are two water cleansers with slightly different actions. When added to the drinking water they help to keep canary flocks healthy and strong. See page 92 for details of these water cleansers.

Good Nutrition

These nutrient groups must be balanced:

- Protein
- Vitamins
- Minerals and Trace Elements
- Fats

Protein

Most realise the importance of protein in the diet. It is the correct balance of protein rather than the total protein that is most important for the breeding canary. The protein balance refers to the essential amino acids in the seed mix.

For fast growth rates and good breeding results it is necessary to provide essential amino acids in the correct balance. To achieve this goal it is necessary to calculate the amino acid content of each seed type and to design a mix that exactly balances the amino acid requirements.

Lysine and methionine are the most difficult amino acids to balance. These are known as the "breeding" amino acids because of their importance for breeding success. Groats, wheat and rape are the most important natural sources of lysine. Sunflower and safflower are rich sources of lysine and methionine. Turbobooster also incorporates high levels of lysine and methionine.

Sources of Breeding Proteins (Lysine and Methionine)

Quality Protein Sources

Hulled oats, rape, wheat and sunflower are the best seed sources for sprouting when looking to improve protein quality. Eggs and Turbobooster are also excellent sources of quality protein.

Lysine-Rich Sources

Groats, wheat, rape and Turbobooster.

Mr Sant's soaked seed mix contains the ideal combination of grains (groats, wheat, rape and sunflower). The addition of Turbobooster makes this an ideal protein source for breeding canaries.

Methionine-Rich Sources

Sunflower and Turbobooster.

There are continuing advantages for the flock provided with a well-designed protein balanced seed mix. The youngsters reared on a multi-grained seed mix thrive in the aviary because they already accept the taste of many seed types. This ensures that their protein needs are met during the high protein demands of the moult and other stress periods, such as breeding.

Turbobooster is a rich source of the breeding proteins, lysine and methionine.

Vitamins

The vitamin concentrations in seeds are highly variable, with vitamin A (corn provides carotenoids), vitamin D, vitamin E and vitamin K levels being extremely low. Among the B vitamins, riboflavin, niacin, and pantothenic acid are often low and vitamin B12 is not present at all.

Dufoplus is an ideal vitamin choice for canaries as it is potent and sugar free.

Vitamins must therefore be added to the diet of canaries. Dufoplus and Turbobooster are rich sources of vitamins A, D and E. Old timers understood this vitamin need from seeing the benefits of giving endives and carrots to their birds and most fanciers continue this practice although the availability of fresh produce is declining. Nowadays it is a more common practice to add vitamins to the soft food mix or water.

As with minerals and trace elements, there is an increased need for vitamins during the breeding season. Breeding birds tire easily and become more susceptible to illnesses when vitamins and minerals are not provided.

Canaries produce their own vitamin C and Inositol, but all of the other vitamins must be given to them via the feed or water. Most vitamins occur naturally in foodstuffs, but it is difficult to give canaries the correct amount and balance during the breeding season. Most of the vitamins play an integral part in the development of fitness and health. The omission or malabsorption of one vitamin can alter the metabolism and result in a deficiency disease.

The signs of a vitamin deficiency in the canary are subtle. Often vitamin deficiency is related to a bowel infection and can be confused with an illness. An important part of the recovery process after illness is the addition of vitamins.

Vitamin A

Vitamin A is a particularly important vitamin for canaries. It is responsible for the yellow colour of feathers of non-coloured varieties. The signs of a deficiency are subtle, but look carefully at the feather colour intensity and body condition. The feathers become pale, rough and lack lustre with a vitamin A deficiency. It promotes appetite and digestion. It also increases resistance to infection as well as to some parasites. Green vegetables and Dufoplus are rich sources of vitamin A.

Vitamin D3

Vitamin D3 is produced by natural sunlight. Vitamin D3 has an intimate relationship with the metabolism of calcium. Calcium is vital to fitness and vitality through its role in muscle and bone health. Vitamin D3 is incredibly important for egg laying, strong babies and vitality in the young

Mr. Dowling grows and provides his own greens as a rich source of vitamin A.

Vitamin B
The B vitamins are energy vitamins and are used to combat stress. E-Powder is a very rich source of B vitamins.

B vitamins are all involved in the metabolism of energy and as cofactors in enzymatic reactions. They are extremely beneficial when the energy expenditure increase nine fold during the heavy feeding of the chicks. These vitamins "oil" the energy pathways, aid in the continuing vitality of the feeding parents and maximise the growth of the chicks.

Thiamin (vitamin B12) is an extremely important vitamin. Although seeds are a rich source of thiamin, it is destroyed in canaries with enteritis. Thiamin supplements are given to accelerate the recovery of canaries during an enteritis outbreak.

birds and breeding flock but an excess of vitamin D causes kidney damage and retards growth. Vitamin D is naturally formed by the action of direct sunlight and breeding birds do better when the aviary is flooded with natural light. Egg binding and soft shelled eggs are rarely encountered in sunlit aviaries.

Artificial light must produce ultraviolet B emissions between 290 and 310 nm to produce vitamin D3. In many cases, vitamin D3 deficiency is indistinguishable from calcium deficiency. Bent keel bones, splayed legs and slipped toes are signs of a vitamin D3 deficiency. It is almost impossible to reverse these abnormalities. Over supplementation of vitamin D can cause breeding failures associated with dead in shell.

Vitamin E
Vitamin E promotes natural health and vitality. Turbobooster is a rich source of vitamins D and E. Vitamin E functions as a biological anti-oxidant that protects cell membranes against damage from free radicals. This function may be important during the stress of overcrowding and during breeding when the formation of free radicals is increased. Vitamin E also has a positive effect on immune function and any improvement in immune functioning must potentially benefit the breeding canary and stressed young bird in an overcrowded aviary. Vitamin E deficiency may occur when rancid oils are fed excessively to the breeding pairs. All oil preparations must be refrigerated and tightly sealed.

Signs of deficiency in canaries include twisting of the neck, stiff legs and leg weakness.

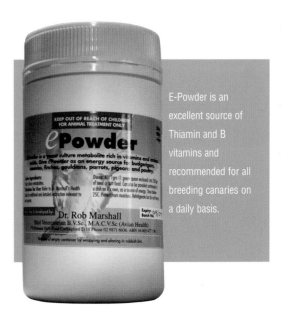

E-Powder is an excellent source of Thiamin and B vitamins and recommended for all breeding canaries on a daily basis.

Minerals and Trace Elements

Minerals and trace elements are the most neglected part of good nutrition for canaries. Calcium, phosphorous, iodine, iron, zinc, sodium and chloride are the most important minerals that must be provided to canaries if they are to enjoy continuing good health.

Fanciers have failed to pay attention to the role and necessity of minerals and trace elements for breeding and show performance, believing that grit provides their flock with all the minerals and trace elements required for good health. This is not so.

Regular grits contain calcium but are deficient in iodine, iron and most other trace elements. Shell grit provides the canary with a source of digestive stones and contains calcium, but is a poor source of mineral salts and trace elements. Cuttlefish Bone is a source of calcium, but lacks other minerals.

Mineral supplementation is necessary for canaries because seeds, shell grit and cuttle fish are poor sources of sufficient minerals. Seed is very low in calcium (0.01- 0.20%) and sodium (20-600ppm), and contains only marginal levels of phosphorous, copper, zinc, manganese and selenium. Shell grit is not the best form of calcium supplementation for egg laying birds. Egg laying hens need more than twice the calcium of the non-laying bird.

A concentrated mineral supplement (e.g., F-Vite) is the best and safest method of providing calcium, which is largely unavailable in shell grit. Far too much shell grit has to be eaten to satisfy the calcium needs of breeding hens that may then as a result, fall ill and die from gizzard obstruction after engorging on the shell grit.

A wide variety of calcium supplements are available, each with varying calcium/phosphorous ratios and vitamin D3 content. Calcium carbonate (blocks, cuttlebones, oyster shell and eggshell) is very high in calcium but contains no phosphorous and is poorly absorbed into the body. Diseases associated with calcium deficiency are potentially very serious.

An abnormally high incidence of egg binding, cloacal prolapse, leg paralysis in breeding hens, deformities in babies or poor eggshell quality suggest a low level of calcium in the diet or a poor absorption of calcium into the bird. Vitamin D3 is needed for the calcium to be properly absorbed.

Direct sunlight is the natural source of vitamin D. The breeding canary is particularly susceptible to Vitamin D3 deficiency and related egg binding problems when they are housed indoors. Vitamin D3 is needed for the bird to absorb calcium from the intestine and if not having direct access to sunlight, must be added to the diet of all breeding birds kept indoors.

Shell grit, cuttlebone and mineral supplements must remain dry. Wet grit creates a major health hazard because the moisture in the grit promotes harmful bacterial growth and contamination.

E.coli and other related bacteria are commonly found in wet grits. These infections originate from the dead and decaying molluscs that inhabit the grit shells. Some of the bacteria produced by these decaying marine animals are toxic. Wet and contaminated grit is a common cause of nesting diarrhea, nestling deaths and poor breeding performance in canaries.

Canaries balance their own mineral needs. They search for minerals and trace elements when the levels in the body are depleted. They often fly against the wire or approach the fancier when they crave minerals.

Depletion of minerals occurs mostly when the hens are laying eggs and parents are feeding young. Mineral deficient parents become agitated and may reject their young.

Mineral powders should be provided on a daily basis during the breeding season and can be added to the soft food or placed in finger

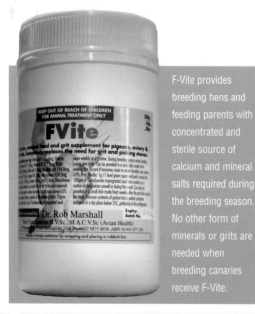

F-Vite provides breeding hens and feeding parents with a concentrated and sterile source of calcium and mineral salts required during the breeding season. No other form of minerals or grits are needed when breeding canaries receive F-Vite.

drawers. Specialised mineral powders (F-Vite) should be given on a daily basis to prevent many of the behavioural problems of breeding canaries. They provide the breeding birds with all the necessary minerals, mineral salts and trace elements in a concentrated, clean form. Because they are in a concentrated form, there is no wastage and the birds consume every last portion.

Mineral deficiencies are a common cause of egg binding, tired adults and stunted chicks. There is no more important time for minerals than when the birds are laying eggs or feeding the young. Hens search for the minerals soon after mating and while laying eggs. Feeding parents also crave mineral salts and electrolytes. It is amazing how much of the minerals they consume at this time. Iodine is the most important trace element for breeding. Trace element supplementation is best added to the water or soft food mix during the breeding season.

Ioford provides breeding canaries with an additional source of iodine, iron, trace elements calcium and vitamin D.

Fats

The fats of most interest are the fatty acids and the fat-soluble vitamins.

Polyunsaturated fatty acids play a significant role in the continuing health and vitality of canaries.

Turbobooster is a finely balanced and potent source of immune system modulating fatty acids.

The fatty acids are intimately involved in the growth and quality of feathers and the development of healthy and robust immune systems in young birds. They play a vital role in the prevention of disease.

Fatty acid supplementation on a daily basis during the breeding season promotes strong and resilient youngsters and is particularly useful as part of preventing diseases in the young birds. Fatty acids (Turbobooster) are often combined into a soft food mix with cultured yeast by-products such as E-Powder.

Turbobooster provides the perfect balance of fatty acids that help stimulate the immune system.

Fitness

Exercise improves circulation to muscles and organs that ultimately improves bodily functions. A heightened level of fitness accompanies regular exercise and also enhances the health status of canaries. They are then more able to cope with stress. The health benefits of fitness are enormous.

The placement of seed and water dishes on the floor of the aviary or flight is a clever way to improve fitness levels. The upward flight from a standstill requires sustained effort and is a most strenuous exercise for canaries. They become fit within a very short time, thus increasing disease resilience. However stress from such flight must be monitored to ensure birds are not overworked, leaving them more susceptible to disease.

Canaries housed in cabinets are more likely to become sedentary and more likely to fall ill. I believe weaker or inherently inactive varieties such as the Yorkshire and Borders would benefit enormously from an exercise regime that enhances fitness.

The placement of seed and water dishes on the floor in this tall aviary stimulates strenuous upward flight. This is a clever way to improve fitness levels.

Sunlight, Warmth and Dryness

Canaries do best when exposed to sunlight. The importance of sunshine becomes obvious when we see them bask in the sun in shear delight after having been deprived of sunshine for a period of time. Sunlight provides canaries with a natural source of vitamin D. Vitamin D is essential for the utilisation of calcium and for the health and performance of breeding hens, for strong bones and male virility. Breeding birds do better in a breeding room that is flooded with natural sunlight.

Canary rooms and aviaries must be designed to prevent drafts, extremes in temperature and the accumulation of moisture, as canaries are susceptible to fluctuating moisture and temperature. Canaries form part of the finch family of birds and have adapted to grassland habitats where conditions are dry. Canaries are consequently susceptible to the diseases associated with moisture, wet weather and fluctuating temperatures.

The detrimental effects of wet conditions can be counteracted without affecting the natural resistance of the flock by using products such as Megamix (see page 95) that naturally increases the acidity of drinking water and prevents infections arising from a contaminated environment.

Regular Baths

If allowed, canaries will take a bath in all weather conditions. Baths are best provided in the morning in order to give plenty of time for the birds to dry off. Take care in cold weather as they take longer to dry and may become chilled. Hang-on baths are practical when canaries are housed in breeding holes as they lessen the opportunity of wetting the cage floor. Wide, shallow baths (1-2cm/1/2-3/4 inch deep) are best suited for the flights. Young and aviary birds should receive a bath at least once a week.

This type of bath is usually placed on the aviary floor and any spillage is cleaned up following the bath.

Canaries love to bathe and must be provided with regular baths if they are to remain happy and healthy. This is a typical bath used by Mr Sant. It hangs on the outside of the cage. This type of bath prevents any moisture from entering the cage during the bathing process.

Some fanciers believe baths should not be given to breeding birds. However, bathing should be encouraged as it stimulates health and happiness. Happy breeding canaries feed and nurture their young in a vigorous fashion. Baths should hang off the cage door and not be given inside the breeding cabinet. Bathing should take place just prior to lunchtime, after the parents have finished their morning feeding. This allows adequate time for the birds to dry completely before nightfall. Breeding birds often enjoy a bath each day.

Avoid Overcrowding

Overcrowding usually occurs towards the end of the breeding season when there are many young birds. This is a time when young birds are especially susceptible to illness because the stress of overcrowding suppresses the immune system. Germ levels within the aviary and drinking water will increase with overcrowding and this is best kept under control with KD Powder. When there is an obvious overcrowding problem, it is recommended that KD Powder is added continuously to the drinking water to promote a clean, germ free environment that will help protect the overcrowded flock against illness.

Overcrowding is unhealthy for canaries and the most common underlying cause of illness in juvenile canaries.

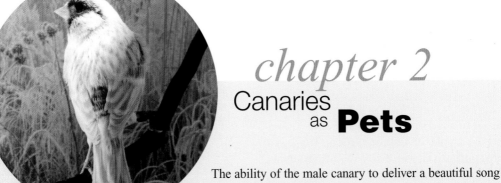

chapter 2
Canaries as **Pets**

The ability of the male canary to deliver a beautiful song makes it a very popular pet around the world. Canaries are the most popular pet bird in the USA. They are the easiest of pets to keep and have simple care requirements. With the correct care, a canary will reward its keeper with hours of song throughout the day.

Choosing Your Pet Canary

A male canary is the best choice as a pet because adult males deliver the best song. Females chirp rather than sing.

It is, however, very difficult to identify a male canary unless it is actually heard singing. As well, it is not until maturity that the male, is able to develop its song fully. Furthermore, canaries stop singing during their summer moult and many of the birds found in pet shops are juveniles. Because of the difficulties in selecting a male it is best to seek the help of an experienced pet shop owner or canary breeder to help identify a male as your new canary although it is not always possible for them to guarantee the sex and singing ability of your pet bird.

The sex of canaries is determined most accurately from their ability to sing during their natural breeding season (late winter until the beginning of summer) and as adults. It is difficult to determine their sex during their natural moult (summer months) and as juveniles because they do not sing at this time. Generally speaking the cock canary is more masculine in appearance than the hen; his carriage is bolder, his posture more erect and lively in his actions. The cock's head is larger and fuller than the hen's and the plumage is richer in colour. The voice of the cock is deeper in tone and more mellow and stronger than the hen's. The whistle of female and young canaries is a very restricted chirp or short twitter. The sound they produce is neither melodious nor long-lasting.

The male canary is the best choice. It has a bold appearance and its song is melodious and long-lasting.

It is easy to select an adult male when its song is heard but male canaries do not sing yearlong. They stop singing during their summer moult because of the great energy drain of replacing long feathers during their annual moult. Without this singing ability it is difficult to accurately determine the sex of a canary during the summer months.

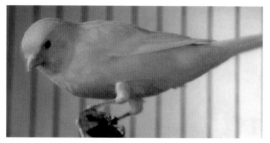

The female canary is small and feminine. It produces a soft whistle rather than a melodious song.

The age of a canary can be determined by examining the amount of scale on the legs. The legs of young birds are cleaner than old birds and quite free of scale. Young birds are more energetic than old birds. Young birds are easier to train and tame, but more difficult to "sex." Both sexes of young canaries look the same and they do not develop their song to a degree where sex can be accurately determined until they have matured at about nine months of age. Young canaries do continue to whistle throughout their first (juvenile) moult because they do not replace their long feathers (flights and tail) during this time.

Selecting a Healthy Canary

Visual examination in the pet shop is the first step in selecting your new canary. It is often difficult to determine the health status of a bird through visual means and some canaries may mask the signs of illness. All birds have this ability (known as preservation reflex) and it is thought to be a protective mechanism in the wild. Visual examination and consideration of the following physical attributes provides the prospective canary owner with a basic understanding of the health condition of the bird.

Selection of a male bird can be difficult. In this selection, the bird second from the left, facing forward, exhibits signs of a male bird; an upright posture and bold appearance.

'Eyeball' examination of the canary through the wire of an aviary or cage will not give a clear indication of the health of the individual. Below is a checklist of physical attributes that should be examined thoroughly.

1. Alertness & Activity
The canary should look bright and alert, move around actively, stand evenly on both feet (when awake) with an upright posture and pass a physical health examination. It should be quick moving in the cage and fly in a darting motion from perch to perch. The ideal pet bird should be heard singing from a distance. This indicates the most vital birds in the cage.

2. Feathers
A healthy canary has richly coloured and lustrous feathers that lie tightly on the body. Birds that are fluffed up (in a ball shape) are attempting to conserve body heat and are unwell.

The wing and tail feathers should be examined for mites. Quill mites often live along the quills at the base of the long tail feathers and are a frequent cause of ill health in canaries.

3. Eyes
The eyelid should be round without any pinching. Pinched eyelids indicate a sinus infection. There are many causes of sinus infection, the most common being Ornithosis.

The perfectly round and sparkling eye of this Fife canary is an indication of good health.

4. Breast Muscle
If possible, get the pet shop owner to pick the bird up and feel the keel bone as an indication of the bulk of the pectoral muscle and of wasting (going light). Birds with a prominent keel bone have a chronic illness, the most likely cause of which is a Megabacteria infection.

5. Feet

The age of a canary can be roughly determined by the amount of scale on the legs and feet. Older birds have more scale on the feet. Check for "tassle foot", where skin hangs off in threads from the feet. Tassle foot is usually caused by mites or poor nutrition. The ball of the feet should also be examined for pressure sores that appear as localised red areas. These sores result from incorrect perches or poor nutrition.

6. Vent Feathers

Look for pasting or wetness around the vent as a sign of illness. The feathers around the vent and under-tail region are perfectly clean in the healthy canary. White urate streaks smearing the feathers in this region are a reliable sign of a stressed and unhealthy bird.

7. Beak

The beak of the healthy canary is smooth and shiny. A rough surface or an excessively long beak is often a sign of an underlying and long-standing health problem.

The beak of a healthy canary is smooth and shiny.

> *Note: Canaries with abnormalities of any kind should not be purchased. Crossbred canaries make the most hardy pets. Birds from inbred flocks are not recommended as these birds are often poor physical specimens and more likely to succumb to illness.*

Preparing a Home for Your Pet Canary

Cage Design

The best canary cage is rectangular in shape with a size and dimension of a double breeder (see pages 39 & 44) .This allows the bird plenty of space for the bird to fly freely.

Fitness plays a large role in the health of the canary and it is necessary to provide adequate space for free flight and exercise. The wings of a canary should not be trimmed as it has adverse effects on their health. Instead, adequate room for flight enables the canary to achieve a high level of fitness and strength. Perches should be placed at either end of the cage so birds can fly from one end to the other.

The cage should be of a design that promotes exercise and fitness. It should be placed in an area where it can interact with the family.

Cage Location

The location of the cage in the home is important. Pet canaries thrive in areas where they receive lots of attention but away from heavy traffic flow. The kitchen and laundry must never be used to house birds as they promote fungal infections. The greatest enemy to your pet canary is moisture in the cage that allows bacteria and fungus to breed. These infections are harmful to your bird's health.

The best location for your canary cage is a well lit position with plenty of fresh air. The cage must not be exposed to drafts (e.g., near opened windows or doors) or cold temperatures as this makes the bird susceptible to illness. At the same time, extreme temperatures or an inability to escape strong sunlight can lead to overheating and a poor physical condition. Canaries appreciate the warmth of sunlight during the day and can often be found singing and bathing in the sunbeams. It is important to ensure the birds are able to escape from direct sunlight if it gets too hot. This can be achieved by placing the cage in partial shade or by providing a nest box.

Place the cage up off the ground with the perches at eye level. It is best placed in an area of the house with a clear view of the normal household activities and sounds, but not in the direct line of traffic flow. When your bird is well adjusted to the household it can be moved closer to the action.

When canaries are placed outside during the day it is important to provide protection from predators and extreme temperatures. Dogs, cats and wild birds (e.g., magpies, currawongs and butcher birds) can injure or kill a canary through the wire of the cage so it is important to cover the cage with a lightweight fabric while outdoors. This also protects the canary against extreme temperatures caused by the heat of the direct sun or the chill of a draft. The cage is best hung from a secure hook as this helps protect the bird from dogs and cats that may otherwise claw at the cage.

Perches

Close attention must be paid to the correct selection of perches for canaries. To accommodate the shape of a canary's foot, perches must be oval in shape. The canary has three toes forward and one back and an oval perch best accommodates this shape. The best size perch is 5/8"/1.5 cm wide and 3/8"/1 cm thick with rounded corners. Soft wood perches are less harsh on the feet, with soft pine woods making the best perches. Hardwood or plastic perches are liable to irritate the feet of canaries and are not recommended. The cage should be furnished with a variety of perches of all shapes and sizes and it is best to place them at either end of the cage to promote flight and fitness.

Birds with overgrown toe nails are likely to strain and dislocate their toes if they become caught in the wire. Overgrown nails should be trimmed on an angle with the long point of the angle being on the upper side.

Perches should be kept clean as dirt will irritate the bird's feet, causing picking and swollen sores. Feet sores are particularly distressing for birds. If a canary develops sore feet, the centre of the perch should be hollowed into a groove to prevent further rubbing. Special rubberised tape (e.g.,

Long nails can get caught in the wire, causing pain and damage to the foot.

vetwrap) should also be placed around to soften the perch. KD Cleanser is particularly useful in maintaining a clean perch as it removes any harmful germs that may be present.

Daily exercise is recommended for pet canaries. A large cage door with a landing enables the canary to easily exit and re-enter the cage for daily exercise..

Water and Seed containers

The most suitable water container is a clear cylinder that can be fixed to the outside of the cage with a feeder tube placed through the wires. These water containers help keep the water clean and allow the owner to see if the bird has plenty of water at a glance. The drinking vessel should not be too large as this often leads to a failure to refresh the water on a daily basis and an ultimate loss of water quality.

The drinking water should be refreshed daily and, at the same time, the water vessel should be cleaned. A pet bird becomes quickly upset and often unhealthy as a result of impure water or a dirty drinking container. The use of a water cleanser (KD Cleanser) once a week promotes clean drinking water and containers and is an important component of maintaining the health and well being of the pet canary.

Food and water containers in cage.

A D-shaped feeding vessel that can be fitted to the inside of the cage is a suitable means for providing canaries with seed and health additives. The container should be placed away from the drinking vessel and it is best to clean the container each day as the seed is replenished.

Finger drawers are also helpful for providing minerals and other supplements to the pet canary. Greens and millet sprays may be hung from the side of the cage using a clothes peg.

Cage Floor

Ideally, the floor of the cage should have a wire base suspended above a metal tray which can be slid out for cleaning. The use of paper, sand or shell grit as a floor covering is not recommended as this can be harmful to the health of the canary. Ingestion of sand, grit or paper from the cage floor can sometimes lead to a blocked gizzard, a

very serious condition that is easily avoided. The cage floor should be cleaned each day and disinfected once a week with KD Cleanser. A clean cage floor also allows the canary owner to monitor changes in the droppings each day and to gain a better understanding of the overall health status of their bird.

Cage Cleaning

Cage hygiene is a critical component in the ongoing care of the canary. A clean cage is free from germs that are often harmful to the health of canaries. The cage should be cleaned out each day and disinfected once a week with KD Powder. The feed and water containers must also be cleaned daily.

The surfactants in KD make it an ideal cage cleaner that easily removes dirt and droppings.

Physical and Emotional Security

It is true that at times birds must be restricted. However, permanent confinement is unhealthy for birds selected as pets. The prime purpose of the cage is to improve the physical and emotional security of the bird at all times.

Daily contact outside the cage is important for the emotional health of the pet bird. Canaries housed indoors can be trained to be let out of the cage and into a closed room for daily exercise. Pet canaries may also be trained to fly to their owner and perch on the shoulder. It is important to ensure the area in which the canary is allowed to fly is free of any object that may cause it harm. Windows should be closed and covered with a curtain and the room thoroughly inspected for any object that may become a hazard (e.g., heaters, gaps between the wall and furniture, fans etc). The health advantages of allowing the well-trained canary to have free flight each day are tremendous. The bird develops a strong fitness level and a greatly improved overall health condition. Canary owners can develop a strong bond with their pet and the process of training a canary to fly freely within a closed room helps in the development of this relationship. This relationship also promotes happiness and emotional security in the pet canary.

All birds should be confined to cages while their owners are away to avoid accidental injury and other misfortune. An unsupervised pet bird allowed the run of the house eventually gets into trouble.

The First Days at Home

The time it takes for your canary to "settle in" varies with age. Younger birds (recently weaned) settle within a few days but older birds may require three weeks to finally adjust to their new surroundings. During the first few days in its new home, your pet canary may be easily alarmed and it is important to ensure it is exposed to as little stress as possible in its new environment. Handling and loud noises should be kept to a minimum, allowing the bird to familiarise itself with its new surroundings without being overwhelmed. It should be introduced to its cage and other family members at this time. The cage must be elevated on a table or have the perch at eye height and should be positioned in a protective corner, away from drafts. Gently talk and whistle to your new bird as this activity will accelerate the taming and bonding process.

Quick movements will scare your new bird and it is recommended to keep your dog and cat away from it for at least two weeks.

Too much stress during these important first days may cause illness in your bird just as people under stress become ill. The most notable disease

is Ornithosis. This disease becomes active in birds under stress and may be transmitted to humans.

The following recommendations will limit the stress experienced by your new bird and should be adopted from the time of collection and continued for its entire life.

- **A suitable cage**
- **A clean cage**
- **Correct dietary requirements**
- **Sufficient rest time**
- **Health check by an avian veterinarian**

Vet Check

An appointment with an avian veterinarian should be scheduled to coincide with the purchase of a new canary. Find an avian veterinarian who has the facilities to perform in-house diagnostic testing. Pet canaries retain the survival instincts of their wild counterparts and are able to hide illness or weakness. An examination by an experienced avian veterinarian is required to determine the exact health status of your new pet. A thorough examination is performed to identify illness or health flaws with further tests being performed on the droppings and throat to check for diseases that are difficult to detect visually.

A complete health examination within 24 hours of purchase is recommended for every new canary. This is a very good health insurance policy for the bird, you and your family. A clean bill of health at this time means that under the correct care your bird should remain happy and healthy. This is also a good time for you to discuss feeding and the proper care of your canary with the avian veterinarian.

Health Signs

Beak

The beak of a healthy canary remains clean. Rubbing the beak quickly onto the perch is a common activity in canaries but excessive rubbing may indicate a sinus infection.

Behaviour & Activity

An enduring change in the behaviour of your canary is a reliable sign of a health problem although emotional, hormonal and environmental disturbances may also initiate an alteration in behaviour. Look carefully at the health of your bird if it does not want to come out of its cage, whistle or wants to stay close by rather than explore or fly.

A change in the voice and ability of your pet bird to sing is a sign that your pet canary is unwell or unhappy. A squeaky or soft voice may indicate a potentially fatal windpipe fungal infection that needs immediate veterinary attention. The sudden and complete stoppage of singing or chirping behaviour is also a reliable sign of a health problem requiring early attention.

Droppings

Changes in the consistency and colour of the droppings of canaries are not a reliable indication of a health problem because of the varied diet they eat. A change in smell or colour to (black, red, yellow or orange) and an increase in size are reliable signs of a health problem that requires veterinary intervention.

Eye Signs

The eyelid should be round without any pinching. Pinched eyelids indicate a sinus infection.

Feather Signs

Healthy canaries have a bright coloured, lustrous plumage. Changes in the intensity and shine of the feathers may appear rapidly (a matter of days) after the onset of illness. Healthy feathers remain perfectly clean and repel dirt and the accumulation of droppings. Pasted vent feathers and dirty feathers are signs of illness. Feather picking should be investigated immediately as it is often a sign of a health problem such as lice and mites.

Feet Signs

Good health and blood circulation keeps the feet of the canary warm and dry. Poor environmental conditions (low temperatures, high humidity, poor hygiene), nutritional imbalances and illness are common causes of cold and dirty feet.

Mouth Signs

Excessive stretching open of the mouth of the canary should be considered grounds for veterinary advice or intervention.

Weight & Body Condition

Canaries are prone to obesity and must receive plenty of exercise to remain fit and healthy. It is wise to know and monitor the weight and body condition of your canary. A sudden loss in body condition is a reliable sign of a health problem. Birds that are eating less may lose significant weight within a single day.

This Australian Plain Head Canary shows all the signs of perfect health. Notice its beautiful lustrous feathers that are held tightly on the body, clean feet and robust, upright stance.

Ongoing Care and Health Programme

Feeding

Apart from seed, the canary enjoys and needs variety in its diet. When refreshing the seed each day never just top up the dish. The husks of eaten seeds must first be removed or they may stay on the top and cover the heavier seeds, causing the canary to starve if it cannot find the seed. It is best to provide clean, fresh seed each day and clean the feeding container at the same time. It is important to ensure the feed remains perfectly dry at all times.

The pet canary should receive a basic seed mix (e.g., Plain canary 50%, two or three types of millet 35%, rape seed 5%, groats 5%, soft wheat 5%) in a D-cup container made fresh daily. As well once or twice a week a tonic seed/soft food treat (e.g., equal parts maw, linseed, lettuce, polenta, grated carrot, hulled oats) should be included and is a highly anticipated part of the pet canary's diet.

This tonic seed mix contains maw, rape, niger and plain canary seeds.

A canary needs a daily supply of fresh green food. (e.g., endive, silver beet, chicory etc). They love to eat greens although this often exposes the birds to harmful germs and fungal infections. Birds without access to greens need a vitamin supplement (Dufoplus and Ioford) for two days each week in the drinking water.

Do not over feed canaries fatty foods such as oil seed if they are not free flying. A bird in a small cage gets very little exercise and cannot burn off excess fats. The daily requirements of canaries are simple: A small amount of clean seed, a piece of fresh green food, a mineral supplement and clean water. The ongoing care of canaries incorporates two health programmes - the Singing Programme and the Moulting Programme. The daily care for your canary and is a simple process that will ensure the health and happiness of your pet.

Water Hygiene

Fresh water every day is essential for a healthy bird. Do not just top up the container as it must be thoroughly cleaned before being refilled. KD water cleanser should be mixed into the drinking water for one day each week and whenever a bath is given.

KD is given once a week in the drinking water to promote overall strength and vitality. In high humidity, KD can be given for three consecutive days to protect against illness.

Cage Cleaning

It is advisable to clean the cage once a week as the healthiest birds are found in the cleanest surroundings.

Bathing

Canaries love to bathe and it is best to provide it in the morning. The bath should be given to canaries at least three times a week. KD water cleanser should be added to the bath water to keep the feathers perfectly clean and help repel insects. Bathing is a vital part of continuing happiness for canaries and helps to keep them fit and well. When a bath is given do not let the birds soak themselves with water to such an extent that

Regular bathing plays an important role in maintaining the health, happiness and fitness of the pet canary.

they cannot fly on to the perches. Do not leave the bath in all day as the soiled water will often be used for drinking.

The bath should be hung over the door of the cage which is opened and the bath placed opposite the opening. The dimensions of a bath are 8" (20cm) long, 6" (15cm) wide, 5" (12.5cm) deep and the top is covered with a piece of glass in place of the ordinary wire to prevent water from getting on the bottom of the cage. About 2" (5cm) depth of water is sufficient for bathing. This can be placed on the floor inside the cage or hung over the door. After a bath clean the cage and replace the paper with a dry sheet.

KD or S76 should be mixed into the bath water at drinking water strength once each month to help eradicate lice and mites and keep the feathers clean (see Health Programmes).

Lice, Mite and Worm Control

Lice, mites and worms are an underestimated cause of ill health in canaries. Routine treatments to control infestation are necessary for continuing good health in pet canaries. These treatments are generally given each three months, although during the heat of summer it may be necessary to provide monthly treatment.

S76 is given in the drinking water for one day each three months to control lice, mites and worms. KD baths each week also form an impor-

S76 is added to the drinking water each three months to protect against lice, mites and worms.

tant part of the lice and mite prevention programme. These baths help remove dead mites that otherwise irritate the birds.

Exercise and Training

To promote strength and fitness in your pet canary, it is recommended to allow daily exercise in the form of free flight within a closed room. Over time, your bird can be trained to fly freely for a period of time and then return to the cage for feeding. Canaries can also be trained to fly to their owner's shoulder with a simple command. Before any training can begin, the bird's confidence must be gained.

Pet canaries can be trained to fly to the hand or shoulder of their owner.

- **Avoid sudden movements or noise when near the cage.**
- **Catch the bird frequently but do it quickly.**
- **Do not chase the bird around the cage.**
- **Gently hold the bird for a few minutes then return it to the cage.**
- **Allow the bird to hop from your open hand to a perch.**

Talk to the bird frequently and give a short "greeting" whistle or sing to it. This "greeting" call eventually becomes a signal for the bird to answer back. Canaries can learn to understand key words such as "come" to fly to a shoulder or "cage" to return to cage.

Talking to a canary at eye level is very important during training. Sitting on the shoulder is one of the easiest tricks for a canary as the bird is as confident and comfortable here as it is at eye level. Canaries orientate themselves by sight and sound and identify others by sight.

Pet canaries should be trained so that they can be let out of their cage for daily exercise. The bird must first be tame and unafraid of its owner before starting exercise training. First let the bird come out of its cage on its own accord. All food and water must be removed from the cage a couple of hours before opening the door to allow your pet canary out for free flight hand. When the bird is out flying free then the food and water should be returned to the cage after which time you should leave the room. Eventually the bird will return to the cage to eat. The door must be closed as soon as the bird returns to the cage so that it cannot escape again after eating and drinking. Never have food or water elsewhere in the room apart from inside the cage. This food training reward system encourages the bird to return to the cage.

Never try to catch your pet bird with your hands or a net when it is outside the cage enjoying a free-flight session or your bird will associate freedom from the cage with recapture and not want to leave its cage when the door is opened. Close and cover all open windows before letting your bird out and provide the bird a perch (t-stand) or safe zone where the bird can land and rest while it is out flying free. Paper can be placed on the floor beneath the perch to collect droppings.

Repetition is the basis of training and success at training depends upon the amount of quality time spent with the bird each day. Without regular attention canaries become untamed.

Canaries have a well developed communication-based intelligence. They soon recognise and "talk" to their owner by emitting a "sweet-sweet'" sounding contact call. Canaries do not share the talking abilities of parrots but when encouraged by human singing do enjoy responding in their own song-language. Communication through human voice and song is the best way to "talk" with pet canaries.

The intelligence of pet canaries is often underestimated as they can be easily taught to fly from and return to their cage on command. Canaries do not enjoy being held in the hand but may be trained to sit on a shoulder.

Pet canaries make the best pets when they are encouraged to learn and interact with their owner. This is best achieved through songs and voice. They are able to be trained and are known to be highly intelligent although they may not be able to talk.

Cutting Claws (nails)

Pet canaries need to have their claws cut occasionally when they are obviously long. Sharp human nail clippers are ideal to clip their claws but great care must be taken that too much is not snipped off. Bleeding, pain and a week or two of depression will result when too much nail is removed. It may be necessary to consult an avian veterinarian if your canary has fast growing nails that become excessively long or deformed. Long nails in canaries may indicate poor perch selection or a nutritional or liver disease.

Trimming of overgrown nails helps prevent accidental injury from the nails becoming stuck in the wire of the cage.

Song Training

From an evolutionary perspective, researchers believe that patterns of vocalization have become more complex over time, with the most recently evolved species (songbirds e.g. canary) having the most complex vocalizations.

The communicative value of the song may be:

1. "Choose me because I am healthy." and, furthermore, may indicate;

2. "I am experienced and will, therefore, make a good partner."

The singing male may convey a bird that has plenty of exposure to learning a repertoire.

The chief sound-producing vocal organ of a bird is the syrinx. Researchers are still debating the role of the trachea, larynx, tongue, sinuses and airsacs in the modification of sounds. Songbirds have a very complex syringeal system in which the syringeal muscles and internal membranes interact to produce nearly pure tones (singe-frequency tones, similar to human whistles). Canaries have well developed syringeal muscles and full song is produced only when the syringeal muscles are fully grown. The canary is able to produce sounds from each side of the syrinx simultaneously and independently.

The acquisition of song in individuals is determined by an interaction of learning and inheritance. In different species, the proportion of each is largely responsible for the variation from totally learned to totally unlearnt and presumably inherited. The song of canaries is both inherited and learnt. The quality of the song production markedly improves when they are able to learn from other canaries, especially their fathers.

The function of the song of canaries is primarily to attract a member of the opposite sex. The breeding season is often accompanied by the onset of an elaborate song for the purpose of attracting a female. The connection between song and breeding is strong. Song requires a lot of energy and it is believed that prolonged and strenuous singing advertise good health and fitness (vitality) in males. A high energy diet (rolled oats, rape, linseed, maw and a little soft food daily) has been found to play a great role in the development of song in Roller canaries (undoubtedly the best singer of all canaries) and a canary in full song requires an energy rich diet. The following "Singing Programme" helps maintain the pet canary when in full song.

Singing Programme for Pet Canaries

This Programme extends for about 9 months and should start in first week of autumn and extend to the beginning of the moult in summer.

Day of Week	Water Supplements	Food Supplements	Additional Advice
Friday	KD[1]	Turbobooster E Powder, F-Vite[3]	S76 should be administered in the drinking water each three months to control lice, mites and worms. During summer, this treatment should be given each month.
Saturday	Dufoplus & Ioford[2]	Turbobooster E Powder, F-Vite[3]	
Sunday	Dufoplus & Ioford[2]	Turbobooster E Powder, F-Vite[3]	
Monday	Fresh Water	Fresh Seed	
Tuesday	Fresh Water	Fresh Seed	A KD bath should be given one week following S76 treatment to help remove dead lice and mites.
Wednesday	Fresh Water	Fresh Seed	
Thursday	Fresh Water	Fresh Seed	

The dosages and instructions described here are recommended for the pet canary health Programme. Some dosages appearing on the product labels may vary slightly. These are to be used for birds with illness or nutritional deficiencies.

[1] KD Water Cleanser is prepared by adding 1gm (1/4 teaspoon) into one litre of water. The drinking vessel is filled from this litre and the remainder used to clean out the cage. KD cleanses the bowel of harmful food and water related germs, promoting a stronger natural health.

[2] 5 drops of Dufoplus and 10 drops of Ioford are mixed together into 100ml (see reverse side of standard U.S. cup measure) of drinking water and safely left for two days, as they are sugar free. They provide the vitamins and trace elements necessary for vitality and good health. An increased intensity of plumage colour should be noticed within three weeks of using the products mentioned in this Programme.

[3] 6 drops of Turbobooster is mixed thoroughly into 100 grams (2/3 cup) of dry seed, sprouted seed or soft food mix. 1gm (1/4 teaspoon) of Epowder and 1gm of Fvite are then added to the Turbobooster impregnated seed. The Turbobooster provides canaries with the fatty acids, protein and minerals necessary for good health.

Another important aspect of development of song in birds is the existence of a critical period during which the young bird must be exposed to the correct song if it is to develop its own normal song.

The ability of Rollers to sing is improved when a good singing father "teaches" his youngsters his repertoire of songs. Similarly, the quality and complexity of song produced by birds bred purely for song such as Canary-Goldfinch mules (Goldfinch bred with a Border or other canary variety) may be improved in a similar fashion. Goldfinches have the ability to mimic and they start to do so from an early age. The mules, as well, retain their ancestral ability to mimic and should follow the same song training processes as Rollers. The ability of song birds to mimic is thought to improve their ability to attract a female. Mimicry is another form of song learning and the tendency to mimic is most likely inherited. Mimicry is also used by some song birds to mark their territory.

Song training should start as soon as the young bird starts chattering (about 6 weeks of age). The birds must be in the best of health to learn new songs. To prevent any form of outside distraction during the training phase, the cages are blinkered

The Goldfinch is a wild bird which is crossed with different varieties of canaries to produce a mule bird that combines the beautiful tones of the Goldfinch with the singing ability of the canary varieties.

with curtains so that they can see only the tutor birds. They must receive regular feed times (9am and 4pm) and time to bathe, preen and sun. Outside this time they quickly settle into a routine of listening, learning and singing when the curtain is drawn. Young mule cross-bred Goldfinches should follow a similar form of schooling at this young age as they quickly pick up the songs of nearby birds (e.g., sparrows). Above all the success of song learning requires a healthy well-fed fit canary.

The singing ability of pet canaries may be improved by:

1. **Good Health; achieved by good hygiene and KD water cleanser**

2. **A high energy, balanced diet; achieved through the Singing & Moulting Programmes**

3. **Fitness; achieved by daily free flying**

4. **Regular baths**

5. **Sunshine if possible.**

6. **Accelerating the moult; achieved by applying a summer Moult Programme**

Canary-Goldfinch mules are ideally suited and much sought after as pet birds because they are tireless singers of beautiful song. They are difficult birds to breed and are only available from specialist breeders.

The Moult

Canaries must shed their old feathers and regrow new ones once a year. Young birds change their body feathers only and start to do so from six to eight weeks of age. In adults the moult should commence in summer but the start may vary a little depending upon weather conditions. There is a noticeable lack of vigour and reduction in singing at the onset of the moult. Soon after, a few feathers will appear on the floor of the cage. This is the time that the Moult Programme should commence. The addition of nutritional additives (e.g., Turbobooster, E-powder and F-vite) to the food during the moult period as well as implementing treatments to guard against mites and daily baths are very helpful in accelerating the moult and shorten the "non-singing" period of male canaries. The moult should be completed between three and four months.

This bird has almost completed its moult.

Pet Canary Moult Programme

The moult programme should commence during the first week of summer and extend until the first week of autumn.

Day of Week	Water Supplements	Food Supplements	Additional Advice
Friday	KD[1]	Turbobooster E Powder, F-Vite[3]	Tonic mix should be given for two days each week.
Saturday	Dufoplus & Ioford[2]	Turbobooster E Powder, F-Vite[3]	S76 should be administered in the drinking water each three months to control lice, mites and worms. During summer, this treatment should be given each month.
Sunday	Dufoplus & Ioford[2]	Turbobooster E Powder, F-Vite[3]	
Monday	Fresh Water	Turbobooster E Powder, F-Vite[3]	
Tuesday	Fresh Water	Turbobooster E Powder, F-Vite[3]	
Wednesday	Fresh Water	Turbobooster E Powder, F-Vite[3]	A KD bath should be given one week following S76 treatment to help remove dead lice and mites.
Thursday	Fresh Water	Turbobooster E Powder, F-Vite[3]	

The dosages and instructions described here are recommended for the pet canary Health Programme. Some dosages appearing on the product labels may vary slightly. These are to be used for birds with illness or nutritional deficiencies.

[1] KD Water Cleanser is prepared by adding 1gm (1/4 teaspoon) into one litre of water. The drinking vessel is filled from this litre and the remainder used to clean out the cage. KD cleanses the bowel of harmful food and water related germs, promoting a stronger natural health.

[2] 5 drops of Dufoplus and 10 drops of Ioford are mixed together into 100ml (see reverse side of standard U.S. cup measure) of drinking water and safely left for two days, as they are sugar free. They provide the vitamins and trace elements necessary for vitality and good health. An increased intensity of plumage colour should be noticed within three weeks of using the products mentioned in this Programme.

[3] 6 drops of Turbobooster is mixed thoroughly into 100 grams (2/3 cup) of dry seed, sprouted seed or soft food mix. 1gm (1/4 teaspoon) of Epowder and 1gm of Fvite are then added to the Turbobooster impregnated seed. The daily administration of Turbobooster, Epowder and Fvite provides canaries with the fatty acids, protein and minerals necessary for fast and good moult.

chapter 3
Breeding
Behaviour

Knowledge of the canary's breeding behaviour and its nutritional requirements during the breeding cycle is essential for breeding success. Health is also necessary for breeding success.

In the aviary situation, where all ages and both genders fly together, the natural forces for breeding success move spontaneously from one stage to the next. Exhibition canaries, however, are separated by gender into flights or cabinets and only introduced to each other when they begin to show signs of breeding condition. It is more difficult to breed birds using this type of system.

Breeding Season

Canaries breed during a set breeding period that is triggered by warm weather and an increasing length of daylight. Breeding may naturally begin early during the last month of winter, but more often, spring heralds the beginning of the breeding season for canaries. The normal breeding period for canaries kept in open aviaries begins in the spring (April-May in Northern Hemisphere and August- September in Southern Hemisphere).

Across Europe and USA, canary breeders have changed this natural breeding period to fit in with their cultural lifestyle. They use a method of breeding that artificially extends the daily photoperiod (length of daylight hours). Many fanciers pair their birds in the month of February, two months before the beginning of the normal breeding season, so that breeding will be completed before the summer holidays. They also breed early so that the moult period is completed before the exhibitions that are commonly held toward the end of the year. Additionally, some want to breed as many clutches as possible. This artificial system of breeding invites breeding failures, so special knowledge of all aspects of canary care must be taken to ensure success. The challenge and the skill required to achieve success are what attracts many fanciers to the hobby.

Special knowledge, planning and attention to detail is necessary in order to achieve success when breeding canaries.

Breeding Requirements

Canaries require several conditions before they will successfully breed. The pre-requisites are as follows:

- **Maturity**
- **Good Health**
- **Breeding (photoperiod) Stimulation**
- **Minimum Temperature & Humidity**
- **Breeding Condition**
- **Nests and Breeding Holes**

Maturity

Most canaries will reach sexual maturity at approximately 10 months of age. Sometimes fertility problems occur when birds born in the last clutch of the previous year are used to breed too early in the following year.

Good Health

Before the onset of the breeding season, physical examinations should be performed to determine the health and body condition of the birds. Birds lacking the correct nutrition or carrying a disease will lack the vitality necessary to come into breeding condition or complete the breeding cycle.

Breeding (Photoperiod) Stimulation

The natural breeding behaviour of canaries is determined by an ancient biological clock that is set in motion by the increasing day length that occurs in the latter part of winter. These ancient natural forces also control the onset of breeding activity for many other birds.

With the increasing day length following the shortest day of the year (June 23rd in Southern Hemisphere; December 21st in Northern Hemisphere) the sex organs of cock birds are activated and as long as the weather is not too cold, they come into "breeding condition" within 4 weeks. Hens do not respond as quickly to the increasing day length. They require a day length of at least 10 hours, sometimes as much as 12 hours, to attain "breeding condition."

This apparent asynchrony is beneficial to the breeding outcome as it protects the energy reserves of the hen. She must preserve her energy for egg production as well as for the rearing of young. Strong hens carry this considerable burden with ease when in breeding condition and fed appropriately. Less vital "weak" hens may fail to come into proper breeding condition. When permitted to breed, such birds often succumb to illness and sometimes death. A hen in breeding condition must also receive appropriate courtship activities from a breeding-ready cock bird if she is to successfully complete her nesting and egg laying response.

Artificial lighting and heating is often used to initiate breeding activity throughout the world because most exhibition canaries are housed and bred indoors. This is known as Photoperiodic Stimulation.

Artificial Daylight Manipulation

It is possible to manipulate the breeding cycle of canaries by regulating the number of hours of light they receive each day. This is known as Photoperiod Stimulation. Accurate light regulation strategies must be applied in order to stimulate breeding activity.

The photoperiod is the ratio of light to dark time. A 15:9 ratio means 15 hours of light and 9 hours of darkness. The photoperiod is very important in those species of birds living in zones with seasonal changes. In temperate-zone birds such as canaries, ovarian development and testicular growth are synchronised by a combination of increasing day length, the stimuli provided by a partner and an available nesting site.

Artificial lighting and heating used by enthusiasts to manipulate breeding activity can improve breeding potential and the survival chances of newly hatched birds during cold spells. Up to fifteen hours of daylight should be provided for canaries because if longer when breeding, they may not receive enough rest. Automatic timers must be used to switch the light on and off. A second source of low intensity light, the nightlight, should come on 15 minutes before dark and go off 15 minutes after day break. Its dimming effect prevents plunging the birds into sudden darkness at night or daylight in the morning. If the length of the daylight is too long or fluctuates, the birds may go into an early moult and may cease to breed altogether.

Experience demonstrates that male canaries need slightly longer preparation time with respect to the extension of daylight than females. This additional time can be obtained by placing the males in isolation 2 weeks earlier, so that light stimulation may begin earlier. The reason that males need a longer preparation period is probably because in nature, males receive extra competitive incentives, such as the song of another male while they mark out their territories trying to attract a partner. These incentives are often not present in an artificial breeding situation.

Most problems in canary breeding are due to errors in the manipulation of the light cycle. Canaries need a minimum of 14 to 15 hours of daylight to begin breeding (nest building and production of eggs). With this amount of light, they are also able to sufficiently feed their youngsters to raise them properly. The cycle of light is also a major determining factor in whether breeding is sustained.

There are 2 methods of manipulating the length of daylight: gradually increasing the daylight length and immediately increasing the daylight length to the full period.

Gradually Increasing Daylight Length

With this technique, the amount of daylight is gradually increased each week. Depending on how quickly the daylight period is lengthened, 2 months may be required to extend the 8 to 10 hours of naturally daylight to 15 hours. If a weekly addition of 30 minutes (5 additional minutes per day) is used, it will take approximately 10 weeks to obtain this result. This means that the fancier needs 2 to 3 months to prepare for breeding. Gradually increasing the length of the day more closely resembles the natural light stimuli and is used by more than 80% of fanciers. Fifteen hours of daylight appears to be ideal. Poor annual breeding results and high numbers of chick deaths occur when the daylight length exceeds 17 hours.

Immediate Increase to Full Daylight Length

Daylight length can also suddenly be increased from 10 to 15 hours. In this case, the birds reach breeding condition after 3 to 4 weeks, but most are unable to maintain good results throughout the full breeding season. However, some fanciers do have good results with this method. A sudden increase, used by approximately 10% of the breeders, often leads to poor fertilisation of the first clutch (which normalises afterwards) and a higher mortality rate of females.

Technical Aspects of Light

The spectrum of optical radiation lies between 102nm in the ultraviolet (UV) and 106 nm in the infrared (IR) spectrums. This wavelength range is subdivided into 7 bands: UV-C, UV-B, UV-A, visible light, IT-A, IR-B and IR-C. The UVB band in natural sunlight allows the multi-step conversion of 7-dehydrocholesterol into 1,25-dihydroxycholecalciferol (vitamin D3), which is then reabsorbed by the skin or ingested during preening. Vitamin D3 is very important for calcium metabolism. If there is a lack of incoming sunlight, full spectrum lamps can be used to induce the internal vitamin D production in the skin. In addition, environmental contamination can be reduced with UV light. If artificial light is provided for breeding birds, the kind of radiation produced by the lamps plays an important factor.

Frequency

Normal fluorescent lamps do not give continuous light but flicker on and off like a stroboscope at approximately 50 times per second (50Hz). The stroboscopic effect of fluorescent light may lead to stress and may negatively influence the birds' general condition. If many lamps are used at the same time or a combination of bulb lamps and fluorescent light is used, the stroboscopic effects will be less marked. The latest development is the high frequency or HF lamp which has a frequency of 28,000 Hz, have a longer lifetime and make dimming possible.

Ambient Light Temperature

Fluorescent lights give their highest output at a temperature of 20°C/68°F. These lamps are very sensitive to temperature. At a low ambient temperature, the buffer gases inside the lamp will deteriorate, and there will be less light output. It is recommended to use multiple lamps simultaneously in case of defects and to provide a small amount of light (17 W) during the night in case of nocturnal commotion.

Temperature and Humidity

Most fanciers maintain the temperature in the breeding room at approximately 15°C/59°F at the start of the breeding season. Breeding problems should be anticipated at the beginning of the season when temperatures fluctuate or drop below 10° C/50°F.

Humidity levels within the breeding room should be kept within a range of 55% to 70%. Levels above 70% increase the likelihood of bacterial, fungal and yeast infections that could lead to the sudden deaths of breeding hens. Maintaining the humidity at the lower end of this range minimises the development of pathogens within the breeding room. Too dry an environment may create infertility and hatching difficulties. It may be necessary to place water beneath the nests in rooms with humidity levels below 55% to aid hatching. The introduction of water tubs during excessively dry weather may also help. Some breeders "moisturise" eggs immediately prior to hatching with a little spray of warm tap water into the nest, or by plunging the eggs for a second into a cup of warm water. This is thought to improve hatchability.

Breeding Condition

The combination of sex hormones, good health and physical fitness brings the birds into top physical condition. This is known as "breeding condition." The most important facet of breeding exhibition canaries successfully is an understanding of the meaning of "breeding condition."

In the wild, a spring flush of energy rich seeding grasses stimulates finches to breed. The increased energy and protein available at this time activates hormonal changes that bring hens and cocks into "breeding condition."

The onset of breeding condition is hormonally

To achieve the best results, both the hen and cock must be in perfect breeding condition.

controlled but its intensity relies upon good health, natural vitality and the genetic background of the canaries. The best time to allow canaries to breed is when they are bright and active and in top breeding condition. They must not be placed into breeding cages unless in "breeding condition." Breeding condition is the main key to breeding success.

Sex hormones provide canaries with the strength and vitality needed for breeding. Without this hormonal preparation they will not be able to withstand the extremely high energy and nutritional demands of the breeding season. These huge energy requirements are essential for courtship, egg laying, incubation and rearing young, and therefore, it is important for breeding pairs to be in optimal physical condition. Poor breeding outcomes result when canaries are not in breeding condition before being introduced to their nest boxes. For wild birds, it is the availability of nutritious foodstuff (directly related to day length) that determines the time and duration they are in breeding condition. For the captive bird it is the environmental conditions and nutrition provided by the fancier that maintains breeding condition in breeding pairs.

For canaries, the hen determines the start of the breeding cycle for she alone carries the burden of laying eggs and accepts most of the rearing responsibilities. She must be in very good physical condition if she is to endure the hardships of breeding. Most fanciers move the hen into the breeding cabinet when she shows signs of coming into breeding condition. Here, nest making activities and courtship from the cock should further stimulate her breeding activities. The coordination and time at which she is placed into the breeding hole (cabinet) and the cock introduced to her, is critical to the success of breeding exhibition canaries. Knowledge of the different and subtle stages of breeding condition allows the fancier to achieve the best breeding results. The release of female sex hormones associated with the onset of the breeding season prepares hens for the complexity of laying eggs. These hormones are responsible for the mobilisation of calcium from the body tissues to be deposited inside the long bones. The calcium stored in the long bones is essential for the production of hard-shelled eggs because dietary calcium alone cannot meet her massive requirements. Similarly, body stores of protein are essential to create the yolk as dietary levels of protein are not sufficient even when in increased amounts. The body must mobilise protein from the liver, muscle and other organs under the influence of sex hormones to produce yolk protein. The release of the sex hormones is incomplete when canaries are allowed to breed "out of breeding condition." The result is poor fertility, small clutch sizes, egg binding, and weak, sick breeding hens.

Hens may carry nest material in their beaks and search for a nest as they come into breeding condition. Cock birds in breeding condition become virile and more aggressive due to high levels of circulating testosterone (male hormone). Assertive behaviour towards other cocks, protective courtship activities around the nest and the presence of nesting material carried by the hen stimulate the full release of testosterone, which further improves fertility.

The observant fancier easily identifies the most vigorous and fit birds in the aviary and it is these birds that are usually the first to come into breeding condition. For the best breeding results, both the hen and cock need to be maintained in their breeding condition.

Fighting between cock and hen, sudden illness and rejection of eggs and young may result from a loss of "breeding condition" in canaries.

Breeding Condition Essentials

The canary should come into breeding condition:

- By spring (March in the Northern Hemisphere and September in the Southern Hemisphere).
- When physically fit, healthy and psychologically primed to breed.
- When the aviary is healthy, active and noisy.

The canary may not come into breeding condition:

- When it is too cold.
- Until the day length is at least 10 hours long.
- When it is carrying an illness or has a disease.
- When nutrition is poor.
- Under fluctuating environmental conditions.
- When mite infestation causes the canaries to become restless at night.

Important facts about breeding:

- Some birds never come into breeding condition.
- Overweight or underweight canaries may not achieve breeding condition.
- Canaries carrying a disease may not come into breeding condition.
- Quality show birds often fail to come into breeding condition or quickly fall out of breeding condition because they may be from genetically weak families.

Breeding Condition Signs in Hens

The outward signs of breeding condition are more obvious for hens than for cocks. Even so, careful observation is needed. Most birds must be picked up individually to check for physical changes in the abdomen and vent that signal "Breeding Condition."

Breeding condition in the hen is identified by behavioural changes, swelling around the vent. The abdomen also appears to bloat and becomes visible as it parts the feathers.

The early signs of breeding condition in hens reflect the influences of her sex hormones. Their presence indicates she is ready to be moved into the breeding cabinet. Here, her sex hormones are then further stimulated by the presence of the nest, nest making and courtship from a cock. The cock must also be in "Breeding Condition."

First Signs of Breeding Condition in Hens

There is a strong relationship between day length, warm weather and breeding cycles of canaries. It is the hormonal and metabolic changes associated with spring that primes the canary to breed. The recognition of the appearance of the early signs of breeding condition helps the fancier to identify the best time to move the birds into double breeders.

Renewed vigour is an early sign of breeding condition in hens. She may "butterfly" or "ping." "Pinging" is a rapid and repeated flight from one end of the double breeder to the other or flying up and down on a perch. The appearance of "pinging" in hens and cocks are hallmarks of breeding condition signaling that they are ready to breed.

This hen is ready to move into a breeding cabinet as she is showing signs of wanting to make a nest.

The hens then become intensely interested in cocks and frequently peer through the drinking holes in search of them. At this stage, the hen should be moved to a breeding cabinet where she must be regularly picked up and carefully examined for the more advanced signs of breeding condition.

More Advanced Signs of Breeding Condition in Hens

The advanced signs indicate hens are ready to receive a nest, nesting material and soon after, the cock. At this time they pluck feathers from their own breast or feathers from other hens and shape a place for nesting in a corner. She may be seen carrying green food or shavings in her beak and may squat while lifting her tail, calling for a cock bird. At this time she should be caught and closely examined. She is in an advanced stage of breeding condition and a nest should be introduced when the abdomen is full, rounded, the skin tone rose pink in colour and with a yellow line down the centre of the abdomen.

At this time, Stan Nichols recommends, "introducing the cock to the adjacent hole of the double breeder." He further states "the pair must be separated by a slide with holes 2.5cm/1 inch in diameter at the base so they can become acquainted. Then during the next four days, the cock bird is allowed to run free with the hen for an hour or two under supervision. The nest pan with nesting material is provided immediately after the hen calls him and he treads her. They can then be left alone to breed in peace." Maurice Hunt recommends introducing the cock under supervision a day or so after the nest has been introduced.

When the hen comes into breeding condition she is moved to a double breeding cabinet which is separated from the cock by a slide or wire.

Signs of Breeding Condition in Cocks

The cock bird in breeding condition is potently virile because of the high level of the male sex hormone testosterone, and is physically in the peak of condition. The courtship activities of the cock bird around the nest further stimulate the full release of the male sex hormone with the effect of improving fertility. Infertility is more likely when cocks are interrupted after pairing occurs. However, many fanciers believe the most virile cocks are stimulated more by the separation. Cocks come into breeding condition before hens and must be maintained on a high energy and nutrient rich feeding regime (see Nutrition during breeding on page 59) to preserve their vitality and potency. Cocks are much more susceptible to illness when in breeding condition because of the negative effects that heightened levels of testosterone have on the immune system.

Fighting or clear eggs are signs that the cock, hen or both birds are not completely in breeding condition.

When in breeding condition the cock will sing in an attempt to attract the hen and will become more active. Stan Nichols notes the following as a sign that his Yorkshire cocks are coming into breeding condition: "When the cock sights a hen, he pulls his feathers in until his shape is more like a long pencil rather than his normal shape of a carrot."

Essential Signs of Breeding Condition in Cocks

- **An increased frequency, volume and intensity of song.**

- **Whistling to the hens, swaying from side to side in full song.**

- **Keen interest in the hen.**

- **Looking keenly through the drinking holes for the hens.**

- **Dancing on the perch.**

- **Regurgitating food onto the perch or feeding the wire fronts.**

Falling Out of Breeding Condition

The breeding process is physically strenuous for both the hen and cock and weaker birds may fall out of breeding condition at any stage of the breeding cycle. Wild canary-type finches abort breeding when food or water supplies dry up. Similarly, exhibition canaries fall out of breeding condition very quickly when conditions for breeding become unfavourable.

Canaries may fail to come into breeding condition during prolonged dry or cold weather conditions and when humidity levels or temperatures indoors are excessively low, high or fluctuating. Canaries weakened by disease, poor genes and incorrect nutrition become sensitive to the hardships of breeding with resulting poor breeding outcomes.

Physical examination of the abdomen and vent of the hen is necessary to determine when she is in breeding condition. The hen out of breeding condition fails to develop the bloated abdominal signs of breeding condition. The photo of the bird on the right is in breeding condition and that on the left is out of breeding condition.

Signs of Loss of Breeding Condition

Cabinet Signs

- Failure to pair up.
- Failure to lay.
- Sudden death of or illness in cock or hen.

Cock Signs

- Less singing.
- Decreased activity.
- A loss of feather colour.
- Loose feathers.
- Eyes lose their sparkle.
- Accumulation of watery droppings below the perch.

Hen Signs

- A loss of feather colour.
- Loose feathers.
- The eyes lose their sparkle.
- Egg binding or egg-laying paralysis.

Causes of Loss of Breeding Condition

- Incorrect Pairing Time (e.g., pairing too early or when it is too cold).
- Physical Problem
  - Birds are too fat or too thin.
  - Cock bird too young or too old.
- Disease (especially Ornithosis, Megabacteria, E.coli or contaminated food related diseases).
- Poor Nutrition
  - Insufficient energy, protein, vitamins and minerals. Contaminated food also reduces nutritional value.
- Birds Unsettled
  - Poor photoperiod stimulation via a faulty or incorrect lighting system, cold, draughts, mites, lice or flies.

Nests & Breeding Holes

Breeders use several different types of nest pans. Plastic nest pans have a very smooth surface that is easy to clean but may result in movements of the nest. Ventilation holes can be drilled in the bottom of the nest pan in order to fix the nests and prevent movement. Stone nest pans can be very well impregnated with a water-soluble insecticide. Sometimes, self-made wooden or bamboo nest pans are used.

Breeders use several different types of nest pans.

Metal nest pans are excellent in well managed aviaries that are free from humidity and remain perfectly dry. In moist conditions where E.coli infections become a problem, they may predispose the breeding birds to Sweating Disease.

Several types of nesting materials are available: "Sharpie" consists of small white cotton fibres that are washed and cut in small pieces approximately 3 to 4cm/1-1/2 inches. "Sisal", the fibres of the plant Agave rigida, is a very fine, organic nesting material. Care is needed, as constriction of a digit may occur from entanglement in the fine fibers.

Nesting material is usually placed in a container on the inside of the cage. Here it is readily available for the hen to make her nest. Nest making is an essential part of enhancing fertility in the female.

Nowadays, canaries are mostly bred indoors. The birds are kept in pairs in breeding cages (50 x 40 x 40cm/24 x 16 x 16 inches) and require artificial lighting. In canary vernacular, each breeding section is referred to as a "hole." Each cage should have drinking water, seed mixture, soft food, cuttlefish bone, grit, nesting material, conditioning seeds and bath water that is changed on a regular basis. The most suitable substrates for the cage bottom are plain brown paper or small pieces of wood. Some breeders use wire on the cage bottom. Wire is easy to clean but can be dangerous for the youngsters sitting on the bottom of the cage because entanglement of the feet may occur.

Some breeding facilities have cages with the nest boxes inside the breeding cage while others have breeding cages with the nest boxes outside. To collect or candle the eggs and to leg band the youngsters, one may find it easier to have nest boxes hanging outside. Some breeding rooms use so-called "baby cages." The youngsters of the first clutch are put in a cage next to the parents and are separated from them by a wall containing holes 2cm/3/4 inches in diameter, or by cage wire. The parents can prepare the next round peacefully while they are still able to feed the former clutch through the holes until the babies are completely weaned. There are breeding facilities where the youngsters of the first clutch can stay together with their parents after the start of the second round. This may, however, interfere with mating and lead to poor fertility of the second clutch.

After weaning, the youngsters are put together in large cages so they can exercise and develop their flight. Individual perches are very important to prevent picking. Often an older male is placed together with the youngsters to feed those that still beg for food.

Double breeding holes are best for breeding canaries as it allows adequate room to separate the cock from the hen . It also provides room to separate the babies from the hen when she is ready to lay eggs again.

These hybrid mule youngsters have been placed into a larger cage with older birds to teach them to eat properly.

chapter 4
Breeding
Systems

Because exhibition canaries use a different breeding system, they are supplied with individual breeding boxes, known colloquially as "breeders" or "holes", in which to breed. Breeding success or failure depends largely upon the canary fancier's ability to co-ordinate the sexual responses of both the cock and hen.

There are many possible ways to breed canaries. The breeding systems described here have been collated from the experiences of some of the best fanciers in Australia.

Improved Breeding Results are More Likely to be Achieved by Knowing:

- More about the natural breeding cycle of canaries
- The notion of "breeding condition"
- The time when the hens are best introduced to the cocks
- The additional nutritional needs of canaries during the breeding season
- The best methods for managing disease

Natural versus Controlled Breeding

Canary breeding is a difficult challenge. The challenge is lessened when canaries are allowed to breed in open aviaries in a purely natural way. In cold climates and with modern day exhibition varieties it may, however, be impossible to breed in this way. Instead, intensive methods must be employed to breed the more delicate varieties. The success at breeding these varieties depends upon the skill of the fancier in manipulating nature.

More experienced fanciers use a highly "controlled" breeding system that introduces the cock to the hen at her most receptive time. Knowledge of the breeding cycle is imperative for success when using this technique. The "controlled" system follows a similar process as that used for infertility in humans where the woman is impregnated with donor sperm at the time of ovulation. It also assumes the health of the hen is perfect and that she has come into breeding condition naturally in response to her natural biological clock. This system may be refined further to include a "bull system" where the hens are introduced to the cock purely for copulation. She must then either rear the eggs herself or her eggs are "run" under other pairs.

Alternative and more "natural" approaches may also be employed. A "natural" system gives the pair time to come into breeding condition and pair up naturally in an aviary setting. They may also be allowed to choose their own mates. The birds are protected from each other until they are compatible and then allowed to make a nest and rear their young. This is a successful way to breed the more hardy varieties as long as they are healthy and well fed. The "natural" system is, however, not applicable to exhibition quality canaries where the fancier must control the breeding outcome if show quality offspring are to be produced. The selection of breeding pairs must then be based upon their genetic background and show quality.

In natural breeding all the cocks and hens are placed together in a large breeding aviary for them to select their own partners. "Natural systems" allow the birds their own time to pair up.

Natural Systems for Breeding Canaries

"Natural systems" allow the birds their own time to pair up and are more successful than those that control the mating process. This latter type "controlled system" requires careful observation to ensure the birds are introduced to the breeders (holes) at the most appropriate time and when they are in breeding condition.

"Natural systems" provide those fanciers with time restrictions the best chance of breeding success. The hen and cock should be introduced to adjacent holes of a double breeder when they exhibit signs of breeding condition in the flight. They should not be introduced prior to this time because of the likelihood of becoming too fat in the confines of the small breeders. The divider must be removed and nest and nest material introduced immediately after the hen and cock are seen feeding each other.

Controlled Systems for Breeding Canaries

For safety reasons, the birds must be housed in double breeders and separated by a screen until they are known to be compatible because hormonal based aggression is common. This system places more strain upon breeding hens than an aviary system where free flight and natural sunlight enhance breeding activities. They must receive more exact amounts and ratios of the best quality nutrition and husbandry resources to remain healthy and fit. Further difficulties should be expected because of the inherent "breeding" weakness of exhibition quality canaries. Some of the best quality birds fail or are slow to come into "breeding condition" and are often infertile. To overcome this inherent problem, a health and breeding system that mimics nature must be adopted.

Such a system also requires a flock to be in perfect health, to receive good nutrition and the use of strong virile birds as breeding stock.

Under controlled breeding systems, strong breeding hens form the backbone of any breeding Programme and must be nurtured. For studs experiencing breeding problems, it is better to breed from the strongest hens of known successful bloodlines, even at the expense of show quality, because they produce more offspring and there is a far greater chance of breeding show champions from the increased numbers of young produced. They must also be closely related to the best show birds. Such hens retain the genetic qualities of their champion brothers and sisters and are more likely to produce champions purely from a numbers game. They also pass an innate breeding strength onto the next generation. More than anything else, it is the introduction and maintenance of these quality strong hens that will lay the foundations for breeding success in the future. Although a system that uses exhibition individuals of a known successful genetic background improves the chances of breeding champions, the "trial and error" breeding of these birds still remains the only method for determining success.

The canary fancier must take over the role of nature. Pairs must be selected and all stages of the breeding cycle must be controlled and synchronised. This is an extremely difficult task for those without experience. Canaries that are housed and breed in aviaries also survive and breed according to the laws of the natural environment, namely "survival of the fittest."

However, canaries also live and die in an artificial man-made environment. Their breeding success is ultimately dependent upon the decisions, knowledge, experience and diligence of their keeper. Some families and varieties of canaries, especially Borders and Yorkshires, have an inherently poor fertility record and to achieve the best breeding results, fanciers must pay special attention to their special needs. Attention to detail is imperative to breeding success. Even then, breeding difficulties may remain with Yorkshires.

Controlled systems of breeding allow the fancier to develop a complete understanding of the needs of each particular pair. The above hen is very content in her own private breeding hole. A controlled system also allows the fancier complete control over how each bird is paired.

Step by Step Details of a Controlled Breeding System

There are many variations of the same breeding theme. The following is one possible system:

Most commonly the hen is placed into a breeder hole from the flight when she shows the first signs of breeding condition. With the "controlled system", the time the birds selected for breeding are moved from the flights and placed into the breeders has a significant effect on their breeding performance.

After moving to the breeder, the most vital hens should lay their first egg by the tenth day,

although it takes only five days from copulation to egg-laying. This five-day leeway period is necessary for the courtship activities focused around the nest to bring the breeding hens into full breeding condition. The female sex hormones released during this time are responsible for the mobilisation of calcium from the body into the bone ready for egg production.

When the canaries coming into breeding condition are left too long in the breeding "holes" without access to nesting material and nest, the release of the sex hormones is diminished, resulting in poor fertility and small clutch sizes.

For the best breeding results, it is important to move the birds into the breeders before they are in "full" breeding condition. Most fanciers introduce the hens to the breeders at the first signs of breeding condition for this very reason. Some fanciers introduce the cock into the adjacent hole of the double breeder at the same time because he is naturally in a more advanced state of breeding condition than the hen.

At this time, the hen should be closely examined for more advanced signs of breeding condition. Nest and nesting material should then be introduced to stimulate her hormonal levels further. When she accepts food from the cock, the divider is removed and mating should be successful. This "controlled" system is adopted to maximise breeding success.

In canaries, "pinging" is the best sign of impending breeding condition and the ideal time to move the hen or pairs into the double breeders.

It has been noted that the best breeding results occur at the time the hen shows advanced signs of breeding condition. This pair is obviously happy and in full breeding condition, ready to produce many healthy young.

For the best breeding results, both the hen and cock should be in breeding condition at the same time.

Bull System — Mr. Stan Nichols

Mr. Nichols is a world renowned Yorkshire Breeder from Melbourne, Australia. His system can be used equally well with all varieties of canary. He states "The very best quality champion cock bird can be used as a stud bird. Even with a successful winning strain of Yorkshires, this type of bird is not bred very often, perhaps three to five years apart. So it is important that full use be made of such a bird's superior qualities, and if he proves fertile and produces well, he should be a major influence in improving the standard of your birds for the next 3 to 4 years.

As the three to four hens, chosen for the suitability in quality and breeding background, come into breeding condition, they are placed in their individual breeding cages and the stud bird is run with each hen for approximately half an hour (no more) daily. He is then returned to his own cage. When a hen has completed her nest, the cock bird is run in with her for 10 to 15 minutes only. In fact, if the hen calls him and he treads her fully, I take him out immediately and run him in with another of the chosen hens. The stud bird is run in with each of his hens until their first egg is laid and after that he does not go back with her until she is ready to commence her second round. It does not take long for the stud bird to learn his responsibilities, and as soon as the show cage is taken to this cage, he will be down near the door ready to go to the hens. He is never allowed to be with a hen for more than half an hour at any one time, and this seems to prevent him from becoming attached to one hen and behaving badly with another."

Breeding Cages

The location and design of the breeding cages is an important component of breeding success. There are three kinds of breeding cages available - single, double and triple. The fancier must select the system that best suits his/her particular needs.

The single breeding cage is generally no smaller than 60 cm long, 40 cm high and 30 cm wide (32x16x12 inches) and consists of a single compartment. This system is not commonly used nowadays with the double cage being preferred.

The most commonly used breeding cage is the double cage which consists of a larger box cage into which a slide partition can be inserted. The slide can be either solid or wire. When the slide is inserted, the cage is divided into two breeding sections to allow the hen to start her next clutch while the babies are weaning next doorr. Following the breeding season, the slide can be removed and the cage used as a larger flight cage. The double breeder is generally no smaller than 120 cm long, 40 cm high and 30 cm wide (48x16x12 inches), although when the divider is inserted, each breeding cage is the same size as one single breeder.

The triple breeder is generally 170cm long, 45cm high and 30cm wide (72x18x12 inches). It works on the same principle as the double breeder, although it allows the fancier to insert two sliding partitions to form a cage with three breeding sections. These three sections are also used to wean and train young birds for the show season as described by Mr. Nicholes. This type of cage is particularly useful when running one cock with two hens as it allows easy separation with the sliding divider.

Notes

chapter 5
Breeding
Details

Starting Point of Breeding

February should be chosen as the starting point for breeding in Northern Hemisphere countries. Even in Australia and other Southern Hemisphere countries, where natural light enters the bird rooms, artificial lighting and heating are used to stimulate breeding activity. Throughout the world the onset of breeding condition is naturally determined by the longer days and warmth of Spring-time weather. In Victoria, Australia, with their cooler weather, the majority of fanciers pair up their birds at the earliest during the last week of August, but usually in September (the first month of Spring). In Queensland and northern New South Wales, where the weather is appreciably warmer, some fanciers may pair up much earlier. Irrespective of the location, it is ultimately the "condition" and behaviour of the birds that should determine the start of breeding.

Pairing birds too early when they are not ready to breed often results in poor breeding results (clear eggs, dead in the shell, hens leaving eggs or parent birds not feeding the young). The most vital old birds and "early-bred" young birds come into breeding condition first. Late bred young birds may be too young to breed themselves until late in the breeding season, and the "weakest" birds, either genetically or diseased, may never come into breeding condition. The more robust varieties, Glosters and hybrids may start breeding as early as July in New South Wales, whereas the weaker varieties such as Borders and Yorkshires wait until September before showing signs of breeding condition.

The extraordinarily high physical demands that breeding places on canaries require them to be in perfect physical condition prior to mating. Poor breeding results are inevitable when at the time of mating the birds are not in breeding condition. The production of robust and healthy babies requires that the parents are both physically and mentally in the best health at the time of pairing. When there is a delay or failure to pair up or to lay eggs, the fancier must first look for the reasons why the birds are not in breeding condition. Any illness or condition lowering the physical well being of the breeding bird will lower the breeding performance of that bird. In order to breed successfully, not only must the birds be in top physical form, but they must be emotionally sound as well.

Selection of Breeding Pairs

The selection of fit, disease-free breeding birds is the single most important part of breeding healthy canaries. The observant fancier easily identifies the most vigorous and fittest birds in the flight. These birds are the first to come into breeding condition. This requires that the strongest and most healthy birds are selected for breeding, the breeding starts at the appropriate time, the best nutrition is used and the birds are not carrying a disease. It is wise to handle the selected pairs to double-check their condition prior to moving them to the breeding cabinets.

Maurice Hunt spends a lot of time observing his birds prior to selecting the breeding pairs.

It is important to predetermine the sex of individual birds to ensure they are paired appropriately. In males, the caudal end of the ductus deferens forms a mass called the sinal glomerulus. During the breeding season, the sinal glomerulus pushes the cloaca walls into a "cloacal promontory." Females do not develop this projection and have a flatter vent.

Obese hens may fail to come into breeding condition and are susceptible to egg binding and sudden death while laying or incubating eggs. They must lose weight before breeding. This may be achieved by placing them in a flight with elevated perches and feeding them on the ground with a weight reduction seed mix. A suitable weight reduction mix may include up to 70% millets and 20% canary seed. Obese cocks are more likely to be sterile. Fat birds develop fat depots that can be easily felt as two oval masses on either side at the base of the crop. Fat depots also appear around the vent, resulting in normal, small droppings becoming caked around the vent.

Underweight birds are "light" in the hand, have dry feathers and are usually carrying an illness. They are usually lifeless and lack the strength of the bird in top breeding condition. They may also have a wasted pectoral mass and prominent keel bone. Take care as some healthy, strong canaries also have deep keels and are not underweight.

Underweight canaries are poor breeders. Hens have egg-laying problems and often produce abnormally shaped, clear eggs. Megabacteria, Mould Disease, E.coli enteritis and Ornithosis disease are the most common causes of "going light" and poor breeding performance in canaries.

For breeding success, it is far wiser to select a smaller, energetic hen rather than the largest, lethargic but good show quality hen. The best show birds may fail to possess the vitality and character needed to breed successfully. It has been found that there is a high rate of infertility and breeding failure among the very best show cocks and hens, although these superior birds are paired up optimistically at the beginning of each breeding season. It is wise to keep this in mind when purchasing new breeding birds.

This Red Factor Mosaic hen is in perfect breeding condition.

The best breeding outcome occurs when the canaries selected for breeding are in breeding condition at the time of mating. There are several factors that determine the right time to pair the birds, but foremost is the health and vigor associated with breeding condition. Both the cock and hen must be in 100 percent breeding condition when paired. Birds that are not full of vitality and vigour are not ready to breed and will fail to be productive breeders. They may also die suddenly at any stage of the breeding cycle.

Before pairing birds, each bird should be physically examined and "trimmed." Nails, beak and vent feathers may need trimming. Often current year stock does not need to be touched. Long nails may puncture eggs soon after they are laid.

Not every fancier trims the vent feathers. Others trim buff birds only. Because of the heavy plumage of some canary varieties (especially the type canaries), the plumage surrounding the vent area (peri-cloacal region) is cut approximately 1cm/3/8 inch above the cloaca and horizontally before breeding. This reduces the potential for excrement to cake around the vent and may increase the possibility of copulation. Loose perches should be repaired before nail trimming. Trimming of the eye feathers can also be important so that the male can see the female. Sometimes there is an overgrowth of the upper beak that may also need trimming.

The breeding cages should be disinfected before introducing birds. Protector is recommended (see page 160). In addition, prevention of infestations of red mites, northern mites and lice is achieved by spraying the nest boxes and cages with Coopex (or another pyrethrin based insecticide). Mosquito netting is necessary to reduce mosquitoes in areas that experience Canary Pox.

Breeding cages should be disinfected and sprayed for mites before introducing the birds.

Some of the best fanciers take complete control of the breeding cycle and use a "bull" system where the cocks are introduced to the hens for copulation alone, after which time the hen accepts sole responsibility for incubating and rearing the young. This system reaps the reward of producing more young of show quality standard but also places enormous strain upon the breeding hen. She must receive the exact amount and quality of nutritional and husbandry

resources to remain healthy and fit. Other fanciers introduce the breeding pairs as they show signs of breeding activity allowing them to pair up and breed in a more natural manner. Difficulties remain, however, with either system because of the inherent "breeding" weakness of some varieties of exhibition quality canaries. Many of the best quality birds fail or are slow to come into "breeding condition" and are often infertile. To overcome the breeding weaknesses of canaries, a breeding system that mimics nature must be adopted.

Disease Resistant Birds

The most vital birds are invariably the first to come into breeding condition and are the most fertile. They are also the healthiest birds and consistently resistant against diseases such as Ornithosis (Chlamydophilla), Black Spot (Circovirus, Atoxoplasmosis) and Canker (Trichomoniasis). These birds should be the first to be chosen as breeding stock just as they would be first to breed in nature. The offspring from these pairs should also be used as future breeders. The most experienced and successful exhibitors agree that the selection of breeding pairs must combine quality and vitality.

Selection System — Mr. Stan Nichols

1. The first consideration must be given to the pair of birds that produced the outstanding exhibits of the current season. These proven pairs are the backbone of the stock.

2. The cock, buff or yellow, young or old, that has proven his value by siring champion youngsters, particularly major award winners from different hens, should be given the first choice of two or three hens.

3. A proven stock cock rates very importantly. His main purpose is to maintain size and substance of future stock. Hens that have type, elegance and feather are selected for him.

4. Each bird is thoroughly checked to ascertain its health and vigour. If there is any doubt

about it being 100 percent fit, it is put aside. To breed with a bird having a respiratory ailment such as asthma (due to Mycoplasma or Ornithosis) means taking a risk of weakening the strain as a whole.

This is a proven stock cock that Stan Nicholes rates very highly. His main purpose is to maintain size and substance

Preparations for Breeding — Mr. Stan Nichols

The preparations for breeding Programme start after the shortest day of the year. The check list below starts early in August (Southern Hemisphere) for Yorkshires and Borders.

1. Transfer the hens from the indoor flight into double breeding units.

2. Trim the feathers around the vent with scissors. Cut any overgrown toenails and beaks.

3. Treat hens for mites and lice. Administer S76 in the drinking water for two consecutive days, spray with Avian Liquidator or apply dusting powder.

4. Artificial heating: Start artificial heating when fluctuations in temperature may create breeding problems. This occurs quite often in August and early September (Southern Hemisphere) when daytime temperatures drop from 22°C/72°F down to 4°C/39°F overnight. Set the temperature thermostati-

cally at 16 degrees Celsius/61 degrees Farenheit. Fluctuations in and temperatures below 10°C/50°F in the bird room are a common cause of early season breeding failures.

5. Artificial Lighting: Start artificial lighting from the middle of August with an automatic dimmer. Commence with an extra half-hour in the morning and at night, then increase this time by half an hour each fort-night until there is a total of 12-13 hours of light each day. The dimmer takes half an hour to fade out, giving the feeding hens plenty of warning to find their roosting place. Ensure there is back up power in case of an energy blackout.

6. The treatment and change in environment from the flight to the breeding units often sets the hens back a little. Cock fertility may also be affected. They may take two weeks before they show signs of coming into breeding condition. The hens in the flight should be monitored carefully as they too may come into "breeding condition." Not all hens will come into breeding condition simultaneously. The abdomen of hens that fail to come into breeding condition is flat with a wrinkled and leathery skin. Such hens may lay eggs but not fully incubate them (leave the nest).

7. Introduce the pair to sprouted seeds and supplements according to Dr. Rob Marshall's Spring Breeding Programme.

Pairing Process

The onset of breeding condition in the hens determines the ideal time to start pairing the birds, and it is the hens themselves who will determine this process. Fanciers use slightly different techniques of pairing.

The male is placed into the female's cage when the birds are ready for pairing. In a classic situation, one male and one female are kept together for the whole breeding season and allowed to rear the youngsters together. Alternatively, one high-quality cock may be used to pair with several females. After copulation, the male is separated, and each female rears her youngsters alone.

Fertile sperm may be stored in the females' sperm glands (tubular glands within the oviductal wall located at the uterovaginal junction) and may fertilise eggs for approximately 8 to 10 days. The regulation of sexual behaviour is altered through the effects of social interactions, notably the song of other male birds. Sexual competition of this kind can exert powerful effects on the reproductive success and overall well-being of the individual.

Mr. Maurice Hunt prefers to wait until the hen is nest making before introducing the cock. Mr. Stan Nichols looks closely at the vent and abdomen before introducing the hen to the breeding cabinet. The principle aim is to have the hen in full breeding condition (ovulating) when the cock is presented to her. Mr. Stan Nichols' methods of pairing his birds is outlined below.

Method of Pairing — Mr. Stan Nichols

Mr. Nichols introduces the cock to the breeding cage after the hen has been placed there. The breeding cage should be divided with a slide that has 1" diameter holes approximately 3" from the

The hen is in full breeding condition and ready for the cock when she consistently carries nesting material placed in the wire front This is the best time to introduce the nesting pan and a sufficient supply of material for her to start building her nest. The divider is removed to allow the cock to be introduced to the hen for mating.

floor. This prevents any damage to the hen. Within a day or two they should become friendly and the cock will feed the hen through the holes in the slide. The slide can be safely removed when the hen consistently carries nesting material placed in the wire front. This signals the time to introduce the nesting pan and a sufficient supply of material for her to start building her nest because she is now in full breeding condition and ready for the cock.

Egg Care and Synchronised Hatching

During the egg-laying period, eggs are collected and replaced with artificial eggs while the female continues to lay her clutch. As they are laid they are removed. They are kept in a cool place (15°C-20°C/59°F-68° F. in numbered boxes in a bed of seed and replaced in the nest after the fourth egg has been laid. Any extra eggs are not removed. This is done to achieve a uniform growth of the youngsters. The average clutch size of type canaries is 4 eggs. Colour canaries often have a clutch of 4 to 7 eggs.

Mr. Sant uses this type of artificial egg.

The obvious advantage of removing eggs as they are laid and replacing them when all eggs have been laid is that the youngsters all hatch out on the same day. The standard process for "synchronised hatching" is as follows.

Each egg is removed immediately after it is laid and replaced in the nest with a dummy egg. The eggs should be placed in a small drawer, lined on the bottom with sawdust for safety and turned over each day as they would be in the nest.

On the fourth day, the eggs are returned to the nest, removing the dummies. This protects the

In order to synchronise hatching, most fanciers move the eggs into specially made drawers lined with sawdust as illustrated above. The sections are labeled according to the nest from which they were taken.

eggs from hens that do not sit (incubate). They may be kept for up to eight days and placed under a feeder hen if necessary. The eggs are candled after the hen has been sitting for five to six days. Eggs that remain clear after a further three days are considered infertile. (Eggs that have died may be identified by egg post-mortem. See page 107). If all eggs are infertile, the nest should be removed and the hen paired up again when she starts carrying nesting material.

Stan Nichols describes his hatching process as follows: "Eggs are due to hatch on the 13th day after being set, but sometimes a hen does not sit as tightly as she should, particularly in the first few days and the eggs may not hatch until the 14th and 15th day. On the morning of the 13th day, a bath is provided and this, as well as being refreshing for the hen, provides essential moisture for the nest and eggs. If the hen does not bathe, a fine spray of water should be applied over the nest and eggs. Also on the morning of the 13th day, the eggs should be carefully placed in a cup of warm water. This should activate the youngster

and cause the egg to bob up and down. If the egg does not move, the youngster is probably dead in the shell. When this happens, repeat the procedure on the 15th day and still no result, the nest is removed and replaced when the hen is again carrying the nesting material."

Running Eggs

It is advisable to have three to four pairs of feeders when breeding the larger type of canaries such as Yorkshires, Norwich and Crests. Reds, Lizards, Glosters and common canaries make the best foster parents as they are smaller, more vital and energetic in their feeding duties. Select the best feeders each year and raise a few of their young for future use.

Feeders are used to rear the young of the very best breeding pairs. This technique increases the likelihood of breeding champions. By using feeders, four rather than three rounds can be produced from the very best pairs without them being burdened. The quality breeding pair is allowed to raise the first and third clutch of eggs with the second and fourth rounds being fostered. The eggs are taken away and put under feeders. The hen must be allowed to sit on dummy eggs for seven days after the laying of the last egg before the nest and eggs are removed, allowing her time to recuperate. Within a week she will be nesting again. This system allows the champion Yorkshire hen to lay four rounds of eggs but restrict the heavy feeding responsibilities to two rounds only.

Canaries will foster the eggs of other canary varieties. Here, Yorkshire eggs have been placed under Glosters.

Notes

chapter 6
Seasonal **Health Programmes**

A plan is needed in order to be successful in any walk of life. Canary breeding is no different and the health programmes outlined in this chapter should provide the diligent fancier with a reliable and simple method for keeping canaries healthy and productive. The Seasonal Programmes provide support for canaries at critical physiological stages.

Seasonal Health Programmes

Introduction

The programmes are divided into seasons that follow the natural biological cycles of canaries.

The focus of the programmes is to stimulate a strong natural resistance by providing the correct nutritional balance and is used to protect the health of the flock by using preventative medicines in such a way that enhances vitality and breeding performance. For the best results, the seasonal health programmes are usually initiated in autumn in preparation for breeding, but they may be started at any time of the year.

Each programme is similar but varies in the amount and frequency of nutritional supplements, soft food and sprouted seed provided. Ongoing routine disease prevention is similar throughout most of the different programmes. Special disease prevention treatments may also be required in aviaries with special or ongoing problems.

At first, it is best to apply the General Health Programme described on page 57 to all birds. Within a short period of time (2-3 weeks) on the programme, you will notice an improved vitality and feather quality in the birds. This programme is then simply adjusted to cater to the needs of birds according to age and time of

year as outlined in each seasonal programme. Recipes for successful soft foods and sprouted seeds, together with the frequency and amount they should be fed, are described under each programme. For example, soft foods and sprouted seed are not provided to hens after they start incubating their eggs, although prior to laying eggs they must be fed in large amounts twice each day.

The Seasonal Health Programmes rely upon an understanding of the natural breeding cycles and exhibition routines of canaries. Additional programmes are described to enhance fertility (Autumn or Winter Cleansing Programme), protect young bird health (Spring Young Bird

Mr Sant monitors each bird as part of his daily rounds. Attention to detail and providing the birds with their exact needs is an essential part of continuing good health and breeding success for canaries.

Programme) and to accelerate the moult (Summer Moult Programme). The ultimate aim of these programmes is to produce a naturally resistant family of birds capable of breeding robust young that also consistently remain healthy.

The Autumn or Winter Cleansing Programme is recommended for all canary breeders because of the impact Ornithosis has on breeding outcomes and the inherent weakness of canaries to this disease. Lice, mite, coccidiosis and worming prevention should be an ongoing process for all canaries. Wet and cold weather programmes must be introduced to canaries kept under natural conditions. Additional nutrition must also be provided to those housed indoors under artificial lighting and heating conditions.

The Disease Programmes are discussed in the next chapter. They detail Emergency First Aid procedures and treatment strategies. Because of their high genetic value, individual treatment is sometimes as important as the protection of the entire flock. Sick individuals should be treated in isolation and water cleansers administered to the rest of the flock while a diagnosis is confirmed. Antibiotic treatment is often required for the birds affected through contact with others, but only after diagnosis.

In terms of feeding canaries, the choice between using a purely natural feeding system and a scientifically based one depends upon the time fanciers have to spend with their birds, as both produce comparable breeding results. The natural system provides breeding birds with the benefits of fresh produce. It does, however, take considerably more effort and time to maintain than through the use of the nutritional supplements described in this book. A natural system is potentially more hazardous to the health of young canaries because of an increased chance of contamination in fresh produce.

Stan Nichols notes the difficulties in providing a balanced diet to canaries: "Of course, wild seeded grasses and thistles etc are excellent. However, it is important that they have not been contaminated in any way. For this reason, I grow my own green food in a small vegetable garden, which is well fenced against dogs and other pests. Insecticides are never used in my garden. I feed these greens most of the year and the birds eat them readily. I have found, when introducing a green food they

have not had for many months, in most cases they pick at it but seem to prefer their regular greens."

The General Health Programme

The General Health Programme forms the basis of all of Dr. Marshall's health programs. This programme introduces the fancier to the methods for administering his health products.

Spring Programmes

The Breeding Programme

The Spring Breeding Programme provides the nutrients required for breeding and stimulates a strong, naturally occurring and enduring level of health in breeding pairs. Disease prevention recommendations are also included in this programme.

The Young Bird Programme

The Spring Young Bird Programme has been designed to protect susceptible young birds from illness during weaning, adolescence and the juvenile moult. This programme also outlines the special nutritional needs of young canaries from weaning up until the start of their first moult. Disease prevention programmes play a vital part of this programme as canaries within this age group are particularly vulnerable to illness.

Summer Programmes

The Moult Programme

The Summer Moult Programme has been designed to accelerate the moult in canaries of all ages and simultaneously to protect the most susceptible (juveniles and breeder hens) from illness.

The Disease Cleansing Programme

The Summer Disease Cleansing Programme should be introduced to young birds that respond favourably to a Doxycycline/Megamix Treatment Trial or show signs of Ornithosis towards the end of the moult. The first week in February (in the Southern Hemisphere) and August (in the Northern Hemisphere) is the best time to start the trial, and thereafter the treatment for Ornithosis in young birds.

Autumn Programmes

The Show Programme

The Autumn Show Programme should immediately follow the moult. It marks the beginning of the show season and is an ideal time to start a fitness programme. It is used to prepare the birds for exhibition success.

Winter Programmes

The Disease Cleansing Programme

The Winter Disease Cleansing Programme should be introduced to flocks that have previously experienced infertility and poor breeding results. Autumn is the ideal time to implement this programme as flights are often overcrowded with young birds. It uses medicines to identify the health status of the flock and to clean the flock of diseases that affect fertility and future breeding performance.

The Mid-Season Fitness Programme

This programme keeps birds fit and prevents laziness in preparation for breeding. It should continue until the start of the winter Pre-Breeding Programme.

The Pre-Breeding Programme

The Winter Pre-Breeding Programme is a conditioning programme and has been designed to improve breeding outcomes by ensuring the birds are in their best possible condition by the start of the breeding season. This programme promotes fitness and strength but also prevents the birds from becoming fat. It is used to prepare productive flocks for the hardships of breeding and must begin after the shortest day of the year or 10 weeks prior to the intended start of breeding. Under special circumstances a cleansing programme may be necessary during winter.

The General Health Programme

The General Health Programme forms the basis of all programmes and introduces the fancier to the method and frequency options for using Dr. Rob Marshall's health products.

Day of Week	Water Supplements*	Food Supplements**	Hygiene Instructions	Additional Advice
Friday	KD[1]	Turbobooster E-Powder, F-Vite[4]	Use KD[2] to clean the soaking seed, seed sieve and containers.	Dufoplus, Ioford and Turbobooster are often added to the soft food or sprouted seed. F-Vite and E-Powder are provided in finger drawers or sprinkled on top of the sprouted seed. NV powder may also be sprinkled on top of the sprouted seed. See page 64 for various soft food and sprouted seed recipes.
Saturday	Dufoplus & Ioford[3]	Turbobooster E-Powder, F-Vite[4]		
Sunday	Dufoplus & Ioford[3]	Turbobooster E-Powder, F-Vite[4]		
Monday	Fresh Water	Fresh Seed		
Tuesday	Fresh Water	Fresh Seed		
Wednesday	Fresh Water	Fresh Seed		
Thursday	Fresh Water	Fresh Seed		

The dosages and instructions described here are recommended for the pet canary health programmes. Some dosages appearing on the product labels may vary slightly. These are to be used for birds with illness or nutritional deficiencies.

[1] KD Water Cleanser is prepared by adding 1gm (1/4 teaspoon measure) into one litre (reverse side of standard US 4 cup measuring cup) of water. KD cleanses the bowel of harmful food and water related germs, promoting a stronger natural health in the flock. For further information on KD usage please refer to the article written by Mr. Swaveley, champion border breeder. He uses it each day for his breeding and young birds. KD can be used together with colour additives such as **canthaxanthadine**.

[2] KD soaked seed cleaner. 4gms (1 level teaspoon) into one litre of water is used for sprouting seed hygiene. (See page 63) for further details).

[3] Dufoplus (2.5ml) and Ioford (5ml) are mixed together into one litre of drinking water and safely left for two days, as they are sugar free. They provide the vitamins and trace elements necessary for good health, fertility and quality eggs. The signs of improved health are visible by the increased noise and activity within the bird room. An increased intensity of plumage colour, even in colour fed birds, should be noticed within three weeks of using the products mentioned in this programme. Dufoplus and Ioford may also be added to sprouted seed or into the soft food mix. This system frees up the water for KD.

[4] 3 mls (30 drops) of Turbobooster is mixed thoroughly into 500 grams of dry seed, sprouted seed or soft food mix. Choose the system that suits you best. Two level teaspoons (10 grams) of E-Powder is then added to the above mix. F-Vite is best provided in finger drawers or open dishes. The Turbobooster provides canaries with the fatty acids, protein and minerals necessary for good health, a fast moult, excellent fertility and superior breeding results.

* Turbobooster, E-Powder and F-Vite may be fed daily during many programmes.
**Many fanciers use KD for three consecutive days.

Spring Breeding Programme

Day of Week	Water Supplements	Food Supplements*	Disease Control
Monday	Fresh Water	Turbobooster[3] E Powder[4], F-Vite[5]	**Mites / Lice** — S76 in drinking water for one day each month. Nest treatment (Coopex) may also be necessary.
Tuesday	Fresh Water	Turbobooster[3] E Powder[4], F-Vite[5]	
Wednesday	Fresh Water	Turbobooster[3] E Powder[4], F-Vite[5]	**Black Spot (Atoxoplasmosis)** — Carlox for three days while hens are sitting on eggs.
Thursday	Fresh Water	Turbobooster[3] E Powder[4], F-Vite[5]	**Black Spot (Circovirus) & Nestling Diarrhea** — KD in drinking water for three consecutive days each week.
Friday	KD	Turbobooster[3] E Powder[4], F-Vite[5]	**Wet Weather Enteritis** — Megamix mixed with Ioford for two days each week.
Saturday	Dufoplus[1] / Ioford[2]	Turbobooster[3] E Powder[4], F-Vite[5]	**Bathing** — Weekly KD bath during warm weather.
Sunday	Dufoplus[1] / Ioford[2]	Turbobooster[3] E Powder[4], F-Vite[5]	

[1,2]Dufoplus (1ml/1/4 tsp.)and Ioford (2.5ml/1/2 teaspoon) are mixed together into 500ml of drinking water and safely left for two days, as they are sugar free. They provide the vitamins and trace elements necessary for good health and vitality. Dufoplus and Ioford may also be added to a soft food/sprouted seed recipe for two days each week.

[3] The Turbobooster provides canaries with the fatty acids, protein and minerals necessary for good health and excellent fertility and breeding results. Glossy strong feathers, strong babies and increased vitality are the health changes you will notice. Provide once a day in a soft food/sprouted seed recipe.

[4] E-Powder is an energy supplement that may be added to every meal of soft food, sprouted or tonic seed*. It may also be made available in finger drawers.

[5] F-Vite should be made available in a finger draw continuously. F-Vite may also be added to tonic seed.

*1/2 cup E-Powder & 1/2 cup F-Vite mixed through 2Kg/4.5 lb. tonic seed.

Notes: The Spring Breeding Programme should be introduced after hens are placed in their breeding holes. The success of the breeding programme relies upon the selection of vital individuals as breeders, providing the best possible nutrition and being particularly fussy about hygiene.

The most vital birds are invariably the first to pair up, the most fertile and the best parents. These traits are hereditary and the offspring of these birds should be retained as future breeders. There is also a strong link between vitality and natural resistance against disease. A strong and naturally resistant flock will be achieved in a much shorter time when youngsters from strong pairs are selected as future breeding stock. The young born to weaker pairs and the weaker pairs themselves should be culled from the flock.

Tonics seed containing niger, rape and other delicious seeds help stimulate the canaries into breeding condition. E-Powder and F-Vite can be mixed into the tonic seed.

The fragile and delicate nature of exhibition canaries necessitates a planned approach to their breeding season. Knowledge of breeding behaviour and nutritional requirements during the breeding cycle is essential for breeding success.

To overcome the breeding weaknesses of canaries, a breeding system that provides the best resources for successful breeding outcomes must be adopted. The Spring Breeding Programme is one such breeding system that has been designed to stimulate a strong, natural occurring and enduring level of health in breeding pairs, especially the hens, to help them rear strong robust young without tiring. This programme should improve breeding performance.

Essentials for a Successful Breeding Season

Protein and Energy

Soft foods, sprouted seed, Turbobooster and C-Powder must be added to the flock's diet. The frequency and amount fed varies according to the stage of the breeding cycle.

Good Hygiene

Stan Nichols notes "From the day that the young-sters hatch, the soft food and sprouted seed are changed three times a day. Small amounts should be offered up to three times a day to avoid the possibility of spoiling."

Clean Drinking Water

KD should be added to the drinking water for two or more days each week to clean the water and prevent disease originating from contaminated foodstuff.

Vitamins and Trace Elements

Dufoplus and Ioford should be added to the drinking water, soft food or sprouted seed for two days each week. The best results may be seen when the vitamins are given the day after KD.

Minerals

F-Vite mineral powder must be made available at all times

Disease Prevention

Mites/Lice Ongoing Prevention:

Add S76 to the drinking water for one day each month. Nest treatment (Coopex or Avian Liquidator) may also be necessary.

Black Spot (Atoxoplasmosis) Prevention:

Add Carlox to the drinking water for three con-secutive days while hens are sitting on eggs.

Black Spot (Circovirus) Prevention:

Add KD Powder to the drinking water for three consecutive days each week.

Nutrition for Breeding

Nutritional supplements must be given to canaries because their enclosed environment cannot pro-

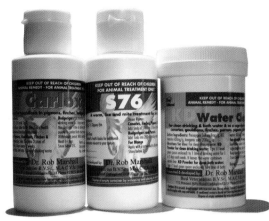

KD Powder, S76® and Carlox® are the three products that are used as part of an ongoing disease prevention programme.

vide them with the variety of nutrients required for breeding success. Seeds and seeding grasses on their own do not provide the nutritional diver-sity required for their sustained breeding activity.

In addition to the general requirements for good nutrition during breeding as set out in Chapter One, it is important to stress the added energy necessary for successful breeding. Breeding hen birds use much more energy than non-breeding birds and above all, it is the energy content of the food that determines breeding success or failure. More than anything else, a successful breeding season requires a constant supply of energy. The popular process of feeding sprouted seed to canaries provides their babies with an instant source of energy. This concentrated form of ener-gy is a good means of achieving breeding suc-cess. However, there are real potential dangers associated with sprouted seed as a source of ener-gy and strict soaking protocols must be followed. Additional sources of protein and energy should be provided to help canaries cope with the efforts of breeding.

Over the years, many methods and recipes have been devised to provide canaries with a good diet for breeding but with varying degrees of success. Although we are now able to provide a better, more precise level of nutrition to breeding birds, gaps in our knowledge of good bird nutrition remain. Very high quality nutritional supplements are available that may be added to the drinking water, soft food mix or as a dry edible powder, ensuring the best nutritional balance is met for

F-Vite, Ioford, Dufoplus, Turbobooster and E-Powder are examples of Dr Rob Marshall's high quality nutritional supplements. These products form a basis for many of his health programmes for canaries. They may be added to the drinking water, sprouted seed or soft food mix.

higher levels of oil in their diet than other birds. Sprouted rape is an excellent choice as it is high in protein and favoured by many fanciers. Canaries relish this oil-based seed when feeding their young.

Energy Requirements

Additional sources of protein and energy must be provided to breeding canaries. Historically, egg food have provided the extra protein but the importance of additional energy during breeding has not previously been a topic of great interest.

Energy is a most necessary ingredient for breeding success because of the extremely high metabolic rate and small size of canaries. Energy must be provided to help canaries raise their young. Carbohydrates, fats and protein are all sources of energy. Carbohydrates provide an instant source of energy, fats a concentrated form of energy and protein provides energy when all else fails. Soaked seeds contribute a reliable source of energy. Additional sources of energy in the form of food supplements (e.g., Turbobooster, E-Powder) or soft foods offer a convenient method for topping up the energy needs during the breeding season.

Breeding canaries burn up nine times as much energy as a non-breeding bird. Young and ill bird need up to three times the energy of a non-breeding adult to remain healthy. Above all else, a constant supply of energy is needed for good breeding results.

Although the popular process of feeding soaked seed provides chicks with an instant source of energy, there are potential dangers associated with it. Sunflower, hulled oats and corn are recommended when looking to improve energy levels during the breeding season.

Traditionally, seeds rich in carbohydrate (millets, hulled oats and corn) have been used to provide the extra energy required during the breeding season. Additional sources of energy (Polenta, E-Powder, Turbobooster) are now available to help with rearing of young.

those unwilling, unable or without time to provide fresh grasses and foodstuffs each day.

Knowledge of the nutritional requirements of canaries is the foundation for improving breeding results because breeding canaries need a precise level of nutrition. Additional energy, vitamins, minerals and trace elements are known to benefit the breeding performance and health of canaries. Seeds and seeding grasses on their own are not enough for sustained breeding activity in canaries and additional foodstuffs must be provided. Soft foods, soaked seed and nutritional supplements provide the additional nutrition required for canaries to remain healthy and productive. The quantity and frequency to which they are added to the diet varies from one season to the next. The nutritional requirements of hybrid canaries are less exact and they are far easier to manage than the refined exhibition quality canaries. Greater amounts of protein, vitamins, minerals and energy must be provided in order for these birds to achieve comparable breeding results.

Energy for Breeding

The importance of providing additional energy during breeding cannot be overstated. Energy must be provided so that canaries can raise their young. For breeding success, additional sources of energy in the form of sprouted seeds, soft foods, Turbobooster and E-Powder should be made available. Fats offer the most efficient conversion to energy and canaries can tolerate much

Corn on the cob is highly recommended for breeding canaries. Corn on the cob given each day is a favourite. Take care with the selection of the cob as it is susceptible to mould contamination when wrapped in plastic. Corn forms a rich supply of the important breeding amino acid methionine and is very high in energy. Cans of sweet corn or Polenta provide good alternatives when fresh corn is out of season.

Fats offer the most efficient conversion to energy and oil seeds (e.g., sunflower, rape, niger, maw and lettuce seeds) and are a rich source of energy. These seeds are also old sprouting favourites but must be restricted in quantity. Canaries can, however, tolerate excessively high levels of oil seeds in their diet. Some of the oil seeds, notably rape and sunflower, are susceptible to mould toxins that may poison baby canaries and weaken adult birds. "Clean" oil seeds are also rich in protein and make an excellent choice for soaking or sprouting.

E-Powder is an excellent source of energy that can be included into a soft food mix.

Maurice Hunt's polenta based high energy soft food mix (see recipe page 64, 159).

Sources of Energy

- Soaked seed (Hulled oats/Sunflower/Rape)
- Corn kernels or Polenta
- E-Powder
- Turbobooster

Protein for Breeding

In nature, insects provide the additional protein requirement during the breeding season. Protein can be provided in the form of an egg or soft food mix. Traditionally, soft foods were called egg food. Initially, they consisted of a crushed boiled egg mixed with bread or biscuit crumbs, and were given to the birds during the breeding season as an additional source of protein. Over time, additional protein sources became readily available (Farex protein cereal, powdered eggs, wheatgerm and so on) and were added to the egg food. Observant fanciers changed the soft food recipe further by adding more bread or carbohydrate products based on their experiences of feeding parents leaving some of the egg food uneaten in preference for the biscuit or bread crumbs. Others combined the soft food with soaked seed producing further improvements in breeding outcomes. Lysine and methionine, are especially important proteins for breeding canaries. Turbobooster and sprouted seeds should be added to the diet of canaries because they contain these important "breeding amino acids."

Soft Foods, Sprouted Seed, Energy Protein for Breeding

From a nutritional point of view the soft food/sprouted seed recipes must contain both protein and carbohydrate for the feeding parents. The addition of protein and energy supplements (Turbobooster and E-Powder), vitamins (Dufoplus), minerals (F-Vite) and trace elements (Ioford) to these recipes completes the nutritional needs of canaries. Soft foods and sprouted seed are considered a treat for all canary varieties and provide a perfect vehicle to which these nutritional supplements may be added. These are simply mixed into the soft food or sprouted seed immediately prior to feeding time. They are usually devoured within a matter of minutes, providing feeding parents with a most hygienic and convenient form of soft food. Sprouted seed may also be used as a source of protein for breeding birds but its most important role is as an energy source. It provides instant energy during every part of the breeding cycle (courtship, nest making, egg laying, incubating and feeding), but unfortunately, is often the cause of breeding failure when contaminated with mould or bacteria.

Frequency of Soft Food/Sprouted Seed/Supplements During Breeding Programme

The supply of soft foods/seed and nutritional supplements must be adjusted throughout the different phases of the breeding cycle to ensure the nutritional needs of each phase of the breeding cycle are properly catered to.

The amount and frequency of soft food and sprouted seed that is provided to canaries varies throughout the breeding season and must be adjusted according to the birds' requirements. Vitamins (Dufoplus) should be restricted to two meals a week, trace elements (Ioford) to three times a week and protein supplements (Turbobooster) to once a day. Energy supplements (e.g., E-Powder) may be mixed with every meal.

Soaked seed is highly beneficial to breeding canaries, although special attention to hygiene during the soaking process is vital in ensuring the food remains clean and free of contamination. The frequency to which soaked seed is fed varies according to the time of year.

Maurice Hunt places the hens into the holes as they come into breeding condition. Here they are further stimulated by nest making activity and courtship activities by a cock into the best possible condition to produce eggs. At this time the hen should be receiving a daily portion of soft food/soaked seeds recipe (a full description of this recipe can be found on page 64 and 159) that has been fortified with additional calcium (Hi-Cal). This should continue until she has laid her last egg and started to incubate her clutch. When sitting on eggs, hens need to receive less soft food/sprouted seed in order to avoid obesity. The

soft food/soaked seeds/supplements recipe should be provided every second, rather than every day. No additional calcium is required until she starts preparing her second round of eggs.

After the young have hatched it becomes necessary to increase the number of times soft foods and soaked seeds are provided. The frequency and quantity of the recipe needs to be increased to 2-3 times a day, depending on the size of chicks and how quickly the food is eaten.

Soft Food/Soaked Seed Hygiene for Breeding

Stan Nicholes emphasizes the importance of attention to detail and hygiene when preparing food during the breeding season. "In all cages where parents are rearing young, a piece of newspaper is placed over half the cage floor, in the opposite side from the nest. Each morning, three clean vessels - the first containing 2 tablespoons of sprouted seed, the second, 1 tablespoon of egg food and the third, a heaped teaspoon of very finely ground seeds (sprouting seed mixture) are placed on the paper, avoiding the area directly under the perch. It is of utmost importance to change the sprouted seed and egg food at least three times a day, particularly in hot weather. Each morning, the vessels are removed and disinfected. The soiled paper is removed and replaced. All food remnants must be removed form the cage floor.

Fresh green food is secured by a clothes peg in an old style, glass cream bottle of fresh water, with another peg secured across the top of the bottle to prevent a bird from getting its head into the water. Several fanciers who have not taken the precaution of using the second peg have reported a bird drowning, possibly trying to bathe in the water. The bottle of greens is placed close to a perch and provides the birds with fresh appetizing green food for the whole day, as well as assisting with humidity. Of course, wild seeded grasses and thistles, etc., are excellent. However, it is important that they have not been contaminated in any way."

Stan continues with his thoughts on the benefits and potential dangers of soaked seed. "Sprouted/soaked seed provide a major food source when the chicks are in the nest and when

Fresh green food is provided in the form of a couple of leaves of chicory (catalonga), Chinese cabbage (wong bok) and a small young rape leaf.

The birds relish in perfectly clean and fresh sprouted seed such as this. From the day that the youngsters hatch, the soft food and sprouted seed should be changed three times a day.

ing process is a very physically demanding process for the parents and the instant energy provided by the sprouted seed allows them to rear clutches without tiring.

However, there are real potential dangers associated with sprouted seed as a source of energy and strict soaking protocols should be followed. Sudden deaths of nestlings with full crops are most often the result of contaminated seed being fed to their parents.

Strict hygiene during the sprouting process must be followed to prevent the potentially harmful effects of fungus and bacteria that often contaminate the seeds used for sprouting. With current scientific knowledge, these recipes can now be simplified by using nutritional supplements.

conditioning stock prior to the breeding season. The sprouting mix is soaked for a few hours, and then transferred to a special sprouting frame. This is a wooden rack containing five trays with wire mesh bases. A piece of clean damp toweling is placed on the tray, then the soaked seed, containing a wide selection of seeds suitable for sprouting, are sprinkled onto the toweling. The seed is covered with another piece of towel and kept moist by spraying as required. A new tray is started each day. Five trays are in use at all times and the towels are washed after every use. Excess sprouted seed can be placed in a plastic bag and stored in the refrigerator.

To avoid the chance of spoilage, small amounts are provided at any one time. The seeds and soft food are placed in small white china dishes and the greens in the half-pint milk bottle. All are placed on newspaper cut to fit the size of the cage floor, in the opposite half of the breeding cage where the nests are. The paper should be changed at least once a day. Good hygiene is a must. Plain canary seed can be placed in hoppers and a variety of seeds crushed in a coffee grinder can be fed via finger drawers."

When seed is soaked in warm water the germinating process transforms the starch inside the seeds into a sweet form of immediate energy. The warmth and moisture changes the sour taste of the starch into the sweet taste of a simple sugar that the breeding birds love so much. Both the growing babies and parents thrive because the increased energy requirements (nine times higher during breeding) are rapidly satisfied. The feed-

The sprouted seed preparation technique described below has been adapted from that of Mr Don Swaveley, champion Border fancier. The seed selected for soaking must be pre-tested for cleanliness by culture testing or sprouting on cotton wool. Seed that bubbles excessively, smells bad or grows fungus must be rejected. For safety, no more than three seed types — preferably sunflower, rape and wheat — should be selected for sprouting.

Soaked Seed Technique

The seed selected for soaking must be pre-tested for cleanliness.

1. Soak the seed mix in a 4 litre/1 gallon glass jar overnight.

   Add 1 teaspoon of KD powder to the water in the container.

2. Wash the seed mix thoroughly using a 25 cm (10 inch) sieve and tap water, then rinse the seeds with KD water. Allow the sieved seed to drain thoroughly before placing them in an oven or on a warm surface for 24 hours.

3. Next morning wash the seeds with KD water again.

4. Wash the seeds again in the evening with KD. Make sure they are well drained. Repeat morning

Soaked seed must be left to drain before placing onto a warm surface for 24 hours.

Soaked seed is allowed to germinate in a warm position. Note Mr Dowling's custom made lid with mesh that allows easy washing and drainage.

and night until seed shoots appear or the seeds are opening wide enough for birds to pull sprouts out. The amount of time to germinate varies upon the air temperature. Make sure the soaked seeds are not too wet or too dry.

5. Seeds should have a short sprout only. Turbobooster, Dufoplus, IofordNF (or NV powder) and E-Powder can also be mixed with the sprouted seed at this time. Soft food may also be mixed into the soaked seed.

6. Sprouting equipment must be thoroughly sterilised between each use.

7. Reject seed that smells "off" or develops a mould at any stage.

Recipes

Dr. Rob's Sprouted Seed Recipe

Seed Mix

Supplements

Dufoplus[1], Ioford[2], Turbobooster[3], Hi-Cal[6]
E-powder[4] & F-vite[5] should be available in finger drawers at all times.

Preparation

After the final rinse, add the following to each kilogram of soaked seed, mixing thoroughly:

Dufoplus[1] . . . . .2.5ml (1/2 teaspoon)

Sprouted seed ready to add food supplements.

Ioford[2] . . . . .5ml (1 teaspoon)
Turbobooster[3] . . . . .5 ml (1 teaspoon)
E-powder[4] . . . . .10 gram (2 teaspoon)
Hi-cal[6] . . . . .20 mls (4 teaspoons)

Hygiene

Uneaten remnants must be removed within 6 hours.

Maurice Hunt's Soft Food Recipe

Ingredients

Bread crumbs . . . . .2 Kg
Stabilised wheat germ .2Kg
Semolina 250gms
Polenta 150gms
Heinz high protein cereal 100gms
Ground rice 100gms
Maw seed (optional) (250grams)

Preparation

To each cup (250 gram) add:

One hard boiled egg, 1 teaspoon E-Powder, 1 ml Turbobooster, 1 teaspoon NV powder and 30ml Canthaxanthadine (Concentratation: 1 tablespoon/Litre)

Hygiene

Uneaten remnants must be removed within 6 hours.

[1] Dufoplus should be added to one meal for two days each week.

[2] Ioford should be added to one meal for two days each week.

[3] Turbobooster should be added to one meal each day.

[4] E-Powder may be mixed into every meal each day. Additional amounts may be used in finger drawers. E-Powder may also be mixed with tonic seeds.

[5] F-Vite may be provided in finger drawers. F-Vite may also be mixed with tonic seeds.

[6] Begin to add Hi-Cal when hens make the nest and continue until the 4th egg is laid.

Dr Rob Marshall's health products dramatically increase the nutritional value of the soft food mix.

Introduction to Young Bird Programme

Because of the stressful nature of the weaning period and adolescence, it is wise to have a special weaning and young bird routine for canaries during Spring. The Young Bird Programme has been designed to entice the young birds to accept a wide variety of foods and supplements. It also protects them from disease at their most vulnerable age.

The Young Bird Programme should continue through spring and summer until the end of the moult. It protects young canaries from the stress of hormonal fluctuations, strengthens their level of natural resistance and accelerates the juvenile moult and onset of maturity. The adolescents glow with health as the programme progresses. Good nutrition, hygiene, weekly disinfecting and water cleansers form the basis of this programme.

Repeat treatments are necessary to control and prevent lice, mites, coccidiosis and Black Spot during this difficult time for canaries.

Weaning birds are inquisitive and eager to try different foods. This is an ideal time to teach the young to accept a large variety of foods and develop good eating habits.

Young Bird Programme

Day of Week	Water Supplements	Soaked Seed Supplements	Mixed in Tonic Food	Disease Control
Monday	Fresh Water		E-Powder/F-Vite	**Mites/Lice** — S76 in drinking water for one day each month. Coopex spray the cabinet or flight. KD baths.
Tuesday	Fresh Water	Turbobooster Dufoplus/Ioford on soaked seed	E-Powder/F-Vite	
Wednesday	KD		E-Powder/F-Vite	**Black Spot (Atoxoplasmosis) & Coccidiosis** — Carlox for three days each month starting the second week after entry into the young bird flight or cabinet.
Thrusday	KD		E-Powder/F-Vite	**Megabacteria, Thrush & Molds** — KD in drinking water for three consecutive days each week.
Friday	KD		E-Powder/F-Vite	
Saturday	Fresh Water	Turbobooster Dufoplus/Ioford on soaked seed	E-Powder/F-Vite	**E.coli & Wet Weather Control** — Megamix on days of rain.
Sunday	Fresh Water		E-Powder/F-Vite	**Disinfect Cage/Flight** — Clean and disinfect the cabinet with KD once a week

Notes: Dufoplus, Ioford and Turbobooster are added to sprouted seed for two days each week. Mineral and energy powders (F-Vite & E-Powder mixed together) should be made available at all times and can be mixed into the tonic food. Use small containers to avoid spoiling & waste.

These products are essential for the continuing health of young birds as these birds are most susceptible to illness.

Essentials for Keeping Young Birds Healthy

Protein and Energy

After weaning has occurred, young canaries should continue to receive additional protein and energy each second day. Sprouted seed and Turbobooster are good sources of protein and energy. E-Powder & F-Vite mixed into a tonic seed is a practical method for providing additional energy to young canaries.

Good Hygiene

KD helps keep the cage and utensils perfectly clean.

Clean Drinking Water

KD should be administered from one to three days each week to clean the drinking water and "self-clean" the water vessels. Due to its action on water, KD forms an important method for reducing Thrush/Mould infections and the spread of Megabacteria among susceptible young birds.

Vitamins and Trace Elements

Dufoplus and Ioford should be added to the drinking water, soft food or sprouted seed for two days each week. The best results may be seen when the vitamins are given the day after KD.

Minerals

F-Vite mineral powder may be mixed with tonic seed or placed into finger drawers.

Weaning: Background Information

It is not exactly known what triggers the weaning process but most canaries are ready to wean between 21-30 days of age. At weaning age, canaries become very inquisitive and develop a huge capacity to learn. They learn through observation of others. This presents an ideal opportunity to teach young to accept a large variety of foods and to establish good eating habits.

Methods for weaning canaries vary somewhat from one fancier to the next. Those disadvantaged by space restrictions must keep their young birds in cabinets rather than allow them freedom in flights.

Experienced breeders believe canary chicks should receive food from their parents until 30 days of age. They consider this the best time to start the weaning process. Border Fancy enthusiasts prefer to remove young from their parents at a younger age — from between 21-25 days of age. Special care must be taken when weaning at this younger age, as weaker individuals may not be able to find the water or eat properly and may fall behind. In this state they become susceptible to illness and may possibly die.

Young canaries must be separated from their mother when she starts to prepare (make a nest) for her next clutch of eggs. Sam Callavaro has his Red factors feed their young until 30 days of age. To prevent feather plucking by the hen, the chicks are removed from the nest to an adjoining cage, separated from the mother by a wire divider. Here, the mother feeds them through the wire until they are 30 days old. To help avoid feather plucking, the hen should be provided with nesting materials when the young are about 21-25 days of age. The father (separated from the hen) may be also placed in with the young for most of the day. Here, he feeds them until they are eating well by themselves. To ensure that the next round of eggs is fertile he is moved to mate with the hen for one hour or so every morning. The young stay with the cock until they are 30-31 days old. Sam then moves them to another cage.

While in the weaning cage chicks should receive a large variety of foods including tonic seeds, sprouted seeds, plain canary seed, soft foods and greens. Receiving egg foods alone at this age results in weak youngsters because too much protein is consumed.

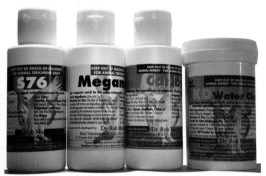

Because of the stressful nature of the weaning period and adolescence it is wise to have a special weaning and young bird routine for canaries. Administering the medicines shown above helps keep young canaries in top health.

Disease Prevention

Mites/Lice Ongoing Prevention

S76 is administered in the drinking water for one day each month. Additionally, Avian Liquidator or Coopex is sprayed the same day S76 is given.

KD baths should be given regularly to clean the feathers and help to remove any dead mites.

Mites and lice are a major cause of sickness in young canaries. They also help transmit blood parasites and canary pox.

Black Spot (Atoxoplasmosis) & Coccidiosis (Isopora canaris) Prevention

Carlox/Baycox®/Coccivet for three days each month starting three weeks after birds have entered the young bird cage.

Mould and Bacterial infections

Mould and bacterial infections are controlled in most aviaries when KD powder is added to the drinking water for two or three consecutive days each week. Start this treatment one week after the young birds enter young bird flights or cabinets.

Wet Weather Protection

Canaries, especially juveniles, succumb to illness most commonly after wet weather. Coccidiosis, E.coli, Thrush and mould infections are the most common wet weather diseases. Megamix has been developed specifically for wet weather problems and should be administered to the drinking water for the duration of the downfall. A five-day course of Carlox treatment should also be introduced when it continues to rain for more than three days.

Frequency of Soft Food/Sprouted Seed During Weaning

Sprouted seed and soft foods must be supplied twice daily to accelerate the weaning process as the beaks of young canaries are not strong enough to crack any hard seed until they are 5 weeks old. They must receive soft foods immediately after being removed from their mother. Tonic seeds are soft seeds that are more easily eaten by youngsters. They should also be provided with a soft food, sprouted seed and green foods during the weaning process. Niger, lettuce and philaris seeds are popular examples of tonic seeds. Some fanciers add maw seed to the soft food as it helps teach the young to break open hard seed.

Young birds should be cracking and eating the hard seeds such as plain canary and rape seeds from 5 weeks of age. Mal Coulston likes to move his birds into a flight when they become strong enough to crack hard seed. He moves the chicks into an adjoining breeder at the first sign that the hen wants to make a nest and leaves them here for one week under careful observation. Here, they may be fed by the hen through the wire. After one week they should be eating and drinking by themselves. Only at this time, when he is sure they are all eating and drinking, are they moved into the flight.

The move to the flight may be stressful to canaries of this young age and many fanciers including Maurice Hunt prefer to leave them in cabinets. Maurice Hunt removes his youngsters from their parent(s) as soon as they are eating soft food/sprouted seed recipe by themselves. They are moved into a 3 to 4 hole cabinet the size of which is determined by the number of birds to be weaned. Here they learn to fly. Mr. Hunt does not provide a feeder parent to the youngsters but moves groups of ten to twelve youngsters of the same age into the multiple breeders. They then receive soft food, soaked seed and greens twice daily and are monitored carefully to see if any are falling behind.

These youngsters are still with their mother and should soon be moved to an adjacent cage so they can be fed through the wire. This allows the hen to settle onto the next round of eggs.

Careful monitoring of newcomers to a large flight is necessary. At first the young will fly up the wire but within a week they should be flying strongly within the flight. Any birds that are not flying should be moved to a cabinet and fed with a variety of foods until they are strong enough to re-enter the flight. Although this system of moving young into the flight at an early age may initially be more stressful, it promotes fitness. Mr Coulston believes young birds in the flight are happier and easier to keep healthy. He also believes his birds moult more quickly.

During the weaning period the youngsters should be introduced to the Young Bird Programme. The weaning stage is the best time to introduce canaries to the new tastes of supplements that are included in the Young Bird Programme. This is an age when all birds are most likely to accept different foods and tastes. The young of birds that have been on the Breeding Programme should immediately accept the tastes of the supplements.

Young Birds: Background Information

Few problems should be experienced during the weaning stage. Canaries, however, become most vulnerable to illness and death after weaning, from between 5-12 weeks of age. During this time they must be monitored carefully to make sure they have found the water dish and are eating and flying well. Canaries experience the most psychological stress within the first two weeks after entering the young bird flight or cabinets. This stress is alleviated considerably by bringing clutches of an equal age in together.

Nutritional supplements and KD powder should be started during weaning and continue throughout the Young Bird Programme. The programme has been designed to improve natural resistance and protect the birds from illness. Ongoing prevention against lice, mites, coccidiosis and environmental germs remain an important part of continuing health during this programme.

The Young Bird Programme should start during weaning and extend throughout summer until the completion of the moult. Soft foods, sprouted seed and tonic seeds should also be used to help the vulnerable young birds through this difficult developmental age.

Many fanciers alleviate stress by keeping young birds in small groups in cabinets. Mr. Hunt keeps the same group of birds together in the same breeder until they are half way through their moult. As young birds, they are provided with a hard seed mix, tonic seeds and fed soft food each second or third day. If they are getting too fat, tonic seed or rape is withdrawn from the diet. Midway through summer he separates the young birds into smaller groups. Two birds are moved into one cage, or four to a double breeder. This again alleviates stress on the young birds at the height of their moult, a most vulnerable time.

Mr. Coulston moves the young directly to a flight where they receive soft food, sprouted seed and tonic seed daily for the first two weeks. The amount of soft food is then gradually reduced. After three weeks they receive soft food three times weekly. By six weeks no soft food is provided at all but sprouted seed is continued every second day until they are moved out of the flights

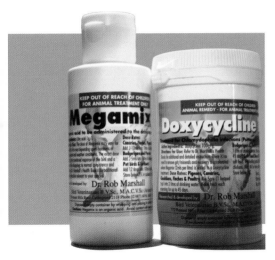

A course of Doxycycline may be required for young birds showing symptoms of ill-health.

towards the end of summer. Most fanciers feed sprouted seed to the young birds, an ideal vehicle to which the health supplements may be added. The gathering of young birds from different nests exposes them to new diseases. This is a time when Black Spot (Atoxoplasmosis), E.coli-type infections, Coccidiosis and Megabacteria infections spread quickly from bird to bird. Ongoing treatments against mites, lice and coccidiosis should begin in the third week of entering the young bird cages. Additional treatments may also be necessary for canker (Trichomoniasis) in varieties (e.g., Red Factors and Glosters) susceptible to this parasite. Ornithosis may also appear during this time, requiring a course of Doxycycline. Any ongoing treatments should continue throughout summer until the conclusion of the moult.

Overcrowding, competition for food and water, aggression from older youngsters and exposure to germs are the main physical factors affecting the health of young birds entering a large flight

Outbreaks of disease should be anticipated when flights or cabinet are overcrowded. Overcrowding intensifies the physical stresses experienced by adolescents due to increasing competition for food, water and perch space. Overcrowding increases the chances of weaker individuals failing to find the water or food as well as experiencing harassment from strong assertive individuals, making them susceptible to illness from E. coli-type infections, black spot and coccidiosis. These

infections spread rapidly and eventually infect even the strongest youngsters. Germs accumulate in high numbers in the drinking water and on the floor.

Essentials for a Good, Fast Moult

The addition of nutritional supplements to the food promotes excellent feather quality. At the same time they protect the birds from the strains of the moult and allow for quick production of new feathers.

Protein and Energy

Soft foods, sprouted seed, Turbobooster and E-Powder must be administered. These should be fed each second day to moulting canaries. E-Powder may also be mixed together with F-Vite into tonic seed.

Clean Drinking Water

KD should be administered from one to three days each week to clean the drinking water and "self-clean" the water vessels. KD is an important method for reducing water based infections that may retard the moult.

Vitamins and Trace Elements

Ioford/Turbobooster can be added to soft food/sprouted seed each second day. These two products are extremely important for a healthy moult. Dufoplus is administered for two consecutive days each week. Dufoplus and Ioford may also be added to the drinking water. If so, Ioford should be administered three days a week.

Summer Molt Programme

Day of Week	Water Supplements	Food Supplements	Disease Control
Monday	Fresh Water	Turbobooster E-Powder, Ioford	**Mites / Lice** — S76 in drinking water for one day each month. Coopex spray the cabinet or flight KD baths.
Tuesday	Fresh Water		
Wednesday	Fresh Water	Turbobooster E-Powder, Ioford	**Black Spot (Atoxoplasmosis) & Coccidiosis** — Carlox for three days each month starting the second week after entry into the young bird flight or cabinet.
Thursday	KD		
Friday	KD	Turbobooster E-Powder, Ioford	**Megabacteria, Thrush & Moulds** — KD in drinking water for three consecutive days each week.
Saturday	Dufoplus		**E.coli and Wet Weather** — Megamix on days of rain.
Sunday	Dufoplus	Turbobooster E-Powder, Ioford	**Disinfect Cage/Flight** — Clean and disinfect the cabinet with KD once a week.

Notes: When medications are administered they replace the use of KD powder.

The protection offered by the medicines mentioned in this book ultimately strengthens the health status of the entire flock allowing the susceptible juveniles through their especially difficult first moult without harm to natural immunity. In fact, this programme protects and strengthens the immune system and natural resistance of the entire flock.

Dufoplus (1ml/1/4 tsp.) and Ioford (2.5ml/1/2 tsp.) are mixed together into 500ml/2 cups of drinking water and safely left for two days, as they are sugar free. They provide the vitamins and trace elements necessary for good health and vitality.

Ioford is especially helpful for the moult.

Turbobooster provides canaries with the fatty acids, protein and minerals necessary for silky feathers and good health. The fatty acids in Turbobooster promote a strong immune system and are especially beneficial during young bird development. Glossy strong feathers and increased vitality are the health changes you will notice. Turbobooster should be added to one soft food meal each day during this programme.

E-Powder should be added to one soft food meal each day. E-Powder is an energy supplement that also helps to reduce the effects of stress on the moult. E-Powder may also be made available in finger drawers.

F-Vite should be available in finger drawers at all times.

The moult requires substantial energy and nutrient resources. The Moult Programme provides a perfect blend of high quality nutrients required for the production of high quality feathers. On this programme, three months should provide ample time for canaries to complete their moult. A fine balance must be reached where enough energy, protein and other micro-nutrients are provided to promote a rapid and complete moult but at the same time the birds must avoid obesity and laziness during the moult period. Sprouted seeds and soft foods may be fed to birds in large or tall flights that stimulate fitness but may need to be restricted for birds housed in breeding units.

The supplements ensure a rapid moult and production of the highest quality new feather.

Minerals

Mineral powders (F-Vite) should be made available at all times. Minerals are vitally important during the moult. F-Vite may be mixed into tonic seed with E-Powder or placed into small containers to avoid spoiling & waste.

Disease Prevention

Mite/lice Control

Mites and Lice exist at their worst during the hot months of the moult. The use of a combination treatment (S76/Coopex) becomes vital for one day every three weeks until the completion of the moult, as mites and lice may cause permanent damage to growing feathers. KD baths should also be supplied regularly to clean the feathers and help remove the dead mites. Regular bathing also helps to speed up the moult.

Black Spot & Coccidiosis Protection

The administration of Carlox should be continued during the summer month, and has no harmful effect on feather growth.

Ornithosis Treatment Trial

Ornithosis often occurs towards the end of the moult. Its presence may be noticed by a slowing down of the moult, inactivity (birds may stay on the floor of the flights) and an increasing number of loose feathered birds. A three day course of Doxycycline and Megamix should be extended to a full 28- day course when an appreciable positive response to the initial trial treatment occurs.

Wet Weather Protection

High humidity and temperatures associated with summer rains may predispose young moulting birds to coccidiosis, E.coli, Thrush and mould infections. These wet weather diseases may retard the moult and lead to poor feather quality. Megamix has been developed specifically for wet weather problems and should be added to the drinking water for the duration of the downfall. KD powder also helps to control these infections when added to the drinking water for two or three consecutive days each week. KD treatments should start one week after the young birds enter the flights or cabinets.

Moult Programme Information

The summer Moult Programme provides canaries with the nutrition that produces the best possible feathers. This programme also preserves the quality of new feathers by controlling insect attack and other illnesses that may retard the moult.

Moulting is the process of losing and growing new feathers. The emergence of the new feather causes the old feather to fall out (shed). In the first moult the chick replaces its down with pin-feathers. The second or juvenile moult starts soon after fledging. The juvenile moult is particularly troublesome for the health of canaries. The first adult moult occurs a year later. Thereafter, during summer, canaries moult each year at the conclusion of the breeding season. The moult starts during the hot summer months of January and February (in the Southern Hemisphere) and July/August (in the Northern Hemisphere) and should be completed within 10 weeks.

At first, canaries moult body feathers and start to replace their flight feathers sequentially. It is the new adult wing and tail feathers of adult birds that take the longest time to grow. The head and outside primary flight feathers are the last to be replaced. The appearance of pin-feathers on the head heralds the closing stages of the annual moult. A slow or incomplete moult is a reliable indication of poor health or a management flaw. Stress of any kind retards and slows the moult. The stress of a moult may precipitate illness in weaker birds. A record of birds slow to complete their moult or that fall ill during the moult should be kept. These birds should not be selected for breeding, as they are inherently weak. A fast moult reflects good health.

The white fluffy down feathers that are produced continuously in a healthy canary should not be confused with a moult. These down feathers provide waterproofing and feather lubricating "powder" or "bloom" and are a sign of top health and fitness.

Moult & Nutrition

The moult requires substantial energy and without adequate nutrients, poor quality feathers are produced and the process becomes prolonged. The moult is a critical time for the future success

These products are recommended as prevention of illnesses associated with the moult.

of your exhibition canaries because the quality of new feathers depends upon the nutrition and health of the feather as it is growing.

Extra protein, minerals and energy are needed because there is an increased metabolic rate and demand for protein. The moult process is quickest when the high energy and protein needs of the moult are adequately met.

Most fanciers feed soft foods and sprouted seeds during the moult. This is a good idea and useful vehicle for applying the health products (Turbobooster, Dufoplus, Ioford, E-Powder) that are crucial for the production of perfect new feather growth. Fatty acids present in Turbobooster promote a flexible durable feather and should be provided to moulting canaries.

There is also a marked increase in the require-ments of minerals, calcium and phosphorus. These minerals are responsible for the strength of new feathers. The trace element, iodine, plays a crucial role in the initiation and progress of the moult. Consequently the supplementation of the diet with minerals (e.g., F-Vite) and trace ele-ments (e.g., Ioford) should be provided to canaries along with fatty acids present in Turbobooster, which promote a flexible and durable feather.

Moult & Soft Foods/Sprouted Seeds/Tonic Seeds

Soft foods enriched with health supplements (see recipes on page 64) may be provided during the Moult Programme, although many fanciers prefer to use dry seed alone. The additional energy pro-vided by soft foods is of special advan-tage to the health of young birds during their first moult. Soft foods and sprouted seeds are usually given each second day during the Moult Programme, but special attention must be given to any weight gains in varieties such as Glosters and Norwiches, who tend towards obesity when fed high energy soft foods. Weight gain is more likely in birds housed in cabinets during the moult and soft food may be of no added advantage to them during this time. Instead, health supplements may be added to the dry seed and drinking water. The more active Yorkshires and Borders do not dis-play weight gain in a flight or cabinet and should be supplied with soft food every second day dur-ing the Moult Programme.

Without additional nutrients the replacement of feathers will be delayed. Turbobooster, F-Vite, E-Powder and Ioford are supplements which can generate a rapid moult. When the birds are allowed to remain in flights where they are able to exercise freely, these are usually provided in the form of a soft food mix. Mal Coulston says his young birds prefer their E-Powder and F-Vite mixed into a tonic seed. When housed in more confined areas these products are best added to the water and on the seed. Turboboooster may be mixed with a hard seed mix or sprouted seeds. Ioford should be added to the drinking water.

Colour Feeding During the Moult

Feather colour is dietary-dependent in species with carotenoid pigmentation. Red factor and new colour canaries fall into this category. They require exogenous sources of carotenoids or related substances to enable full development of yellow orange and red pigments in their feathers. Foods for these birds should therefore contain carotenoids and xanthophylls to enable their proper colour development.

Commercial diets that contain algae (spirulina) should contain sufficient levels of colour. A xan-thophyll food dye, containing 10% xanthophylls and canthaxanthadine is produced by Roche. This is potentially liver toxic to birds and must always be used in accordance with dosages calculated by experienced canary breeders.

Sam Cavallaro, a Red Factor breeder from Sydney Australia, shares his method of colour preparation. "For red factors canaries, a 4ml (1 tsp. + 5 ml) measuring spoon of canthaxanthadine is first mixed thoroughly with a small amount of hot (30°C/86°F) water. This action dissolves the fine granules of xanthophyll that are coated with fish oil. This working solution must be stored away from sunlight in the refrigerator. It may then be used "neat" in the drinking water. The food colour treatment may also be mixed with the soft food mix (until it is a pale pink colour) of breeding canaries from November when the babies have pin feathers (10 days old). It must then continue through each day until April when the juvenile moult is complete."

Maurice Hunt comments on his use of colour chemicals as follows: "Young birds receive colour in the soft food and drinking water immediately after they are weaned from 5-6 weeks of age. Breeding birds start to receive colour in the soft food prior to laying eggs and continuing through until the end of the breeding season. Old birds should start to receive colour at the end of the breeding season in January. They can receive colour in both the drinking water and soft foods until the moult reaches the head feathers. Colour is then reduced and provided in the soft food alone to prevent 'bronzing' of the new head feathers.

The colour chemicals enter the growing feather via the circulation and must be fed to colour canaries when new feathers are growing during the moult.

A working solution is made by dissolving 1 tablespoon of canthaxanthadine powder in 1 litre (approximately 1 quart) of boiling water. For soft foods, 30mls/6 tsps. of cooled working solution is then mixed into 1 1/2 cups of soft food using an electrical blender. The working solution replaces the drinking water and is refreshed each first or second day."

Food colouring is also administered to Yorkshire (3mls/litre dilution rate) and Norwich canaries, enhancing the colour of birds with yellow-type feathers, but not buffed-feathered birds. Canaries enjoy the taste of the colour additive.

Pollen is another source of the usable carotenoids pigment, apocarotenol, that produces yellow to orange hues in the feathers.

Dufoplus has a positive effect on the colour of feathers. It is rich in a high quality vitamin A. Vitamin A has a positive effect on the naturally occurring yellow pigments found in feathers. It produces a greater depth of colour to the feather without being a colour agent. It produces its effect by enhancing the health and the physical structure of the feathers.

Moult Programme: Additional Information

The Moult Programme has been designed to help the canary to complete the moult as quickly as possible, to produce the best possible feather colour and condition and to protect the health of the flock. Colour food can be added to any of the products in this programme.

The commencement of this programme is largely determined in Australia by the geographical location and seasonal weather conditions of the aviary. Canaries should be allowed to start to moult naturally during January (Southern Hemisphere) and August (Northern Hemisphere) at the conclusion of breeding. At this time, as long as they are provided with the necessary nutrients, the moult will be completed in the shortest possible time. Within three months they should have completed their moult.

The Moult Programme should start at the appearance of stray feathers on the floor of the cage or flights. A heavy moult that is completed within eight to ten weeks is a sign of a healthy flock and an effective moult programme.

Management of the moult can result in the difference between a good show season or a disappointing one. So it serves to pay attention to every detail.

Stan Nicholes reveals his thoughts about the moult in Yorkshire canaries as follows:
"It has been noted that some young Yorkshires, who are below top standard for show birds before the moult, improve tremendously after using an effective moult programme. Young canaries of marginal quality can be transformed into top class birds when they receive the correct care and management during their first moult. At the first sign of moult, all birds should be handled and inspected for vermin. The birds should be dusted with a proven dusting powder, once each day over two days, with the powder being worked into the feathers."

S76 should be added to the drinking water for the same one or two days that birds have been sprayed or dusted with pyrethrins (e.g., Coopex or Avian Liquidator). This process should be repeated each month during the moult.

Stan continues "When young canaries have their first moult, they shed all of their feathers with the exception of tail and flight feathers, and at this time, the term 'unflighted' is used for a young bird. Many fanciers will pull out the tail feathers of young Yorkshires during the moult, as the new tail feathers increase approximately a 1/4 of an inch when they grow again, thus increasing the overall length of the bird. Experience with young Yorkshire canaries having their first moult has shown me that the majority of youngsters bred early in the breeding season do not commence their moult until up to ten weeks, whereas youngsters bred in late December and early January commence at six to seven weeks.

The first signs of the new plumage coming through appear on the wing butts and on the breast. This is particularly noticeable on young Yorkshires that are being colour fed. The shedding of feathers continues in a pattern, gradually extending over the whole body, and finishes with the neck and head feathers."

For moulting out the young Yorkshires and also the show team of old birds, Stan adds that he prefers to use treble breeding units: 2.1 metres (7 feet) long, 30cm (15 inches) high and 38cm (19 inches) deep, housing 10 Yorkshires to each. At all times, a show cage is attached to the breeder and the young birds are quite accustomed to it by the time their show training commences. This is approximately 3 weeks before they finish their moult, but the old birds' training is left until they have completely finished their moult.

This method enables him to keep a close eye on each individual bird, assessing the show potential of each bird as the moult progresses.

The majority of Yorkshire canary fanciers agree that during the moult, a bird's resistance is at its lowest. There should be a minimum of handling

Stan Nichol uses the triple breeding unit for his Yorkshires during the moult. This allows him to train them for the show and assess their potential as show birds as the moult progresses.

Baths are most important and considered important to induce a quick, good moult.

and as little disturbance as possible. Stan Nichols agrees with this up to a point. He adds "I find that with quiet and careful handling in the final 3 weeks of their moult, they quickly respond, gaining confidence and steadiness for the major shows ahead. It is at this stage that I select the most promising show specimens and transfer them to single cages to prevent fighting and damage to their new plumage.

Hygiene is a top priority at all times in the bird room, but especially so during the moult, when the bird's strength and resistance to bacteria and parasites are at their lowest. A spotlessly clean bird room, utensils, cages and bird room floor, together with good ventilation and as much sunlight as possible will go a long way in the prevention of bacteria and parasites.

Baths are most important and I consider their frequent use as one of the main instigators of a quick, good moult. I make the bath available every second day. Half the cages receive a bath one day and the other half their bath the next day. This bathing regime should be continued throughout the moult. It helps to rid the birds of loose feathers and encourages the quick growth of the new ones.

Preening is also increased by bathing and they use the oil from the gland at the base of the tail and run it through the plumage, enhancing the sheen on the new feathers that is so essential in a show bird.

Before hanging the bath on the cage door, I place a face cloth between 2 sheets of newspaper and cover the cage floor. By doing this, any surplus water is absorbed by the face cloth and the cage floor is kept dry. This only takes an extra 30 seconds and prevents dampness that could cause mould and E Coli. It is well worth the extra half minute. I attach the baths usually around 8 am and remove them by midday so that all wet birds can be perfectly dry by roosting time."

Moult and Disease

During the moult, both old and young canaries become vulnerable to illness. Bacterial bowel infections (predominantly E.coli, and Streptococcal infections), Ornithosis, moulds (Aspergillosis), yeast (Candidiasis) infections and parasites (Coccidiosis, Atoxoplasmosis, Trichomoniasis, Airsac mites,) account for most of the problems during the moult. The flock should receive ongoing treatments against lice, mites, coccidiosis, Megabacteria and Black Spot during this time. These treatments do not harm growing feathers and actually accelerates the moult.

The conclusion of the moult should herald an overflow of energy and vitality. When canaries fail to come alive at the end of their moult then one must consider the possibility that the demand of growing new feathers has exposed an underlying health or nutritional problem. Inactivity, a quiet bird room, dull feather colour and a lack of sheen are signs that the moult has placed undue stress upon a canary flock. Canaries that experience difficulties with a moult will not "show" to the best of their ability because they will lack vigour and carry plumage that lacks sheen, becomes loose, coarse and lacks the rich and pure ground colour of a canary in superb show condition.

The conclusion of the moult forms the best time to assess the health of the canary flock because it is a time when the young birds are under the most physical pressure. Symptoms of ill health are therefore most likely to appear at this time. Similarly, it is a time when older birds are likely to become infected from germs spread by younger birds. Ornithosis is a disease most likely to be present in canary flocks at this time. Wet weather, mites and lice are also primary causes of disease at this time.

Moult & Ornithosis-Cleansing Treatment

Ornithosis occurs more often towards the end of the moult. Canaries may be infected with Ornithosis and show few outward signs of illness. A slow moult may be the only indication that something is wrong. Lack of activity may be the only other sign of Ornithosis.

Without veterinary testing, it is difficult to confirm Ornithosis as the cause of these symptoms. A short course of Doxycycline & Megamix becomes a useful and safe method for detecting

Ornithosis. A positive response to a three day long course confirms the presence of disease and the need for a longer treatment.

Canaries with Ornithosis remain "loose in the feather" and are difficult to bring into show condition. Flocks with Ornithosis respond excellently to a cleansing treatment. Their plumage becomes tighter, they complete their moult more quickly and they lose the nervousness that accompanies infection.

A cleansing treatment for Ornithosis should start at least 6 weeks before the first show. This allows the month long treatment to be concluded before intensive show preparation begins. In Australia, Ornithosis treatments must be started by the first week of February, as shows start the second week of April.

Ornithosis Treatment

As stated above, a treatment trial with Doxycycline/Megamix is required to determine the need for further treatment.

Ornithosis: Doxycycline/Megamix Treatment Trial

The symptoms of Ornithosis outside the breeding season are very subtle. A therapeutic trial is often the best way to assess the health status (regarding Ornithosis) of your canaries. During autumn (April, Southern Hemisphere/October, Northern Hemisphere), at the conclusion of the moult, a therapeutic trial using Doxycycline & Megamix should be initiated. No harm can be done by administering this treatment, even when Ornithosis is absent from your flock. A five day

long course is necessary to determine the presence or absence of Ornithosis.

Assessing a Doxycycline/Megamix Treatment

A positive response by the third day indicates that Ornithosis is present in the flock.. Increased activity and noise in the birds is the most noticeable change of a positive response. With time, further positive changes should become more obvious. Brighter feather colour and smaller droppings result. The above changes indicate that the health of the flock would be enhanced by a completed course of Doxycycline/Megamix. There are major benefits on the immediate show and future breeding performance from such a treatment.

The treatment should continue until negative signs appear; an indication that the treatment no longer benefits but harms health.

Positive Signs of Doxycycline/Megamix Treatment

The droppings become smaller and less watery. Birds no longer fluff up and become more active. Increased noise and vitality present in the aviary. Feather quality improves with plumage turning tighter and an improvement of the depth of colour becomes apparent. Pin or down feathers may also suddenly appear on the droppings.

Negative Signs of Doxycycline/Megamix Treatment

Negative signs are directly related to Thrush, a yeast infection that occurs when tetracyclines are administered to healthy canaries. Canaries are

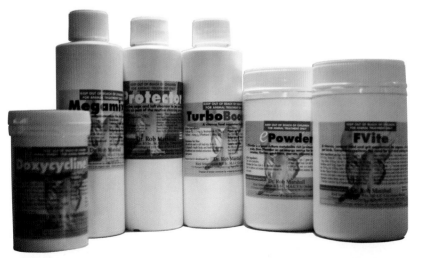

Doxycycline and Megamix are added to the drinking water and are the treatment of choice for Ornithosis in canaries. The health products Turbobooster, E-Powder and F-Vite are given on the seed during this treatment and Protector is used to disinfect the cage each week.

especially vulnerable to Thrush infections. Negative signs indicate the birds are free of Ornithosis. Birds that react negatively may fluff-up and look tired within three days of Doxycycline treatment. They may also develop dark green watery droppings, vomit and become inactive.

Doxycycline/Megamix Treatment Instructions

A Doxycycline/Megamix Treatment should only be completed when the flock exhibits positive signs to a treatment trial. The strongest and older birds may not respond to a Doxycycline/Megamix treatment in flocks where Ornithosis is a not a major problem. These birds may show an initial benefit then become depressed after a week-long treatment. In such canary flocks the Doxycycline/Megamix treatment should be withheld until winter when the show season has ended.

A Doxycycline trial is recommended each autumn or winter. A Doxycycline[1]/Megamix[2] treatment is recommended for flocks with a history of infertility, poor breeding results and for juveniles that are "just not right." Healthy show birds being trained for the show must not be given this treatment.

- Doxycycline/Megamix treatment should be continued until the birds become quiet and fluff up. This may be as short as three days (in aviaries with no Ornithosis) to 30 days (in aviaries with Ornithosis).

- The food should be enriched daily with vitamins[3] and minerals during the course of treatment. These supplements may be added to the dry seed, water or into a soft food.

- The surfaces of cages, aviaries and food stations must be disinfected (Protector[®4]) once a week during a Doxycycline/Megamix treatment.

- After the Doxycycline/Megamix treatment, sugar based vitamins (NV powder[5]) should be added to the drinking water for two days followed immediately by KD powder for one day.

- The show programme should then be applied at the conclusion of this treatment.

---

[1] Doxycycline 10% (1 teaspoon per 2 litre of drinking water)
[2] Megamix (3mls per litre of drinking water)
[3] Turbobooster, E-Powder & F-Vite
[4] Protector
[5] NV powder (1 teaspoon into 500 ml of drinking water

Autumn Show Programme

Day of Week	Water Supplements	Food Supplements	Disease Control
Monday	Dufoplus	Turbobooster E-Powder, Ioford	**Mites / Lice** — S76 in drinking water for one day each month. Coopex spray the cabinet or flight. KD baths. Check for quill mites. When quill mites are noticed Liquidator (spray the birds) and Coopex (apply to aviary) should also be applied.
Tuesday	Dufoplus		
Wednesday	KD	Turbobooster E-Powder, Ioford	**E.coli & Wet Weather Control** — Megamix on days of rain. Megamix should be added to the water whenever it rains (or morning dew is present on the grass) to maintain the vitality of show birds.
Thursday	KD		
Friday	Fresh Water	Turbobooster E-Powder, Ioford	**Disinfect Cage/Flight** — Clean and disinfect the cabinet with KD once a week.
Saturday	Fresh Water		**Bathing** — Weekly KD bath during warm weather. Daily mist sprays to bring to bring the birds into show condition.
Sunday	Fresh Water	Turbobooster E-Powder, Ioford	

Notes: When medications are administered they replace the use of KD powder.

Unhealthy birds are slow to prepare for or fail to achieve "show condition." The Show Programme produces the best results for healthy birds. Canaries that are slow to come into show condition are often infected with Ornithosis.

The Autumn Show Programme uses health additives to help create the very best possible feather quality (sheen and colour). The programme will also provide a well-trained show bird with the necessary energy to perform to its best on the day of the show.

Half way through their moult, Maurice Hunt and Mal Coulston move their young birds demonstrating show quality into smaller groups of between 4 and 6 birds in order to start their show training. At this stage, Maurice sprays the birds 3-4 times a week, instead of avoiding baths.
For young birds that appear loose feathered and listless, this is the last opportunity to initiate a treatment trial of Doxycycline and Megamix.
At the completion of the moult these two fanciers then place birds one to a cage. Here they receive hard seed and tonic seed. Their weight and condition is closely monitored as they are nurtured into show condition. Show condition is achieved by feeding a hard seed diet enriched with tonic seeds together with frequent applications of fine mist sprays and health supplements. Mr. Hunt mixes glycerine with the water sprays to help produce a "tight plumage."

The health supplement, Turbobooster, should be added to the dry seed and Dufoplus/Ioford to the drinking water. When preparing birds for the show, Mr. Coulston prefers to mix the E-Powder and F-Vite into tonic seed that is fed once a week. The combination of these supplements as outlined in the Autumn Show Programme brings feathers into top show condition. Turbobooster helps produce a smooth, glossy, silky and porcelain quality appearance to the plumage. Dufoplus helps create a rich, soft, pure and even ground colour. Ioford helps eliminate frill or roughness to give a tight plumage. F-Vite and E-Powder help strengthen tail and wing feathers.

Adding S76 to the drinking water is a convenient way to treat and protect the birds from lice and mites before and after the show.

Three Winter Programmes

It may be necessary to incorporate three winter programmes into the canary health schedule in the following order:

- The Winter Cleansing Program
- Winter Mid-Season Fitness Programme
- Winter Pre-Breeding Program

The Winter Cleansing Program

The beginning of winter (June 1st in the Southern Hemisphere and December 1st in the Northern Hemisphere) is a very good time to assess the health status of the canary flock. By this time, the show season is concluding and the focus now moves towards the breeding season. Colour canaries usually end their show season by June 1st and type canaries by July 1st in the Southern Hemisphere.

A Doxycycline and Megamix treatment trial should begin for all canaries on June 1st in the Southern Hemisphere/ December 1st in the Northern Hemisphere. This process initiates the Winter Cleansing Programme, and should not harm the type canaries who are still being exhibited.

Although it is best not to use a cleansing programme in healthy flocks, it is often difficult to know whether the canary flock is entirely healthy.

A Doxycycline/Megamix treatment trial offers the best means for identifying health problems in canaries.

The Winter Pre-breeding Programme includes additional protein, energy, vitamins and minerals which are added to proven soft food and sprouted seed recipes. The aim is to improve breeding performance by stimulating the birds into breeding condition as early as possible. This programme is mandatory but does not guarantee breeding success because there are many other reasons why birds fail to come into breeding condition. Weak genes, underlying disease (Ornithosis, Megabacteria or fungal toxins), dry or cold weather conditions and nutritional imbalances also prevent canaries from attaining breeding condition.

A Cleansing Programme should especially be initiated when previous breeding results have been unsatisfactory. An autumn, rather than winter Cleansing Programme, should be applied when Ornithosis has been identified as the cause of poor breeding results. Sufficient time must be allocated to complete an extended treatment before the onset of the breeding programme.

The protection offered by the medicines mentioned in this programme strengthens the immune system and improves the natural resistance of the entire flock.

Lice/Mite Treatment

Lice and mite protection should be initiated prior to the Coccidiosis and Ornithosis treatments. S76 should be added to the drinking water for two consecutive days together with the application of Coopex spray into the cabinets and around the aviary.

Coccidiosis Treatment

A two day period of fresh water should follow the lice mite treatment. A Coccidiosis treatment should then be applied. Coccidiosis and Atoxoplasmosis (Isospora infections) are common causes of disease during the breeding season and in young birds. Autumn is an ideal time to cleanse the flock of these diseases. A primary preventative measure includes a treatment with Carlox. Carlox should be administered for three consecutive days immediately following S76.

Ornithosis Treatment

As stated above, a treatment trial with Doxycycline/Megamix is required to determine the need for further treatment. Please refer to pages 76 and 77 for treatment trial and assessment.

Winter Mid-Season Fitness Programme

This programme should be completed after the Doxycycline/Megamix cleansing programme, but prior to the pre-breeding programme, in order to maintain vitality, health and fitness. It also helps prevent the selected breeding birds from becoming overweight.

This canary is in perfect shape after the winter cleansing programme but prior to the pre-breeding programme. The Mid-Season Fitness programme allows canaries to remain fit and healthy as well as preventing them from becoming fat.

The Winter Pre-Breeding Programme is used to prepare productive flocks for the hardships of breeding. Preparations must start well before (about 10 weeks prior to) the breeding season so that the birds are in their best possible physical condition by the start of breeding.

Canaries follow the same evolutionary breeding cycle as ancient birds. The lengthening of the day after the winter solstice activates the breeding time clock, bringing them into breeding condition as early as a month after the shortest day of the year, as long as the weather is warm.

The first full moon prior to the first of Spring would see most healthy robust canaries ready to pair up. This programme is designed to bring the birds into breeding condition at their earliest opportunity. The Winter Fitness Programme should start 10 weeks before this time. For those who live in the Southern Hemisphere, the last week of June is the best time to start this programme and those in Northern Hemisphere countries should start the first week in January.

Soft Food Introduction

Soft foods should be gradually introduced to the birds still housed in the flight for the first five weeks of this programme. Sprouted seed is then combined with the soft food for the final five weeks. Soft food alone is offered at the beginning of programme so that the canaries do not gain excessive weight prior to the presentation of sprouted seed. They prefer the taste of the fattening sprouted seed and may leave the "protein" soft food uneaten.

The introduction of the soft food to the flights is a perfect opportunity to introduce the birds to the new tastes of F-Vite, E-Powder, Turbobooster and

Winter Mid-Season Fitness Programme

Day of Week	Water Supplements	Seed Supplements*	Additional Instructions
Monday	Fresh Water	F-Vite	**Exercise** — Exercise in long or high flights to stimulate exercise with effort.
Tuesday	Fresh Water	F-Vite	**Bathing** — Weekly KD bath during warm weather.
Wednesday	Fresh Water	F-Vite	**Lice & Mite Control** — Check for quill mites. Each month administer S76 to the drinking water for two days.
Thursday	Fresh Water	F-Vite	**Wet Weather** — Megamix should be added to the water whenever it rains (or morning dew is present on the grass) to maintain the vitality of show birds.
Friday	KD	F-Vite	
Saturday	Dufoplus/Ioford	Turbobooster E Powder, F-Vite	
Sunday	Dufoplus/Ioford	Turbobooster E-Powder, Ioford	

* No soft foods or soaked seed

Winter Pre-Breeding Programme

Day of Week	Water Supplements	Soft Food Supplements*	Additional Advise
Friday	KD[1]	Turbobooster, E-Powder, F-Vite	**Hygiene advise** — Use DK to clean the soaking seed, seed sieve and containers.
Saturday	KD[1]		NV powder may also be sprinkled on top of the sprouted seed as an alternative to Dufoplus.
Sunday	KD[1]	Turbobooster, E-Powder, F-Vite	
Monday	Dufoplus/Ioford		
Tuesday	Dufoplus/Ioford	Turbobooster, E-Powder, F-Vite	
Wednesday	Fresh Water		
Thursday	Fresh Water	Turbobooster E-Powder, Ioford	

[1] KD is safely left in the water for three consecutive days.

* Soft food is introduced gradually over 5 weeks. Sprouted seed is added to the soft food during the sixth week of this programme.

even NV powder, Dufoplus and Ioford. These products should be mixed into the sprouted seed/soft food combination as outlined in the chart opposite.

Winter Pre-Breeding Feeding System — Mr. Maurice Hunt

Respected Melbourne canary breeder, Mr. Maurice Hunt, uses and has recommended a ten week preparatory system for canaries and his system blends in perfectly with the *Winter Fitness Programme*. He has agreed to share his system in this book.

In preparation for the breeding season, Maurice gradually increases the energy and nutrition provided to his old birds over a period of 10 weeks. His conditioning programme starts during the last week of June (10 weeks prior to the intended start of breeding) at the conclusion of a Winter Cleansing Programme. The old birds selected for breeding are removed from the flights and placed in breeding cabinets (holes). Maurice places 10-12 birds in 5-hole breeders where they are carefully monitored during his pre-breeding feeding programme. Others use similar feeding systems but the birds remain in flights. In breeders or flights the birds are monitored and those that are falling behind are removed into smaller cages where they receive greater quantities of soft food. The soft food is provided to the birds for one day during the first week and then for an additional day each week until, by the fifth week, the birds are receiving soft food for five consecutive days. The introduction of soft food to the flights is also a perfect opportunity to introduce the birds to the new tastes of F-Vite, E-Powder, Turbobooster, NV powder, Dufoplus and Ioford. Turbobooster and E-Powder should be mixed into the soft food mix every day. Dufoplus and Ioford should be added to the soft food for two days each week. F-Vite should be made available in finger drawers at all times.

Soft food alone is offered for the first five weeks so that the canaries do not gain excessive weight prior to the sprouted seed being offered. They prefer the taste of the "fattening" sprouted seed and may leave the "protein" soft food uneaten. The technique of blowing the feathers away from

Sprouted seed must be replaced gradually with soft foods so the birds do not put on excessive weight.

the pectoral mass may be used to monitor the birds' weight and body condition during the last 3 weeks of the programme. The pectoral muscle should appear pink and full and adjoin the keel bone at an even level. A prominent keel is a sign of an energy deficit from stress or illness. Underweight birds should be moved to a smaller breeder, receive sprouted seed and soft foods, be monitored and have their weight reassessed. A creamy discolouration of the pectoral mass is a sign of excessive weight. Overweight birds should be returned to the flight where they no longer receive soaked seeds until such time as they return to an acceptable weight (i.e., the pink colour of the pectoral muscle becomes visible beneath the skin).

After five weeks, sprouted seed should be introduced to the soft food mix. By the seventh week the birds in the flights should be receiving sprouted seed, soft food Turbobooster and E-Powder each day of the week. Maurice believes the birds should then be in breeding condition within three weeks if temperatures and humidity remain favourable.

By using a feeding programme that gradually introduces a high energy and protein rich soft food and soaked seed mix and together with adequate exercise, the canaries can be stimulated into breeding condition without becoming overweight. Exercise and fitness may be maintained by housing birds in a tall flight where food and water are placed near the ground. This type of flight stimulates vertical flight which requires effort. This reduces the chances of obesity that causes cock bird infertility and egg binding problems in hens.

Soft foods are used to provide a balanced and palatable protein source for the parents to help prepare hens for egg production and to improve fertility in cocks. It is also used when parents are feeding their growing chicks.

Mr. Hunt's soft food recipe offers an excellent balance of protein and provides a rich source of energy. An excellent nutritional balance is achieved when mixed together with his sprouted seed recipe, Turbobooster and E-Powder. Sprouted seeds provide feeding canaries with an instant source of high energy for the growing chickens.

Stan Nichols describes his winter feeding system as follows. "During the winter months leading up to breeding season, I now use Turbobooster as a substitute for a wheat germ oil and cod liver oil

mixture that was previously used. I add Turbobooster to the hard seed and mix it in well. A calcium supplement Hi-Cal is added to the drinking water five days a week before and during the breeding season. Additional vitamins (Dufoplus/Ioford) are added to the drinking water twice each week during winter."

The addition of Turbobooster will improve the levels of "breeding proteins" lysine and methionine (also provided by sunflower and wheat sprouts). E-Powder should also be added to increase the energy levels further and provide the extra B-vitamins needed to counteract the stressful effects of parenting. The missing vitamins A, D and E are best provided by the addition of Dufoplus/Ioford or NV powder. F-Vite must be provided to meet the extra minerals required for egg laying, feeding and bone formation. With these additions, the nutritional requirements for the pre-breeding and breeding programmes are completely satisfied.

Maurice recommends that "red" birds be introduced to colour (canthaxanthadine) through the combined soft food and sprouted seed mix during the sixth week of this programme. The administration of colour should then be continued each day throughout breeding. This ensures the flight and tail feathers of red birds turn pink (not white) in colour by the time they reach the show bench.

When the weather is warm, the most vital hens may come into breeding condition as early as the eighth week of Mr. Hunt's pre-breeding feeding system. Others may take much longer to show signs that they are ready to breed.

Hens are moved into the breeding boxes when they exhibit early signs of coming into breeding condition. Careful observation of these hens in the breeding box is then necessary to ensure the best timing for the introduction of the nest and nesting material. The nest making activities further stimulate the hen into the heightened level of reproduction that produces the best breeding results. She must, however, be in breeding condition before the nest can stimulate her properly so that she can receive the full benefits from pre-potent cock birds.

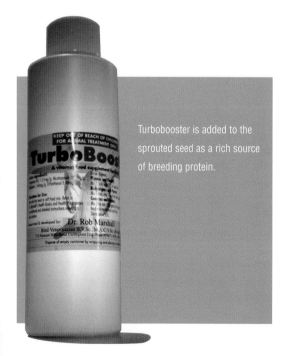

Turbobooster is added to the sprouted seed as a rich source of breeding protein.

The concept of breeding condition is paramount for the successful breeding of canaries. This is the most important notion for canary enthusiasts to understand if breeding success is to be enjoyed. It must be made clear that breeding success is totally dependent upon the birds, especially the hens, being in breeding condition when they are moved to the breeding boxes.

Preparatory systems for breeding, similar to that offered by Mr. Hunt, are a necessary prerequisite to a successful breeding season because they give the birds every opportunity to come into breeding condition at the appropriate time. The Winter Pre-breeding Programme is an excellent programme, but in order to enjoy the best breeding results and enduring health among the breeding hens, remember always to monitor the weight and fitness levels of the birds.

Long beaks, nails and vent feathers may be trimmed during the last 4 weeks of the *Winter Pre-breeding Programme.*

Feeding Regimes	Frequency of Soft Foods/ Sprouted Seed/Supplements
1. Hen introduced to nest in breeding cabinet	Daily Plus Hi-Cal
2. Cock introduced to hen	Daily Plus Hi-Cal
3. Hen laying eggs	Daily Plus Hi-Cal
4. Hen starts to incubate eggs	Soft Food/Sprouted Seed each 2nd day
5. Young start to hatch	2-3 times daily
6. Young develop pin feathers	2-3 times daily
7. Young fully feathered	2-3 times daily
8. Young leave nest	2-3 times daily

The frequency of soft food feeding varies throughout the canary's calendar year. This is necessary to provide the nutritional needs of canaries and to prevent obesity and laziness.

chapter 7
First Aid and Medicines

- Introduction
- Critical Times for Canaries
- Emergency First Aid
- Choosing a Medicine
- Medicine Inventory
- Water Cleansers
- KD vs Megamix

Introduction

For established canary rooms, diseases are best managed by using the same "survival of the fittest" selection processes experienced by wild birds. The healthy birds are retained and the infirm are culled. Hygiene and cleanliness are particularly important for canaries, as they carry no bacteria in their bowel. Attention to breeding selection and hygiene should prevent the more serious diseases from occurring and the need for medicines can be confined to individual illnesses. Repeat treatments to control for worm, lice, mite and vermin infestations remain necessary and should be used with the health programmes as these infestations cannot be controlled through natural resistance. Breeding remains unaffected by these treatments.

There are slight variations in the manner in which medicines may be applied.

In the absence of serious disease and death, antibiotic medicines should be restricted to the treatment of sick individuals in a hospital cage. Antibiotics used in this way should help preserve the long-term health and natural resistance of the remainder of the flock. Only under special circumstances, for example, when many birds are dying during a disease outbreak or when Ornithosis is the cause of poor breeding outcomes, should prescription medicines be administered to the entire flock. Prudent use of antibiotic medicines has also been beneficial in saving nestlings and young birds during disease outbreaks.

Medicines used wisely will save seriously ill individual birds and help them with future breeding. Medicines may also be used to nurture weak individuals and families into breeding condition. With great care the progeny of these weak individuals can become strong enough to breed independently without the help of medicines.

The short-term benefits of administering antibiotics to weak individuals or families should never be regarded as a long-term cure for these birds. Overall, it is the attention to detail, strict hygiene and good management practices rather than the use of medicines that remain the best long-term solution to strengthen and establish families of previously weak birds.

Critical Times for Canaries

An increased incidence of disease at certain times may be explained by a disturbance in the natural cycles of canaries and the existence of overlapping stresses. Problems are more likely to occur during critical physiological stages of young and adult birds. It is during these times that more care should be taken to monitor, identify and remove sick birds for immediate first aid treatment. Canaries remain most vulnerable to health problems at the following times:

Critical Times for Nestlings

0-5 days

Newborns at 1 day of age.

Hatching requires substantial effort. Inherent weakness (disease, brooding failure, etc.) exposes nestlings during their first five days of life to the harmful effects of poor food hygiene (E.coli infections) and Black Spot (Circovirus).

2 weeks (Pin feathers Age)

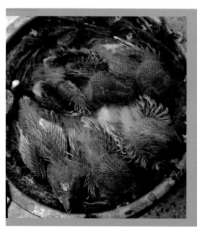

Canaries at pin feather age.

The health of young canaries at the pin-feather age is particularly compromised. Increased food consumption at this age leads to a greater likelihood of food related diseases such as E.coli infections, Moulding disease and Megabacteria.

3-4 weeks (Weaning Age)

Weaning Youngster.

Canaries wean between 21-28 days of age. At this time they leave the safety and warmth of the nest. This represents a significant psychological disturbance to canaries and exposes weak birds to illness.

Critical Times for Young Birds

5-12 weeks (Adolescence)

Canaries become most vulnerable to illness and death after weaning from between 5-12 weeks of age. During this time they must be monitored carefully to make sure they have found the water dish and are eating and flying well. Canaries experience most psychological stress within the

Adolescent Canaries.

first two weeks after entering the young bird flight or cabinets.

The gathering of young birds from different nests also exposes them to new diseases. This is a time when Black Spot (Atoxoplasmosis), E.coli-type infections, Coccidiosis, Canker (Trichomoniasis) and Megabacteria infections spread quickly from bird to bird. This is particularly the case in susceptible varieties such as Red Factors and Glosters. Ornithosis may also appear during this time requiring a course of Doxycycline to be administered.

Critical Times for Breeding Birds

Hens are most at risk during the exertion of producing and laying their eggs. Cocks are at greatest risk to illness soon after courtship begins, as male sex hormones exert a harmful effect on their immune system.

Incubating hens are at particular risk to illness when they are not primed to breed.

Canary hens are at even greater risk of illness when laying their second clutch of eggs while the previous clutch is not yet independent. Virgin breeding pairs are more susceptible to problems than established breeding pairs.

Cock birds are especially prone to illness at the beginning of the breeding cycle. This occurs due to a combination of their androgen (male sex) hormones that are released into the blood stream and the highly energetic nature of courtship behaviour. Androgens are known to weaken the immune system. First time breeders and weak

The male hormones released during courtship weaken the immune system of the cock, leaving it susceptible to illness.

cocks are most susceptible to disease, especially Ornithosis, Megabacteria and E.coli infections.

Virgin hens must also endure energy sapping physical activities of egg production and laying. It is during this stage of their breeding cycle, when the environmental and nutritional requirements are not met, that disease is more prevalent. The problems encountered in virgin pairs are lessened considerably when a nutritional health programme is introduced when they are juveniles and especially during the moult. Health programmes should be introduced a long time prior to the breeding season and a stringent selection and culling policy should also be adopted. Special notice is taken of those birds first to complete the juvenile moult, as they are the strongest and should be chosen first for breeding.

Virgin hens that fall ill during egg production are considered weaklings and are best removed from the breeding programme. Virgin cocks, however, should be given a second chance, as most will perform satisfactorily when held back until the next breeding season. Established breeding pairs rarely encounter contagious illnesses, because their health status and breeding prowess has already been tested or proven during adolescence and as virgin breeders.

Both hens and cocks become susceptible to illness when they are feeding large amounts of food to their young. This occurs when the young are at pin-feather age up until weaning. They also become vulnerable to illness at the conclusion of breeding when they are moved back into a flight and immediately begin to moult.

The majority of problems appear in weaker or older individuals that are unable to cope with the effort required to breed. As part of the continuing selection process, culling is the best option for these weak birds. Enthusiasts, however, must also be able to recognize the different personalities of members within their flock so as to prevent the unnecessary removal of robust productive birds that may fall ill because of poor care and aviary conditions.

Moult is a Critical Time

During the moult, both old and young canaries come under a considerable risk of illness. Bacterial bowel infections (predominantly E.coli, and Streptococcal infections), Ornithosis, moulds (Aspergillosis) and yeast (Candidiasis) infections and parasites (Coccidiosis, Atoxoplasmosis, Trichomoniasis, Air-sac mites,) account for most problems during the moult.

The moult is a particularly difficult time for canaries and a period where weak birds become susceptible to illness.

Emergency First Aid

Emergency First Aid Medicines for canaries may be unrewarding when treatment is delayed because their high metabolic rate and small size exposes them to a rapid death. Early detection of an illness and immediate treatment dramatically improve the chances for an uneventful recovery. I agree with Leaney's and Williams' observations and advice included in their Australian Canary Handbook (1993, p. 219); "Any change from a lively tidy canary with bright eyes, a healthy appetite and a curiosity for anything new is usually the first indication that something may be wrong. It may only be something minor or pass,

but the bird should be watched for other signs and isolated for proper care."

No amount of treatment or intensive care will save a sick canary that has completely stopped eating because canaries die from the shock of haemorrhagic diathesis (acute and massive blood loss into the bowel) within 24 hours of not eating. Consequently at the very first sign of sickness canaries must be removed to a heated hospital cage for treatment. The floor should be lined with clean paper (paper towels are ideal) so that the droppings can be easily monitored.

Emergency treatment administered via the drinking water helps to hydrate the sick canary and must also contain an immediate energy source. Glucose enriched electrolytes (e.g., NV powder) are ideally suited for canaries because they rapidly restore energy levels and stimulate appetite. The danger of haemorrhagic diathesis is immediately alleviated when eating is resumed.

It is also important that heat be provided for the sick bird to restore lost body heat as quickly as possible. A hospital cage heated to 30°C/86°F provides ideal conditions to restore normal body temperature and stimulate appetite in canaries. The ill bird loses body heat very quickly as the energy reserves are depleted by illness. Most sick individuals can be saved when symptoms of illness are recognized early and the normal body temperature and blood sugar levels are quickly reestablished. Antibiotics may be mixed into the drinking water together with the glucose-enriched electrolytes or administered by mouth.

A flat spoon provides the best tool to administer medicines directly to the mouth of sick canaries. A calculated dose of medicine is first placed onto a flat spoon. Leaney and Williams describe the good method of applying a medicine by spoon as follows. "Cradle the bird in the hand. Rest the head on the forefinger and the thumb gently behind the back of the head. Then gently lift the top beak with the leading edge of the spoon. Slide it into the beak and tilt the spoon to allow the medicine to flow into the beak. Canaries resent being handled so this procedure must be performed swiftly to avoid them going into shock." A heated solution of ER formula or NV powder should also be administered by spoon to birds that do not appear to be eating. For birds that are still eating and drinking, NV powder should be added to the drinking water together with a medicine chosen according to the symptoms displayed by the sick bird. Most sick canaries are eager to receive heated fluids. Water cleansers (e.g., KD) should be administered to the rest of the flock while an exact diagnosis is being made. A diagnosis may result in an antibiotic treatment being required for all in contact birds.

The prompt administration of ER Formula to sick canaries can often mean the difference between life and death.

Summary of Emergency First Aid Protocol

Sick canaries must be removed from the flight or cabinet and placed into a heated hospital cage for individual treatment at the first sign of illness.

A hospital cage heated to 25-30°C / 78-86°F provides the ideal conditions to reestablish normal body temperature and stimulate appetite.

The floor of the hospital cage should be lined with clean paper so that the droppings can be easily monitored.

For birds that are still eating, add NV powder to the drinking water together with a medicine chosen according to the symptoms displayed by the sick bird. Birds who are not eating should receive a heated high energy nutrition formula (e.g., ER formula. See appendix).

The hospital cage provides the necessary heat and a quiet spot where treatment can be given while the bird recovers.

Provide a favorite tonic seed, hard seed and soft food impregnated with energy supplements (e.g., Turbobooster, E-Powder, F-Vite) that the ill bird has previously accepted.

Grit, sand and cuttle-bone must be removed until recovery is complete because ill birds often gorge on these, causing an obstructed gizzard and complicating recovery.

The hospital cage should be cleaned and disinfected each day by removing the paper towel floor lining with minimal disturbance to the sick bird.

Emergency Treatment During Breeding

Emergency procedures for illness in the breeding room differ from those employed for birds housed in the flights. Antibiotic treatment should, in most instances, be restricted to individual nest holes and not administered to the entire breeding room. When deaths occur in the breeding room, the medicine treatment should be restricted to the sick individuals, their young and partners. Other breeding pairs should receive water cleansers (KD powder) as a temporary protection while veterinary testing determines the exact nature of the deaths. Medicines should only be administered to the entire breeding room when warranted by the veterinary findings because each pair breeds in relative isolation.

Emergency Procedure for Individual Birds

Sick canaries are susceptible to shock and must receive minimal handling. To prevent death, canaries in shock must be treated as soon as possible. Three or four drops of watery, heated ER formula administered by spoon is an excellent choice to help canaries overcome shock. Canaries in shock may remain motionless on the floor as if dead or fluff up and breathe heavily. Do not attempt to give medicines until they have recovered from the shock of the initial treatment with ER formula. It may take a few minutes to an hour to recover after the treatment, after which time they are ready to receive medicines by mouth. Sulfa-AVS should be the first choice medicine for sick canaries. NV powder should be added to the drinking water until they start eating. When the canary resumes drinking, antibiotics should be administered in the drinking water rather than directly by mouth.

The aviary should be cleaned and disinfected with KD. The healthy birds in the aviary should also receive KD via the drinking water until the diagnosis has been confirmed. The correct choice of medicine (and diagnosis) may be confirmed by a positive response of the sick bird to the selected medicine or from veterinary testing. This medicine should only be administered to the entire in-contact aviary flock when two or more birds have died within a two week period. Otherwise, KD should be added to their drinking water for four consecutive days.

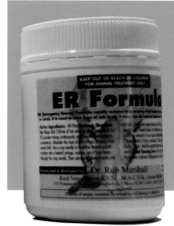

The early administration of ER Formula will save 90% of sick canaries without knowing the exact nature of the disease.

Choosing a Medicine

Selecting and administering the most appropriate first aid medicine at the first signs of illness considerably improves the chances of recovery.

Careful observation of dropping changes and other symptoms when the sick bird is in the hospital cage provides the best means of determining the most appropriate antibiotic.

Changes in the droppings can be used to 'guestimate' the first choice of medicine. The correct choice of medicine can also be determined by the response of an individual sick bird to the medicine. Veterinary testing of the droppings remains the best way to determine the best medicinal choice.

Canaries can show a positive response within 48-72 hours of administration when the correct medicine has been chosen.

The correct choice of First Aid Emergency Medicine may be '"guestimated" from the list of medicine/symptoms options outlined on page 91. The emergency procedures outlined above give seriously ill birds a good chance for full recovery.

The hospital cage should be kept away from human traffic and noise. It must be perfectly clean and prepared with food and medicated water prior to entry of the sick bird. The hospital cage should be cleaned and disinfected each day (by removing and replacing the paper towel floor lining) with minimal disturbance to the ill bird.

Medicine Inventory

Enrofloxacin (Baytril®)

- Baytril is a first choice medicine for treating sick individuals in the hospital cage when the cause of the illness has not been identified.

- Baytril is the first choice medicine for treating the entire flock when Salmonella and Yersinia outbreaks have been confirmed.

Toltrazuril and Vitamins (Baycox®, Carlox®)

- Carlox is the first choice medicine for treating and preventing Coccidiosis (and Atoxoplasmosis).

- Carlox should be used during wet spells (with Megamix) to control Coccidiosis.

Doxycycline Hydrochloride (Doxycycline®)

- Doxycycline is the first choice medicine for treating and preventing Ornithosis caused by Chlamydophila infections.

- Doxycycline should be used together with Megamix.

- Doxycycline may be used to reverse infertility in canaries.

- Doxycycline must not be administered to healthy flocks.

- Doxycycline is the first choice medicine when nestling deaths are associated with infertility.

Amphotericin (Fungilin®)

- Fungilin is the first choice medicine for treating sick individuals in the hospital cage when the cause of the illness is Moulding Disease, Megabacteria or Aspergillosis.

Amoxicillin/Tylosine combination (Moxi-T®, Amtyl®)

- Moxi-T is the first choice medicine for treating sick individuals in the hospital cage when the

cause of the illness is Streptococcus, Staphylococcus or Mycoplasma infections.

- Moxi-T is the first choice medicine for sick canaries when the main symptoms include coughing and wheezing and when the cause of the illness has not been identified.

Nystatin (100,000 unis/ml) (Mycostatin®)

- Nystatin is the first choice medicine for treating sick individuals in the hospital cage when the cause of the illness is Thrush.

Quaternary Ammonium (Protector®)

- Protector is the first choice disinfectant to treat and prevent Ornithosis.

Ivermectin/Homeopathics (S76®)

- S76 is the first choice medicine for treating and preventing gizzard worms, lice, red mites and air-sac mites.

Sulfadimadine/Trimethoprim (Sulfa-AVS®)

- Sulfa-AVS is a first choice medicine for treating sick individuals in the hospital cage when the cause of the illness has not been identified.

- Sulfa-AVS is the first choice medicine for treating the entire flock when E.coli enteritis has been confirmed.

- Sulfa-AVS is commonly mixed with Megamix to accelerate recovery from E.coli and Coccidiosis. Sulfa-AVS is the first choice medicine for treating the entire flock when humidity and rain are associated with death and illness

- Sulfa-AVS is the first choice medicine when nestling deaths occurs with good fertility.

Ronidasole (Turbosole®)

- Turbosole is the medicine of choice for canker and Giardia infections.

Water Cleansers

Water Cleansers play a most important part in the control of canary diseases, especially those of the weaker varieties. They are vital to the success of all health programmes. The main role of water cleansers is to protect inherently strong birds from infection spread by the weak. Antibiotic medicines may be used similarly in a preventative manner but their use does not encourage the flock to develop a natural resistance against disease. Repeated administration of medicines may in fact destroy developing immunity in strong birds and hinder their natural development. Water cleansers enhance the development of a strong natural resistance without affecting immunity. KD and Megamix are two water cleansers with slightly different actions used to promote natural health.

KD powder should be added to the drinking water of all in contact healthy birds immediately after any illness has been identified. At the same time, it should also be used to disinfect the aviary, water and food containers.

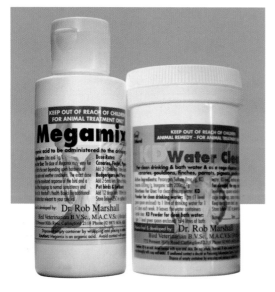

KD and Megamix help prevent most diseases of canaries. They are multipurpose products that function by promoting natural health.

Megamix should be used when a number of birds of different varieties and ages become fluffed up and produce large grey/green watery droppings after overcast weather or rain.

Megamix can be mixed together with all other medicines and health supplements, except KD.

KD versus Megamix

KD is stronger than Megamix.

KD is the first choice acid cleanser for:

- Weaker Varieties
- Canaries housed outdoors

KD is active against Strep, E.coli, Thrush, fungus and virus infections without affecting the immune system.

KD tightens the droppings and lifts the activity in the unhealthy flock, but causes "mushy" droppings when the flock is healthy.

Megamix is the first choice acid cleanser for:

- A strong, healthy aviary.
- Aviaries with problems with moisture or water supply.

Megamix is safe to use for one day or continuously for breeding birds and parents feeding young.

Megamix never depresses or causes bad droppings.

Megamix protects the healthy aviary from stress induced humidity problems such as Thrush and E.coli.

KD Powder

KD contains organic acids that protect the health of seed eating birds by acidifying the water they

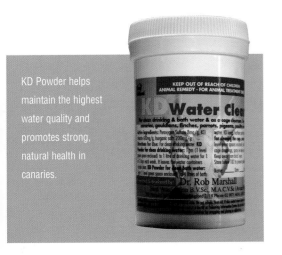

KD Powder helps maintain the highest water quality and promotes strong, natural health in canaries.

drink and thus also the contents of the crop. The blend of organic acids, hydrogen ions and surfactants also helps to keep the water containers clear of sludge and germs.

The KD water cleanser can be used at a high (sanitizing) or much lower (water cleansing) dose. A sanitizing dose is required following disease outbreaks. Low doses should be administered once each week to maintain a clean water system. Most canary breeders use KD continuously to maintain the health of their birds.
KD at sanitizing dose should also be used to disinfect the drinking vessels each week as part of an ongoing cleaning routine.

The very low water cleansing dose is of greatest advantage for canaries. At this dose, KD has a twofold action. Not only is the water vessel automatically cleared of sludge, but the contents of the crop are immediately acidified because canaries drink after they eat. By acidifying the drinking water, KD prevents the contamination of the food and other items stored in the crop and acts in the identical way as food non-buffered acidifying agents (e.g., citric acid).

The young in the nest are most at risk from contaminated food (see E.coli infections on page 122) because it stays in the crop for a prolonged time. KD is especially beneficial in preventing the contamination of the food which is regurgitated by parents to their young. There is no residual effect of KD on canaries because it is immediately neutralized after the food leaves the crop and enters the highly acidic stomach (proventriculus).

Contamination entering the mouth in the form of foodstuff and water is by far the most common cause of disease during the breeding season. KD gives canary enthusiasts the opportunity to recreate the same pristine water, food and environment found in nature without the need for daily cleaning and disinfecting.

KD attacks the heart of health problems, not the disease itself. KD acts by protecting the birds from the germs in the food, water and environment. KD shifts the weaker birds, especially juvenile birds, into good health by allowing the immune system to develop naturally and on its own merits. It protects the birds from germs in the food and water, allowing them to thrive during times of natural stress. This is especially the case for young bird development, during the moult and breeding.

KD for Juveniles and Breeding Birds

Young birds should be allowed to establish their own level of natural resistance. Attention should be placed on the provision of clean water, vitamins, reducing stress and culling rather than using medicines to control health problems. KD is particularly useful when administered once a week.

KD has a positive effect on the immune system and may be used as a Health Stimulant for Juveniles. KD is particularly useful for the aviary crowded with young birds, protecting them from excessive exposure to germs and promoting a stronger level of natural resistance. This process allows the young birds to establish a stronger level of natural resistance. The noise in the aviary intensifies and the activity of the overcrowded young birds lifts the day following the KD. KD accelerates the juvenile moult by promoting good bowel health.

KD kills germs and "self-cleans" the drinkers, removing all traces of sludge automatically. By its cleansing action, KD is used to enhance natural health by lowering the germ count in the water and aviary. This action protects the immune system and nurtures a strong natural resistance in the flock, giving the breeding birds and overcrowded young birds the best opportunity to repel disease naturally and without the use of potentially harmful medicines.

KD helps prevent constipation in nestlings as it has a known purgative effect. KD is preferred to Epsom Salts for this purpose.

KD may be mixed with the bath water in the warmer months as an insect repellent and feather cleanser, repelling red mite, quill mite, scaly face mite, flies and lice. It is not an insecticide.

KD & Health Programmes

When mixed at disinfectant strength, KD is a potent but safe cleanser. It should be wiped or sprayed over the cleaned surfaces of the aviary, nest boxes or breeding cabinet to help repel air born infections, especially moulds and bacterial infections. Unused KD water should be emptied into the soil in the aviary away from plants, as it is harmful to plants, reptiles and fish.

KD as Part of a Health Programme

- KD: Two Consecutive Days a Week.
  The weekend is again the best time to administer KD.

- KD should be added to the drinking water on Saturday morning and emptied Sunday evening.

- Dufoplus and Ioford should then be left in the water until Tuesday night.

- Increased noise, activity and small droppings extending to Sunday evening indicate the need for a two day KD treatment regime.

- Dark green watery droppings and decreased aviary activity on Sunday means KD should be given once weekly unless the weekend is overcast. On overcast, humid or wet days canaries may remain quiet and the droppings may become large and green.

KD Frequency

Each aviary develops its own individual requirements for KD, the frequency being calculated by the flock's response to it.

KD should usually be administered for two consecutive days. More frequent treatments may be necessary for outdoor aviaries or continuously during treatments for diseases associated with contaminated food (White Mould Disease) water (Giardia) or Megabacteria infections.

KD should be used defensively during the early stages of a disease outbreak. Given at the first sign of illness it protects the healthy members of the flock from infection and at the same time improves their natural resistance against the disease.

Response to KD

Positive response to KD:

- Increased activity and noise the day after KD

- Brighter and tighter plumage the day after KD

- Down feathers attached to droppings

Negative response to KD:

- Decreased activity and noise the day after KD

- Fluffed up and large wet droppings the day after KD

- Look at and listen to the flock the morning after KD is administered. There should be an obvious increased noise/activity in the aviary/breeding cage the morning after KD.

KD at the First Sign of Disease

For many "carrier-type" diseases in the aviary and breeding cabinet it may be inappropriate to treat the entire flock with antibiotics. Initially, these diseases that include E.coli, Black Spot, Megabacteria and Strep infections may be the result of a weak family rather than being highly contagious. Even so, when left unattended, these diseases do eventually spread to other birds, infecting even the most robust members of the flock. The role of KD for these diseases is primarily defensive, protecting the healthy members of the flock from contamination via the water, food or environment. The beneficial outcome of KD treatment of "carrier" diseases is to strengthen the flock's natural resistance against them. This enhanced natural resistance does not occur when antibiotic-type medicines are used in the early stages of the outbreak.

KD should be used offensively when the cause of the disease is contaminated food, grit or water. KD must be given to the entire flock when signs of food/grit contamination (deaths in the aviary associated with vomiting and weight loss, breeding hen or cock deaths, soft shelled eggs or feather plucking of chicks, wet nests, smelly wet nests) or water contamination (E.coli or Giardia signs) are recognized as the cause of an illness.

Megamix

Megamix is a blend of unbuffered citric acid and surfactants. The natural acid (citric acid) acidifies foodstuffs and water being stored in the crop.

The activity of canaries may change from day to day depending on the weather and aviary or cabinet conditions. Fluctuations in temperature and humidity have an immediate effect on their welfare. Well-designed and insulated canary rooms offer the best protection from sudden environmental changes. During good weather, they must provide access to direct sunlight and warmth but at the same time offer protection from draughts and excessive air movement. Canaries are happiest and most active during dry, warm weather. They become fluffed up and inactive during humid conditions, prolonged wet or cold spells and when it is overcast. The role of Megamix is to protect the health and vitality of the flock by counteracting the negative effects of poor weather conditions, and may be administered continuously throughout these times.

Megamix protects the birds from the detrimental effects of moisture. It is particularly useful for outdoor aviaries located in "moist" climates (coastal and fog/mist regions) and for those areas using water supplies that have a pH above 7.5. Many canaries in these areas become susceptible to the diseases (E.coli, Thrush, moulds) of high humidity.

Canaries are particularly susceptible to the effects of cold and wet weather. Megamix protects them from the effects of "moisture" related germs on the food. It acts in exactly the same way as acidi-

fying mould inhibitors, which are used to prevent food spoilage in many livestock industries.

Megamix is particularly useful in protecting the health of breeding and young birds during extended wet periods, irrespective of the pH of the drinking water being supplied. During wet weather, juvenile canaries become more susceptible to health problems.

Megamix added to the drinking water during wet weather controls for "moisture" related problems without affecting the developing natural resistance. Megamix is completely safe to administer during the moult or breeding and may be used continuously if need be. Megamix also has the dual action of cleaning the water containers and pipeline systems of sludge.

The Wet Weather Programmes prevent deaths and illness in aviaries susceptible to the effects of moisture. Coccidiosis and E.coli are the main diseases of wet weather, both of which may cause sudden illness and death in one or many birds.

The dose of Megamix is less for canaries than for other birds. The dose may also vary from aviary to aviary, depending upon the humidity in the local area and the "hardness" of the water supply.

The Megamix dose for canaries varies from 2-5mls per liter of drinking water and is calculated by noting the response of the birds and droppings after treatment. Start at 2ml per liter and work up to 5mls until the desired effect is obtained, then stay with that dose. Not only do the droppings return to normal by the afternoon, but the overall appearance of the flock also improves. Look for the return of the glass eye, down feathers on the droppings and a tight, handsome plumage.
The best results occur when Megamix is used at the very first indication of inactivity in a quieter aviary. Previously healthy active birds may suddenly appear tired and fluffed. Megamix invigorates these birds the same day it is introduced. Megamix should then be administered for a further two or more consecutive days during high humidity to maintain vitality in the aviary.

Megamix may be mixed with any other product (vitamins, minerals and antibiotics).

Megamix is particularly useful in protecting the canary from the effects of "moisture" related germs.

Megamix for Wet Weather and Coccidiosis

- A Megamix Programme is used at the first signs of rain.

- Megamix should be provided at the first sign of rain and can continue for three days of rain.

- After three days of rain, Carlox is introduced and administered for as long as the rain continues.

Megamix Programme protects against Coccidiosis and E.coli.

- Given at the first sign of large droppings in aviaries exposed to moisture or wet weather.

- Plays an important part in the control of E.coli, coccidiosis and Thrush in juveniles.

- Used to treat wet nest and sweating disease in susceptible breeding pairs.

- Can be used continuously with no harm.

Megamix Credentials

- First choice water cleanser for a strong, healthy aviary.

- First choice medicine for aviaries with a moisture problem.

- Safe to use for one day or continuously for all birds.

- Never depresses or causes bad droppings in healthy canaries.

- Safe to give to breeding birds and to parents feeding young babies.

Megamix Cocktails

Doxycycline & Megamix Cocktail.

Doxycycline is added to Megamix (2mls per liter) to aid the absorption of Calcium and Magnesium salts during an Ornithosis treatment. This accelerates recovery from illness and also allows breeding to continue during treatment without retarding the growth of chicks or weakening the breeding hen during egg-laying. The Doxycycline/Megamix Cocktail may also be used to treat Ornithosis during the moult where its use accelerates rather than depresses new feather growth.

Vitamin & Megamix Cocktail.

Dufoplus, Ioford and NV can all be mixed with Megamix. This cocktail is often given during a wet weather programme or after a coccidiosis outbreak.

Ioford & Megamix Cocktail.

This cocktail is especially beneficial for moulting juveniles during wet spells. It is also an effective treatment for sweating disease problems in breeding pairs and prevents moisture related health problems. The Ioford/Megamix cocktail is often successful in invigorating "fluffed up" and "just not right" canaries when the cause of the lethargy is uncertain.

Sulfa-AVS & Megamix Cocktail.

This is an extremely popular and effective cocktail for coccidiosis, E.coli & enteritis outbreaks in young birds.

chapter 8
Canary Diseases, Medicines and Problem Solving

Aspergillosis & Moulding Disease

There are two forms of Aspergillosis; inhaled (Aspergillosis) and ingested (Moulding Disease) that may occur together or alone.

Inhaled Form (aspergillosis)

The inhaled form of Aspergillosis is not contagious from bird to bird but originates from contaminated (mouldy) foods, environments and nesting material. The inhaled form of Aspergillosis is relatively uncommon in canaries. Juveniles are susceptible during the moult while feeding parents are susceptible during or soon after wet spells. A moist environment with poor ventilation predisposes canaries to the inhaled form of Aspergillosis. Infection occurs when birds inhale fungal spores present in the nests or aviary. The inhaled spores may accumulate in the air-sac, forming abscesses. Gasping, open mouth breathing and clicking respiration followed by rapid death, are all signs of this incurable form of Aspergillosis.

This disease is uncommon in air-conditioned canary rooms but of considerable danger to canaries housed under more natural conditions, where there is a greater opportunity for foodstuffs to spoil, condensation to occur and moisture to accumulate.

Aspergillosis abscess formation in the air-sacs is not a common finding in canaries. This inhaled form is a likely cause when canaries "go light" and juveniles die during the moult. Infections with Aspergillus may also cause neurological symptoms of head turning, sky gazing and dizziness.

Mycoplasma infections may result from the effects of fungal toxins. Mycoplasma produces the symptoms of open mouth breathing, clicking respiration and death of juvenile birds. Older birds do not show symptoms of Mycoplsma infection. Ornithosis is usually responsible for the death of infected birds. Resfite, or other medicines that combine Doxycycline and Tylosine, is the antibiotic medicine of choice for treating young bird flocks with symptoms of Mycoplasma infection. After the source of the fungus has been removed, a rapid response to Resfite should be anticipated.

The stress of weaning, flights overcrowded with young birds, the presence of inadequate nutrition and underlying disease (especially Black Spot (Atoxoplasmosis and Circovirus) and Ornithosis) predispose young canaries to the effects of an environment contaminated with fungal spores. In weaker young birds, it is a rapidly developing disease of the lungs and air-sacs that causes breathing difficulties and eventual death. Breeding birds with Aspergillosis "go light," may reject their young and rarely regain acceptable levels of productivity.

For individual bird treatment to be successful, Fungilin® must be administered at the onset of symptoms. The disease is incurable once the mould has been established in the lungs or brain. Primary prevention is the best cure as the disease is not contagious. Removal of the source of fungal contamination (sprouted seeds and spoiling foodstuff) combined with the regular use of KD in the drinking water and as a disinfectant should prevent this form of Aspergillosis.

Ingested Form (Moulding Disease)

The combination of Moulding Disease and weak genes is believed to be the most common cause of disease in exhibition canaries.

The ingestion of food contaminated with mould and mould toxins causes the more commonly ingested form of Aspergillosis, known as Moulding Disease. Mould affected food has a lower nutritional value than clean feed and is also capable of producing poisonous toxins. Aspergillosis or other moulds (e.g.,green blue penicillin fungus) found in nest materials and sawdust used on the floor of aviaries, may produce toxins that are capable of harming the health of canaries. The presence of recurrent illness and soft-shelled eggs strongly suggests the presence of Moulding Disease. Ornithosis may also produce similar symptoms.

The primary factors involved in Moulding Disease are immune suppression, weak genes (mutations), malnutrition and a contaminated environment. Nestlings and juveniles, inbred and weaker varieties are most vulnerable to Moulding Disease. Nutritional problems, especially those resulting from an unbalanced diet, also weaken the natural ability of a canary to repel the effects of moulds. Soft-food, soaked decaying seeds left in an aviary and unhygienically prepared foods are common sources of Moulding Disease.

Therefore, the first objective when treating canaries with this disease is to improve cleanliness of the diet. Canaries housed indoors under artificial conditions can be especially susceptible to Moulding Disease. This is because these birds exist without the benefit of direct sunlight and fresh air. Direct sunlight, fresh air and free flight appear to instill a feeling of 'happiness' in birds that cannot be duplicated by artificial lighting, air conditioning or small cages.

Canaries housed indoors are particularly difficult to keep healthy, because of their weak constitution and fragility. It is not surprising therefore that they are the first to be affected by moulding disease, a disease repelled by most strong and healthy birds. Symptoms of 'going light' or 'wasting disease' combined with breathing difficulties or tail bob, especially confined to weaker varieties or inbred families, are signs suggestive of Moulding Disease. Moulding disease is often the underlying cause of recurrent Ornithosis problems in canaries.

Symptoms of Moulding Disease

Flights

- Quiet and low level activity
- Increased thirst (water levels drop quickly)
- Watery droppings from increased drinking
- 'Going light' or 'wasting disease' in young birds
- Leg and wing fractures (from weak bones) while fledging
- Dark green, greasy droppings in many birds soon after the introduction of a new batch of food
- Recurrent illness

Breeding Room

- Soft shelled eggs (despite mineral/grit supplies being adequate)
- Good fertility
- Dying nestlings at pin feather age across many nests
- Pipping deaths, splay legs, panting, gasping and dead youngsters.

The toxic form of Aspergillosis that originates from contaminated soaked seed is however a most significant disease of canary rooms. The toxins produced by fungal contamination harm the immune system and render birds more susceptible to disease, especially Mycoplasma, Ornithosis, Megabacteriosis and Trichomoniasis.

Treatment Strategies

Moulds such as Penicillin moulds produce toxins that are capable of killing young in the nest. Crop stasis, sour crop and vomiting are signs of this type of mould infection. The source of the infection (mould spots in compost heaps within aviaries, contaminated seed, soft food or feeding stations, poor soaking technique) must be removed and the aviary disinfected with KD powder or bleach.

Vitamin, mineral and nutritional support plays a big part in a recovery plan because birds with Moulding Disease are often nutritionally depleted. Prevention should also focus on providing the young birds with exceptionally good nutrition and improved hygiene by using water cleansers and nutritional supplements (see young bird programme).

Flock Treatment

KD powder should be added to the drinking water for three consecutive days.

NV powder should then be added to the drinking water for two days.

Remove the source of infection and disinfect flights or aviary with KD powder.

Mix E-Powder and F-Vite into a tonic seed mix (pages 6 & 158 for tonic seed mix) each day for three weeks.

Individual Bird Treatment

Intensive care is required for sick birds in a heated hospital cage. Those placed in the hospital cage for treatment at the first signs of illness tend to recover in the shortest time. Some birds may die from liver and kidney damage within a day or two. Others may never recover and remain weak indefinitely.

Feed very sick birds with Fungilin and ER formula directly into the mouth using a flat spoon.

Add Fungilin to the drinking water for 10 consecutive days.

Provide nutritional support (sprouted seeds, soft foods fortified with Dufoplus, Ioford, Turbobooster, E-Powder and F-Vite) daily for three weeks.

Do not breed from recovered birds for one season.

These birds may experience problems when they next breed.

ER Formula administered to the mouth of sick birds will help prevent kidney damage caused by moulding disease.

BLACK SPOT

Black Spot is a poorly understood but common finding in canary chicks (1-5 days of age) and juveniles (2-9 months of age). Black Spot refers to the symptom of a black spot on the abdomen of canaries that appears when the spleen, liver or both organs become enlarged because of infection. Black Spot occurs in all varieties of canaries and may spread from one variety to another.

The difficulties experienced in the control of Black Spot in canaries may be a result of the many possible causes of an enlarged spleen and liver.

The two main causes of Black Spot are Circovirus and Coccidiosis (Atoxoplasmosis).

Ornithosis, bacterial septicaemias and other blood parasites (Avian Malaria (Plasmodium), Haemoproteus and Trypanosoma) may also cause Black Spot. German researchers believe Mycoplasma to be the main cause of Black Spot in Europe. Red mites, biting flies, mosquitos and house sparrows spread these blood parasites. Laboured breathing is a symptom seen with these blood parasites.

Black Spot & Circovirus

Circovirus has been incriminated as a cause of the disease that kills nestlings between the ages of one and five days of age. Black Spot caused by Circovirus produces a black spot on the right side of the abdomen in those birds with the disease. Symptoms of Black spot may appear in nestlings as young as one day of age. Infected nestlings are weak and fail to accept food from their parents, have an empty crop and eventually die by three to four days of age. This form of Black Spot is difficult to cure.

Black Spot & Mycoplasma Infection

European investigators believe there is a relationship between Blackspot and Mycoplasma infection. These researchers believe a Pre-Breeding Cleansing Programme using Tylosine cleans the carrier birds of Mycoplasma infection. This treatment is thought to eliminate the Mycoplasma infection from the flock and control Blackspot during the breeding season.

Black Spot & Coccidiosis (Atoxoplasmosis)

A blood form of Coccidiosis called Atoxoplasmosis may cause Black Spot.

See Coccidiosis (page 113) for more notes on Black Spot.

A coccidiosis infection caused by Isospora serini remains the most likely cause of the Black Spot disease in juveniles under a year of age. This disease is also known as Atoxoplasmosis. It is a coccidiosis parasite that differs from the common form of coccidiosis infection caused by Isospora canaria. Coccidiosis is normally restricted to the intestinal epithelium whereas Atoxoplasmosis (a form of coccidiosis caused by Isospora serini) multiplies in the intestine, invades blood cells and

then spreads by the blood stream to infect the liver, lung and spleen.

Atoxoplasmosis infection produces black spots on both sides of the abdomen, a sign that indicates both spleen and liver enlargement. Atoxoplasmosis is thought to be an intermediate form and part of the life cycle of Coccidiosis (Isospora spp).

Symptoms of Black Spot due to Atoxoplasmosis appear in birds under a year old. After this time adult birds may remain infected but show no outward signs of infection. Adult carriers may continue to be contagious for 8 months.

"Carrier" birds are thought to infect their young when feeding. Both cock and hen may be "carriers" but more commonly the hen is the cause. Black Spot occurs more commonly in nests with a first time mother, hens older than three years of age and from a family known to be susceptible to Black Spot. Conditions that weaken the immune system, namely Ornithosis, inbreeding and Moulding Disease, may predispose the canary flock to Black Spot Disease. In previously healthy flocks, Ornithosis and Moulding Disease are the most likely triggers of the disease.

The feeding parent, usually the hen, infects her young as she commonly rears them by herself. She may be continually re-infected by her own Black Spot germs (oocysts) while cleaning the nest of droppings. Cocks may also infect the young when allowed to feed. It is also thought (Roy Dowling Pers. communication 2002) that Black Spot causes "dead in shell" problems, but the mechanism of transmission is unknown. I believe concurrent infection with Ornithosis or brooding failure may account for the dead in shell.

Infected youngsters become listless and huddle, ruffle their feathers into a ball, go light, develop a bloated abdomen, diarrhea and sometimes exhibit neurological signs. Symptoms of the Atoxoplasmosis form of Black Spot appear in young birds under one year of age. Mortality rates (number of birds that die) may reach as high as 80% of the young bird flock. Infection is less common when young canaries are housed in small numbers in cabinets, and conversely, more common in outdoor aviaries and crowded flights.

When Black Spot has appeared during breeding, further outbreaks of it are likely to appear in young birds. Illness and possible death occur in birds between two and nine months of age. The disease spreads from bird to bird via infected droppings. Infected juveniles may remain contagious for up to eight months, causing heavy losses over a long period of time.

Diagnosis is difficult in the live bird because coccidial oocysts are rarely found in droppings or intestinal smears and because of the acute nature of the disease. Special impression smears taken from the lung, liver and spleen of dead birds help to diagnose Atoxoplasmosis.

Black Spot Control and Prevention

There is no medical cure for Black Spot. The best avenue is to eliminate those families susceptible to Black Spot and to control conditions that predispose canaries to this complex disease.

Similar measures must be taken irrespective of the cause of Black Spot. Good hygiene, nutrition and disease prevention help control for Black Spot.

Good hygiene (e.g., F-Vite rather than grit), improved nutrition and disease control (Ornithosis treatments for the resident flock and for new birds in quarantine) play important roles in aviaries where Black Spot is an intermittent problem. The introduction of new birds that carry the disease, poor nutrition and hygiene, overcrowding or contaminated food are

common causes of Black Spot in flocks previously free of the disease. Pre-breeding programmes aimed at eliminating diseases such as Psittacosis and preparing the birds for breeding are an essential part in the control of Black Spot. The use of water cleansers, such as KD, and attention to strict hygienic in the preparation of soft food and sprouted seed also help to control Black Spot. Mr Roy Dowling uses dandelion tea in the water as part of a pre-breeding programme and believes this helps prevent Black Spot in his birds.

Black Spot Symptoms

Nest Signs

Black Spot is more prevalent in the first and third rounds. This finding supports the view that the disease should be able to be controlled naturally in strong individuals when they are housed and looked after properly. Deaths of nestlings between one and five days of age should be assumed to be Black Spot until proven otherwise.

Eggs

Black Spot should be considered as a cause of a green/black coloured, pungent smelling fully developed embryo found in "dead in shell" eggs. Black Spot appears to have little effect on fertility.

Eggs that fail to hatch should be broken open and examined for signs of addling or dead in shell babies.
Eggs that smell when opened carry an infection. Black spot is a common cause of smelly, addled and dead in shell eggs.

Nestlings (0-5 days of age)

Black Spot may be confirmed in nestlings between one and five days of age by the presence of the black spot on the abdomen. Some fanciers believe Black Spot occurs more frequently with poor parents because hand-feeding helps some infected chicks to survive. These chicks, however, remain carriers for life and pose a significant

Repeated treatments with Carlox/Baycox® as part of a Young Bird Programme, Moult Programme and the Pre-Breeding Programme are important for controlling Black Spot.

Nestlings that do not beg for food are weak and should be examined for the presence of Black Spot.

health risk when moved from the nest into weaning cages.

Many nests with Black Spot deaths also rear perfectly normal chicks. Some of these apparently healthy nestlings may in fact be carrier birds and the cause of Black Spot outbreaks that occur in crowded juvenile flights.

Juveniles (2-9 months of age)

Black Spot may also infect juveniles between two and nine months of age. The infected birds become fluffed up, have watery diarrhea and stop eating. Up to 80% of the flock may die from this incurable disease. A black spot (enlarged liver and spleen) and bloated abdomen (dilated bowel loops) are signs of Black Spot that may be seen through the transparent abdomen wall. Outbreaks occur in aviaries crowded with young birds where Black Spot has occurred during the breeding sea-

son. This type of Black Spot is related to Atoxoplasmosis.

Adult birds

It appears that older birds acquire immunity to Black Spot with only carrier birds being susceptible to the disease when their health has been compromised.

Black Spot (Circovirus): Methods for Preventing

Identify and eliminate susceptible individuals and families.

Control diseases (Ornithosis, Moulding Disease from contaminated sprouted seed, soft food or grit) that damage the immune system and predispose canaries to Black Spot.

Practice good hygiene, nutrition and quarantine measures.

Pay strict attention to the hygienic preparation of soft foods and sprouted seed to help avoid Moulding Disease and E.coli infections.

Use Carlox/Baycox as part of a control plan against Black Spot during the Young Bird, Moult and Pre-Breeding Programmes.

Implement a Pre-Breeding Programme that eliminates diseases such as Ornithosis and helps prepare birds for breeding.

Use KD water cleanser on a weekly basis.

Black Spot may also infect juveniles between two and nine months of age.

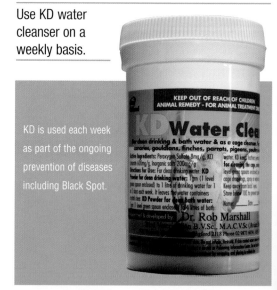

KD is used each week as part of the ongoing prevention of diseases including Black Spot.

BREEDING PROBLEMS

The time breeding commences is critical to breeding success. Infertility should be expected during the first round of breeding when cold temperatures interrupt the breeding cycle or weather conditions are especially dry. It is not uncommon for virgin breeders to experience breeding difficulties during their first round.

The cause of the failure of these two eggs to hatch should be investigated.

Breeding success relies on attention to detail and following a proven strategy.

Infertility

In many ways, the results of the breeding season determine the overall enjoyment the fancier may get from the hobby because there is a far greater chance of breeding show champions when more offspring are produced by the better pairs.

Fortunately, the culture of keeping exhibition canaries has promoted accurate breeding records in which information concerning the eggs and young is recorded. This data is of great value and should be used by the fancier to improve breeding results by selecting fertile individuals for breeding. Eggs offer a wealth of information, enabling the fancier to solve breeding problems and to improve the overall health and breeding performance of the flock.

Egg Problems

- Failure to lay eggs (infertile hen)
- Clear eggs (infertile cock)
- Addled eggs (early embryonic death)
- Dead-in-shell eggs (late embryonic death)
- Soft, thin shelled or malformed eggs (Mineral deficiencies and uterus infections)

Hen Infertility (Failure to lay eggs)

A failure of the hen to lay eggs signals an infertile or barren hen. Hen infertility may be temporary and a failure to lay eggs should not immediately preclude her from future breeding. Canary hens must be in breeding condition before they are capable of laying eggs. It is a failure of the hen to come into breeding condition that is the most common cause of hen infertility during the first round of breeding.

To solve the cause of hen infertility the fancier should:

- Check when the hen was placed in the breeding cabinet. In most instances, hen infertility is the result of an inappropriate breeding starting time and an absence of or poorly defined breeding condition.

- Closely examine the hen for:
    - A loss of breeding condition
    - Obesity (fat hens will fail to come into breeding condition)
    - "Going light" (irrespective of the cause of "going light" these hens lack the strength and vigor to lay eggs)

- Check food quality and latent disease. There may be an underlying disease (Ornithosis, Black Spot (Atoxoplasmosis), Megabacteria) or food contamination (check soft food hygiene, sprouted seed and quality of seed) when a high percentage (higher than 10%) of hens fail to lay eggs.

- Check the breeding records for genetic weaknesses or evidence of inbreeding.

Cock infertility (clear eggs)

Eggs that fail to hatch are not always infertile and each egg must be carefully examined to determine whether it is "clear," "addled" or "dead-in-shell." Many canary breeders use a candling light to determine the fertility of eggs. Candling is the act of shining a light (usually an optic fiber torch) through an egg to observe whether it is clear (infertile), or fertile. It is also used to identify eggshell abnormalities and dead-in-shell problems. Clear eggs indicate infertile eggs but it is not always the cock who should take the blame.

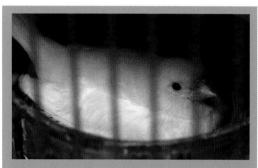

Clear eggs under a perfectly healthy hen in breeding condition are often a result of an infertile cock or a hen who is inexperienced at mating.

In order to solve a clear egg problem the fancier must:

Differentiate the infertile egg from an egg in which the germ or embryo has died.

- Clear (infertile) eggs.
  - Are fresh and clear at the end of incubation as from the first day.
  - Carry no odor at any age when broken open.
  - Show no blood vessel activity when candled.

- Eggs in which the embryo has died.
  - Eggshell is darker. Dark streaks may also be present.
  - Eggs emit a foul odor when opened.
  - Candling reveals blood rings and other signs of a dead embryo.

Physically examine the cock bird for signs of breeding condition, obesity, weight loss or illness as a possible cause of clear eggs.

The size of the testicle enlarges ten-fold as the canary is stimulated into breeding condition by an increasing length of daylight in its environment. Male canaries need three times more energy during the pairing process and up to tens times more energy when feeding young than cock birds that are not breeding. When there is a depletion of the energy available to the cock, he will quickly lose breeding condition and also the ability to fertilize eggs. Processes that inhibit the cock to access and utilize this energy such as obesity, disease and poor nutrition, will result in clear eggs. Cocks that are obese are infertile because they are unable to come into breeding condition. Those carrying disease will quickly lose breeding condition under the energy drain and subsequent stress during the normal process of pairing. Often, male fertility in canaries can be improved with the addition of quality protein, vitamin and energy feed supplements.

Other Causes of Clear Eggs

Inbreeding is a common cause of infertility in cock birds. Male fertility is more hereditary than female fertility and sterility is passed down in the genes from father to son. An unrelated and proven fertile cock should be introduced when a high level of cock related infertility is experienced in an inbred line of birds. There is also a very close relationship between sterility and nutrition. Excessively long or thick feathers around the vent (buff feathered vents) are a common cause of male infertility because they prevent the passage of sperm into the cloaca of the hen. These should be carefully clipped short with a sharp pair of scissors prior to pairing.

Solutions for a high incidence of infertility in the stud

Reassess the time that breeding commences. Do not start breeding when it is too cold.

Identify health problems and "cleanse" the stud with a Cleansing Programme prior to the breeding season. Seek veterinary help when there is widespread infertility in order to identify and eliminate diseases such as Ornithosis, Megabacteria, E.coli and Staphylococcus infections. Fortify the diet to lift the overall nutritional status of the flock.

Change the breeding strategy. "Outcross" when weak lines and inbreeding cause cock or hen infertility.

Addled & Dead-In-Shell Eggs

Addled & dead-in-shell eggs are fertile eggs that fail to hatch. Both addled and dead in shell are fertile eggs in which the embryos have died. Addled eggs represent early (within the first week of fertilization) death, and dead-in-shell a late (a few days prior to hatching) death of the embryo. Eggs failing to hatch should be removed from the nest, cracked open and inspected. This is called "breaking out." Breaking out gives valuable information about eggshell quality and determines whether the egg is infertile, addled or dead in shell.

Breaking out" allows the fancier to understand the exact nature of an egg problem.

"Breaking Out" Findings

Infertile Eggs

- Egg yolk & egg white remains intact.
- No smell.

Addled Eggs

- The egg yolk and white are mixed together.
- Yellow or brown in color
- Usually smells

Dead in Shell

- Fully formed chick is usually clearly visible.

Egg Shell Quality

Check for obvious cracks and stains. Cracked eggs are susceptible to bacterial (Strep. and E. coli) and fungal infections. Fungus usually appears as black marks near the cracks in the shells

Determining the Cause of Egg Death

The age at which the embryo dies must be calculated in order to determine the cause of the dead-in-shell problem. The three important age groups are early, mid term and late deaths.

Addled Eggs

Addled eggs represent early or mid term deaths. Early deaths (less than 7 days), comprising a third of all dead in shell problems, always produce addled eggs. "Breaking out" is the best way to diagnose these early deaths because candling fails to distinguish early deaths from infertile eggs.

A small dead embryo is clearly visible by candling with mid-term deaths (between 7-14 days) but within a few days the egg addles. Candling every second day is a very good way to distinguish between early stage and mid-term dead in shell problems because "breaking out" is not usually performed until all of the healthy eggs have hatched. By this time the eggs may have been dead for up to four weeks and are already addled.

Most eggs in which there are early deaths, remain yellow. Brown addled eggs represent midterm deaths or early deaths caused by infection.

Dead-in-shell and hatching death

Late term deaths (14 days to hatching) are called "dead-in-shell" because the dead embryo is always clearly visible. Late term deaths are easy to diagnose by "breaking out" because they usually occur within three days prior to hatching. Hatching deaths occur for exactly the same reasons as late term dead in shell.

Culture testing of dead eggs is by far the best

The broken open egg contains a baby that has died during hatching. There are a number of causes of dead in shell.

method to determine the underlying cause of addled and dead in shell eggs. Culture testing reveals very quickly whether or not a bacterial disease is involved. A clear culture test reveals the cause of the dead is shell problem to be a management problem or Ornithosis.

Addled or Dead in Shell eggs in one or two nests only

The appearance of dead eggs in one or two nests points towards a weak hen or a hen carrying diseases such as Megabacteria, Atoxoplasmosis or Strep. infection. Treatment is confined to the affected nest(s) only or the hen is replaced.

Addled or Dead in Shell eggs in many nests

The sudden onset of many nests with addled or dead in shell eggs indicates a disease (Ornithosis, White Mould Disease, Salmonella, E.coli, red mite) or a management problem (brooding disease). Appropriate treatment should be administered to the entire breeding flock.

Addled eggs are often mistaken as clear eggs.

Often fanciers mistakenly believe they have a fertility problem because clear eggs and addled eggs look so alike from the outside. "Breaking out" and "candling" are the methods used to distinguish clear eggs from addled eggs.

"Breaking out" and gentle rocking are used to diagnose "addled eggs."

The first week is critical for the development of the fertile egg with a third of all embryo deaths occurring during this time. Addled eggs refer to the death of the embryo within this first week period. The yolk and white of addled eggs mix together, producing a watery, freely moving "addled" egg when rocked or broken open, whereas the yolk and white of fertile eggs are clearly separate. Blood rings visible by candling indicate death within the first week, otherwise known as early embryonic death.

Mid term deaths are uncommon.

Mid term deaths are diagnosed by "breaking out" a mushy brown smelly egg or by candling, where a dark shadow of the dead decayed embryo is seen. The cause of mid-term egg death is usually brooding failure or egg damage.

Many but not all addled eggs smell

Bacterial and fungal infections cause addled eggs to smell. Bacterial infections enter the shell from the ovaries infected with Salmonella or from contaminated droppings (E.coli, Streptococcus) of the brooding hen. Cooling eggs, thin shelled and cracked eggs are more susceptible to bacterial and fungal infections. This may occur when the eggs have been removed from the hen and temporarily stored. A cold spell may kill some of the eggs outright due to brooding failure. These eggs remain odorless but eggs in the same clutch dying later from bacterial or fungus infection may smell when cracked open because cool eggs are less able to repel bacteria. Fungal infections originate from mould in the nest box or from the droppings and are most likely to invade cracked or poorly brooded eggs.

Very dry weather, thunderstorms and brooding failure are common causes of odorless addled eggs.

Odorless, addled eggs are not always necessarily free of infection and Ornithosis and Mycoplasma infections may also be the cause of odorless addled eggs. Excessively dry weather, thunderstorms and brooding failure are also often to blame.

Egg culture greatly assists in determining the cause and treatment of addled eggs.

An egg culture helps identify the underlying cause of addled eggs. No growth on the culture plate points towards dry weather or thunderstorms as the cause of addled eggs in flocks with high fertility and Ornithosis in infertile flocks. Bacteria growth usually reveals a Strep. or E.coli infection. E.coli egg infections are often successfully treated. Staphylococcal egg infections reflect a hen weakened by poor management, Ornithosis or Mycoplasma infections. They do not respond very well to antibiotic treatment. Often it is better to replace the hen.

Dead-in-shell Eggs (Late Embryonic Death)

The time of internal pip is a time of high egg mortality.

Weakened embryos find the three day hatching process very strenuous and die before or shortly after leaving the egg. Disease, poor feeding and brooding failure are the most common causes of

This is a dead in shell baby that has died during hatching, indicating a weak embryo. Ornithosis is the most common cause of dead in shell in canaries.

late stage egg deaths. Dead in shell eggs (late embryonic death) are very obvious when cracking open the egg.

Causes of Dead in Shell Disease
Ornithosis (Infertility), Salmonella (related to mice), Strep. infections, E.coli (good fertility, soaked seed or wet grit) and fungal infections (good fertility, mould on droppings) are common causes of dead in shell.

Strep. and Megabacteria infections affect individual nests while Ornithosis, Salmonella and E. coli affect many nests.

Brooding Failure
In the warmer months, red mites are the most common cause of brooding failure causing dead in shell. A sudden cold spell during brooding causes dead in shell in many weak nests. When

hens are weak with disease or "out of condition," addled eggs are more likely to appear in individual nests. Addled eggs are common in buff feathered birds because they are more susceptible to brooding failure.

Low humidity
Dead in shell occurs in dry seasons. There is also usually a correlating high number of addled eggs. Water sprays and baths are recommended during dry spells.

Atoxoplasmosis Hens
Hens carrying Atoxoplasmosis produce more dead in shell, because they are more susceptible to Mycoplasma, Ornithosis, Streptococcus and E.coli infections that may weaken or kill the developing embryos.

Self Diagnosing Addled or Dead in Shell Eggs

Ornithosis
- Infertility
- Occasional illness or deaths
- Cocks and hens equally affected

E. coli
- Dead in Shell rather than addled eggs
- Many nests involved
- Fertility is good
- Soaked seed, wet grit or sand are often infected with Ecoli
- Occasional illness or deaths in the breeding rooms and flights
- Cocks and hens are equally affected. Cocks are especially at risk during courtship, while the hens become vulnerable when laying eggs
- Stunted growth and deaths of nestlings

Megabacteria
- Mostly addled eggs
- Some dead in shell
- Isolated nests of related birds involved
- Infertility
- Vomiting
- Nesting Diarrhea and Sweating Disease sometimes present

Brooding is an energy depleting process. When the birds are not perfectly healthy they fail to sit tightly on the nest, leading to poor hatching and dead in shell babies.

Strep

- Mostly addled eggs
- Some dead in shell
- Isolated nests of related birds involved.
- Fertility is good.
- Nesting Diarrhea and Sweating Disease sometimes present

Salmonella

- Addled eggs
- Dead in shell
- Many nests involved
- Fertility is good
- Mice always present
- Occasional illness or deaths occurring in breeding rooms and flights
- More hens affected
- Stunted growth and deaths of nestlings

Soft & Thin Shelled Eggs

Calcium and Vitamin D Deficiency

Hens with no access to calcium salts or sunlight may lay soft-shelled eggs. Moulding disease is another common cause of soft-shelled and rough eggs. Small, misshapen, soft, irregular and hard-shelled eggs occur when there is a problem (bacterial infections, fungal infections) with the shell gland, a disturbance in the aviary and with old hens. Soft shelled or thickened eggs rarely hatch.

Thin shelled Eggs

Damaged eggs are more often the result of a calcium deficiency than immature or restless parents. Often the hen in a nest with damaged eggs has lost body condition as a result of calcium problems associated with E.coli, Megabacteria or other bowel infections.

Thin shelled eggs and splay legged offspring.

The quality of the eggshell is vital for the development of strong bones in the hatchlings. Although the egg yolk is rich in calcium, it does not provide enough calcium for normal bone production in the growing embryo and eighty percent of the calcium in the bones of the hatchling is drawn from the eggshell during incubation. The hatchlings from thin-shelled eggs are weak and often develop splay legs.

Causes of Soft or Thin-Shelled Eggs

The "Out of Condition" Hen

The hormonal preparation for laying eggs is critical for eggshell quality. Bowel diseases (Megabacteria, E.coli or White Mould Disease) prevent the hen from absorbing calcium, resulting in the production of thin-shelled eggs.

Inadequate sunlight

The vitamin D from sunshine is essential for the absorption of Calcium.

Inadequate calcium in diet

Cuttle fish and shell grit are poor sources of dietary calcium.

Immediate Treatment for Soft-Shelled Eggs

Collect droppings of hen for veterinary analysis to check for bowel diseases especially Moulding Disease.

Give KD and Hi-Cal together in the drinking water for five consecutive days.

Mix Turbobooster, E-Powder, F-Vite, IofordNF and Dufoplus in a sprouted seed or soft food mix and feed for seven days.

Provide the hen with plenty of direct sunlight to provide her with natural Vitamin D. Dark aviaries predispose breeding birds to health problems and poor breeding results, including bent keels, splay legs, wet nests, poor feather quality and poor egg-shell quality.

Do not breed with this hen for at least eight weeks.

Prevention of Soft-Shelled Eggs

Breeding Season Health Programme.

KD added to the drinking water for at least one day each week.

Pep food cleaner to protect the feed from the harmful effects of fungal infections. The fancier can quickly recognize a potentially harmful fungal infection by the appearance of mould on the droppings in the breeding cabinet.

CANARY POX

Canary Pox is a serious disease of canaries that is transmitted from bird to bird by mosquitoes, mites, other biting insects and through contact with bite wounds. Wild birds, especially sparrows, may infect canaries with other forms of pox.

Canary Pox is a problem for outside aviaries. It is an uncommon infection for canaries housed indoors.

Several forms of canary pox may appear simultaneously. The skin form may first present as conjunctivitis and blinking. These early symptoms progress quickly to yellow-to-brown wart-like sores on the unfeathered parts of the body. The respiratory form presents with a sudden onset of ruffled feathers, breathing difficulties, cyanosis (blue tongue) and death. With this form of canary pox, death rates may reach 100% within three days.

Symptoms of Canary Pox

- Infection spreads very quickly.
- Scabs and pox sores form, especially on the eyelids, feet and toes.
- Open mouth due to diptheric sores in the mouth and larynx.
- Birds of all ages affected.
- Death rate can be very high (20%-100%).

Treatment

It is difficult to save birds once eyelid sores and mouth signs appear.

"In contact" birds should be moved inside to mosquito proof cages in small groups.

KD powder is administered to the drinking water for three weeks.

Turbobooster, E-Powder and F-Vite should be provided each day in sprouted seed or a soft food.

Prevention

Vaccination for protection from mosquito and wild birds is available overseas. Vaccination should be administered one month before the onset of the mosquito season and repeated annually. Canaries will develop immunity three to six months following vaccination.

CANKER (TRICHOMONIASIS)

Canker (Trichomoniasis) is a serious disease that causes illness and death in susceptible families and certain varieties of canaries, especially Red Factors and Glosters.

Most healthy canaries show a strong resistance to canker. It may, however, cause heavy losses in the nest and flights of all ages and both sexes. The protozoal parasite, Trichomonas gallinae, causes this highly contagious disease. It usually enters the flights by youngsters already infected in the nest or from adult carrier birds (newly acquired birds or breeding birds).

Mineral deficiencies and genetic weaknesses brought about by inbreeding susceptible families predispose canaries to canker outbreaks. Canker (Trichomonas spp.) is not only a problem of the upper digestive tract but also a cause of protozoal sinusitis in canaries.

Many of the symptoms (coughing, snicking, respiratory distress and nostril discharge) associated with canker in canaries may be mistaken for a respiratory infection. Other symptoms (gagging, neck stretching, regurgitation, green diarrhea, going light) relate to the severe damage inflicted by the canker organism on the esophagus (food pipe) and crop lining membranes. The pain associated with infection stops canaries from eating. Caseous (cheesy) material may be seen in the crop and esophagus of young (mostly pin feather aged) nestlings that have died suddenly in the nest.

Canker Symptoms

There are Two Forms of Canker
The dry form becomes visible as cheesy deposits in the mouth and at the back of throat of nestlings at pinfeather age (8-10 days old). At this age the

parents change their feeding from milk to large whole grain. The sharp edges of the whole grain can damage the fragile mouth and throat of chicks after which the canker germ produces cheesy deposits that eventually block the opening to the throat and windpipe. The youngsters with this form of canker choke to death. Chicks with open mouth breathing or found dead at pinfeather age should always be checked for signs of dry canker.

The wet form of canker occurs in juveniles and adult birds in the flights or weaning cabinets. Infected birds breathe with an open mouth and have a wet moist wheeze. The canker germ is also poisonous to the liver and the afflicted canaries become ill, do not eat and produce dark green, watery droppings. Vomiting and an increased thirst may also occur. Deaths often accompany this form of canker as it quickly spreads through the flight.

Modern and safe canker medicines (e.g., Turbosole) play a vital role in outbreaks of Trichomoniasis. Canker has a highly contagious nature and often results in a high incidence of carrier birds following infection. Turbosole is the canker medicine of choice for canaries because it is palatable, non-toxic and does not damage the fertility of the breeding flock. Five days on Turbosole, with two days break, followed by another five-day course, brings most outbreaks under control.

Canker begins in the breeders and this is the best place to start eradication programmes. The disease can be eliminated readily from the breeding room without using canker medicines, because individual breeders are used. The best and fastest long term cure of canker in canaries is achieved by removing canker-susceptible breeders from the breeding room and using only resistant birds for breeding. This drug-free approach eliminates canker from the aviary within two to three breeding seasons. Additionally, the administration of mineral powders (e.g., Fvite) and water cleansers (e.g., KD) may successfully prevent canker outbreaks in hardy flocks.

Canker rarely occurs on its own in a healthy, well-managed aviary. Other diseases are commonly involved. There is always a trigger to an outbreak of Trichomoniasis, and to avoid recurrent infections the trigger must be identified. Mineral deficiencies, hard edged contaminated grit and poor hygiene may trigger an outbreak in susceptible flocks.

Young bird deaths are a sign of overcrowding or a stress induced diseases. Old bird deaths indicate carrier birds have introduced a novel strain to the aviary or that the nutrition is faulty. Canker outbreaks occur more frequently where there are pre-existing health problems. Overcrowding, wetness and poor nutrition, diseases such as Psittacosis and Moulding Disease are the most common conditions predisposing the flock to canker outbreaks because they lower the ability of the flock to repel disease.

Turbosole Treatment for a Canker Outbreak

The entire flock should be treated with Turbosole for five days, followed by NV powder for two days, then another five-day course of Turbosole. Flock treatment is necessary during an outbreak to protect the healthy flock from other infections.

Prevention of Canker

KD water cleanser

The effectiveness of the immune system and the maintenance of a strong natural resistance against canker and other diseases depend upon limiting the exposure of the stressed overcrowded young birds to the harmful effects of too many canker germs. A very dry aviary and water cleansers play an important role in the "medicine free" approach to canker control.

Clean Feed & Grit

The feed must be of the highest quality because food contaminated with bacteria, fungus and toxins during breeding spells disaster for the babies. Canker outbreaks associated with poor feed occur because the immune system is weakened, rendering the flock susceptible to the effects of canker.

Balanced Nutrition

Food low in energy and protein also predisposes the flock to canker. During breeding the canaries must be given more minerals, vitamins, protein and energy in their food. Many fanciers give soaked seed for this reason, but often, the soaking accentuates a bad food problem.

Extra minerals help prevent Canker

Minerals are the most under-rated factor of a successful and canker free breeding season. Canker outbreaks are more common in aviaries with a mineral deficiency. It is often the electrolyte imbalance of the feeding adults that triggers a canker outbreak.

Use Canker Medicines with caution

With the introduction of the new canker medicines, the fancier is now able to control most of the canker outbreaks in the aviary, and it is very tempting to use canker medicines on a regular basis. The system of using canker medicines before breeding and in the aviary overcrowded with young birds is useful in aviaries with a known canker problem, but the same system may destroy the healthy flock's natural resistance against canker and actually predispose it to this disease. Many healthy flocks carry a small percentage of canker susceptible birds (nearly always, these birds are from the same family). In these healthy flocks the selective use of canker medicines in the breeding cabinets is a far better option for preventing canker outbreaks than a regular canker treatment that is given to the entire flock. It is better to follow the more natural approach mentioned above and monitor its response, before reaching for canker medicines.

GIARDIA INFECTION AND TURBOSOLE

Giardia infection has been particularly recognized in Norwich canaries. Other varieties appear to be resistant. Symptoms appear in weak individuals only. Squirty, projectile, watery diarrhea in one or two susceptible birds in an otherwise healthy flock signals the presence of a Giardia infection. Giardia is not a fatal infection in canaries. Infected birds may remain carriers. They may also develop a permanent watery dropping, where vent feathers fall out and the abdomen becomes swollen. Infected hens may never return to good health or attain breeding condition, but otherwise look normal and bright. Feather picking is another sign of a Giardia infection.

Administering a five-day course of Turbosole to treat infected and exposed birds is recommended. Giardia may become more of a problem as city water supplies become less reliable.

COCCIDIOSIS

There are believed to be two distinct forms of Coccidiosis in canaries. The first commonly referred to as Coccidiosis infects and remains in the intestine. This form is caused by the coccidial organism Isospora canari,. The other, more serious, form called Atoxoplasmosis and caused by Isospora serini also infects the intestine but then spreads in the blood to other organs (liver, lung and spleen). For further details about this form of coccidiosis, called Black Spot see page 101.

Canaries may become infected with coccidiosis within the first days of life, but not exhibit clinical signs until two months of age. Both forms may cause heavy losses, especially of young birds.

Coccidiosis (caused by Isospora canari) is a disease of wet conditions, dirt floored aviaries and where young birds are weakened by poor genes, fluctuating temperatures, another disease or poor nutrition. Coccidiosis is rarely a problem when the floor of the aviary is kept clean and dry.

Coccidiosis may become a problem when leaking or split drinkers wet the floors of the cage or feed stations. Dry aviary conditions do not always preclude the presence of coccidiosis because outbreaks may appear secondary to other diseases.

Coccidiosis suddenly affects juvenile canaries immediate to a change in weather conditions. Summer (after rain) and Autumn (with increasing humidity) are seasons where canary flights are most crowded with young birds and are the most likely times for Coccidiosis outbreaks.

Symptoms of Coccidiosis

The symptoms of both forms of Coccidiosis appear very suddenly. Symptoms include watery droppings, severe depression, fluffed up look, shaking and weight loss, followed by dark green, tacky, smelly diarrhea, abdominal distension due to an enlarged liver, sometimes nervous signs and death. Coccidial oocysts are rarely found under microscopic examination of droppings or intestinal contents of dying birds because of the sudden nature of the disease.

Treatment and Control

Carlox/Baycox may be used to prevent both Coccidiosis and Atoxoplasmosis. Both forms of Coccidiosis are most dangerous to canaries between 2-9 months of age. Canaries should receive regular treatments with Carlox. Carlox administration should always form a part of the Winter Cleansing Programme to help prevent Black Spot in nestlings. A treatment at this time also helps to protect young birds against infections. Carlox should also be given during the Young Bird Programme.

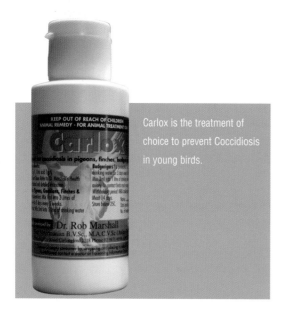

Carlox is the treatment of choice to prevent Coccidiosis in young birds.

The control of Coccidiosis requires strict hygiene practices and regular treatments. Carlox administered at a low dose (1ml per litre) for three days every month prevents coccidiosis outbreaks in young birds and promotes immunity against reinfection, and Carlox is thus the medicine of choice to prevent Coccidiosis in canaries. Resistance of Coccidiosis to Carlox has not been detected. It has little effect on already infected birds, but protects in contact birds within three days.

Prevention of Coccidiosis

Atoxoplasmosis (Black Spot) is a difficult disease to prevent because infected birds may remain contagious for up to 8 months. Infection spreads from parent to chicks and from bird to bird. Young birds are most susceptible to infection.

Carlox treatment, prior to breeding, as part of the Winter Cleansing Programme, should help reduce Atoxoplasma outbreaks.

Treatments for Coccidiosis/Atoxoplasmosis Infections

Individual Treatment
Sulfa AVS is used to stop the spread of coccidiosis throughout an infected aviary during outbreaks. It is also the medicine of choice to treat birds with early signs of Coccidiosis. These birds must be removed from the aviary into a heated hospital cage for individual treatment. Canaries readily accept Sulfa AVS as it is palatable and they are usually thirsty in the early stages of infection. Prevention Programmes must be employed to control Atoxoplasmosis as treatments against active infections have been found to be ineffective.

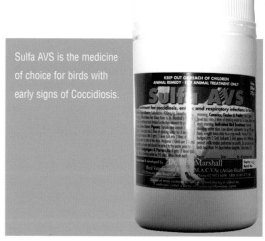

Sulfa AVS is the medicine of choice for birds with early signs of Coccidiosis.

Prevention of Coccidiosis/Atoxoplasmosis

Preventative programmes are recommended against Coccidiosis/Atoxoplasmosis because of the difficulties in curing these diseases.

Prevention for Breeding Birds
An infection with Atoxoplasmosis (Black Spot) in the breeding cabinets is of great concern. "Carrier" birds that infect their young in the nest introduce and perpetuate infections throughout the flock. The disease is spread from the nest to weaning units and then to young bird flights.

The control of Atoxoplasmosis must concentrate on eliminating the infection (breaking the cycle) before the start of breeding. Control, using this technique, may be incomplete as the stress of breeding may cause previously infected but recovered birds to become contagious. A multi-pronged attack is therefore necessary in canary flocks where Atoxoplasmosis (Black Spot) is a problem.

Prevention Treatment against Coccidiosis should be considered for breeding birds when deaths from Black Spot appear in young birds between 2-9 months of age. Carlox administered as part of a pre-breeding cleansing programme should help prevent both forms of Coccidiosis. Carlox may also be administered while the hen is brooding eggs when Black spot has been experienced in her young of between 2-9 months of age. Regular and complete "flame" and chemical disinfection is also necessary because Atoxoplasmosis oocysts may remain infective in the environment for years. Other control options include withdrawing from breeding for a year and complete depopulation.

Prevention for Young Birds
Weaning and juvenile canaries are vulnerable to Coccidiosis because they have not yet developed immunity to this illness. Repeat preventative treatments should be carried out with young birds.

Carlox should be administered at high doses (2mls per liter (75mg/l)) for two days each week for four weeks. Carlox should then be administered at low doses (1ml per 2 liters of drinking water) for five days when hens are brooding eggs.

Carlox for Young Birds
Carlox treatment should start in the weaning unit for two days each week at a low dose and extend for four weeks. Carlox should then be administered at low doses (1ml per 2 liters of drinking water) for two days each month until the conclusion of the moult.

Treating New Birds in Quarantine
Carlox should be administered at the high dose (3mls per liter) for three days each week for four weeks.

ORNITHOSIS & DOXYCYCLINE

Ornithosis (Ornithosis, Psittacosis or Chlamydophila infection)

Ornithosis is the name of the disease in canaries caused by the virus-like bacteria Chlamydia psittaci. In parrots, the same disease is known as Psittacosis. Ornithosis and Psittacosis are now known as a Chlamydophila infection. In this book the name Ornithosis will be used to describe this disease.

Ornithosis is one of the most significant disease of canaries because of its high prevalence and the damage it inflicts on breeding outcomes. Ornithosis must be considered the most likely cause of infertility and poor breeding results in canary breeding rooms. Outside the breeding season, it is difficult to identify the presence of Ornithosis without special veterinary diagnostic testing. After leaving the nest, canaries become quite resistant to the life-threatening effects of Ornithosis, commonly encountered in other bird species, especially parrots.

The effect of Ornithosis becomes obvious during breeding and its highly contagious nature produces widespread breeding failure within the breeding room. Poor natural resistance related to weak genes, moulding disease, contaminated food and poor nutrition are the most common causes of Ornithosis. Ornithosis may also be introduced into a flock by newly acquired birds or after exposure to infected birds at shows. It is a highly contagious disease and spreads through the flock in the air and contaminated droppings. In healthy and well managed flocks its presence may remain hidden until poor breeding outcomes reveal its presence. Ornithosis may be an underlying cause of other problems such as Black Spot, Canker, nestling diarrhea and Sweating Disease.

Infertility, failure of hens to lay eggs, dead in shell, dying babies (from 1-5 days of age) and sudden death in breeding hens are signs of Ornithosis during the breeding season.

Infertility associated with dying nestlings should be assumed to be due to Ornithosis until proven otherwise. Outside the breeding season the symptoms of Ornithosis (one-eye colds, beak scratching, sneezing in juveniles, "pinched" triangular eyelids in adults) are subtle and not always obvious. Ornithosis should also be considered a possible cause of occasional sudden deaths in canaries of any age or sex. Other conditions such as food contamination, overcrowding and nutritional deficiencies may also manifest in this way.

Ornithosis must be considered the most likely cause of eye infections in canaries. Streptococcal and fungal infections are less common causes of similar eye symptoms.

Doxycycline is the medicine of choice for Ornithosis. Metal containers (except stainless steel) and minerals present in shell grits, sand deep litter and mineral supplements have a negating effect on the proper absorption of Doxycycline into the birds' body. In the past, it has been necessary to remove all minerals and metal containers in order to achieve a full therapeutic effect from Doxycycline. However, removal of minerals during Doxycycline treatments has been found to inhibit recovery and create a degree of infertility and egg binding problems in canaries.

The addition of minerals may continue when Megamix (citric acid) is added to the drinking water during Doxycycline treatment. Megamix

A Doxycycline and Megamix treatment trial allows the fancier to determine the status of Ornithosis in the canary room.

has multiple actions. Firstly, recovery is accelerated because there is no need to restrict the mineral supplements that are vital for a full recovery from Ornithosis. Secondly, Megamix contains special surfactants that keep water containers free of heavy sludge that appears to inhibit recovery during antibiotic use. Thirdly, its effect of acidifying the crop contents helps reduce Thrush infections that are associated with Doxycycline use.

Doxycycline/Megamix treatment should be administered to canary rooms that have experienced poor breeding results. Yorkshires and other sensitive varieties should benefit from an annual Doxycycline/Megamix treatment because their weak nature predisposes them to Ornithosis irrespective of the care they receive.

The duration of Doxycycline/Megamix treatment (30 days) required to eliminate Ornithosis in canaries is shorter than that used for parrots (45 days). The Doxycycline/Megamix treatment should continue as long as the birds exhibit a positive response to it.

In canary bird rooms where the status of Ornithosis is unknown or remains unclear, a trial Doxycycline treatment may be used to identify the Ornithosis status of the entire bird room or individual varieties. Some varieties (e.g., Yorkshires) and families (inbred ones) appear more susceptible to the effects of Ornithosis. Individual birds or varieties showing a positive response to Doxycycline treatment are likely to be carriers and should benefit from a 30 day treatment. Previously strong individuals that respond negatively to the Doxycycline treatment are unlikely carriers and will not benefit from further Doxycycline medication. These strong individuals must be potentially considered as the backbone and foundation pairs of the canary stud. Good health is the best control measure against Ornithosis because medicines do not protect the birds from future or repeat infections.

Understanding the Disease

Ornithosis is controlled in canaries by promoting good health through the use of good management practices. Under poor housing and management conditions, re-infection can occur immediately after an Ornithosis treatment has ended.

When carefully monitored, Doxycycline/Megamix treatment for canaries proves very effective in improving breeding performance.

The administration of Doxycycline/Megamix as part of a strategy to improve breeding outcomes becomes beneficial when establishing weak varieties that carry Ornithosis. Inbred families or weaker varieties are vulnerable to the effects of Ornithosis because of their inherent weaknesses. Outside the breeding season, most of these birds infected with Ornithosis may appear quite normal and only show health changes at the onset of breeding. They are referred to as carrier birds.

Carrier birds may remain healthy in a protected and artificial environment but succumb to the effects of Ornithosis when they are exposed to the stress of breeding. Cocks that are carriers are most likely to "fluff-up" and fall out of breeding condition while courting the hen because their fragile immune system fails in response to the suppressive effect of testosterone. Hens that are carriers break down and are likely to become ill during the energy demanding process of laying eggs. The different periods of time during which symptoms of Ornithosis appear should help the fancier recognise the existence of this disease in the bird room.

Doxycycline/Megamix may temporarily render healthy birds sterile. Doxycycline has a very positive health effect when administered to aviaries infected with Ornithosis, but may have serious negative long-term effects when Ornithosis is not present. The benefits of using Doxycycline must be weighed against its potential dangers.

Doxycycline suppresses the immune system, causes Thrush (a serious disease in canaries) and may upset the fine balance of health that often exists in healthy, robust aviaries. The result of using Doxycycline may be worse than the original effects of Ornithosis. Unless there is widespread infertility and nestling mortality across a large number of nests, it is wiser to remove unproductive pairs to a hospital cage for a course of Doxycycline rather than treat the entire flock. Good health promoted by hygienic aviary conditions, health programmes and balanced nutrition form the best control measures against Ornithosis.

The entire aviary should be treated against Ornithosis when many nests fail to go to nest or fertility across the entire breeding room becomes abysmally low. Individual pairs exhibiting signs of infertility can show marked improvements in fertility when Doxycycline/Megamix treatment is administered during the breeding season. No adverse effects from Doxycycline/Megamix should occur when high-energy food, enriched with vitamins and minerals, is provided concurrently during this treatment.

The appearance of symptoms of Thrush infection usually occurs towards the end of a thirty day course of Doxycycline treatment and most commonly in previously robust and healthy individuals. These birds should be removed from the aviary into a hospital cage for Nystatin treatment. Megamix helps prevent untoward Thrush infections associated with prolonged Doxycycline administration. Thrush (Candidiasis) remains the most common outcome of an inappropriate Doxycycline treatment in canary rooms. The rapid recovery following Nystatin treatment confirms a Doxycycline-induced Thrush infection and signals an appropriate time to conclude treatment for the entire flock.

Doxycycline can also be used to diagnose Ornithosis in aviaries where bird health is not right and when the cause of the problem cannot be found without veterinary help. A short three-day long course of Doxycycline/Megamix should be administered to aviaries with respiratory symptoms, ill thrift and where infertility levels are exceptionally high. Ornithosis may be confirmed if the birds improve noticeably within two days. A course of Doxycycline/Megamix should then be continued for up to 30 days. All surfaces must be disinfected once a week during the treatment using a quaternary ammonium disinfectant (Protector).

Birds do not develop immunity to Ornithosis and may become re-infected after treatment. The introduction of new birds is a common source of Ornithosis to canary aviaries. New birds must be quarantined for at least two weeks before being introduced into an existing collection. They should always receive a trial course of Doxycycline/Megamix treatment while in quarantine.

Other diseases may predispose the flock to Ornithosis by weakening the natural resistance and damaging the immune system. Contaminated food, overcrowding, poor aviary design and moisture are the most common causes of recurrent infections. Weak genes, derived from inbreeding and poor breeding pair selection, are also common causes of recurrent Ornithosis in the weaker varieties of canaries. Ornithosis often predisposes these weak birds to other infections such as E. coli enteritis and streptococcal infections.

Doxycycline/Megamix Treatment Instructions

A Doxycycline/Megamix Treatment should be completed when the flock exhibits positive signs to a treatment trial (see page 76 for treatment trial details). The strongest and older birds may not respond to a Doxycycline/Megamix treatment in flocks where Ornithosis is a not a major problem. These birds may show an initial benefit then become depressed after a weeklong treatment. In such canary flocks the Doxycycline/Megamix treatment should be withheld until winter, after the show season has ended.

A Doxycycline trial is recommended each autumn or winter. A Doxycycline[1]/Megamix[2] treatment is recommended for flocks with a history of infertility, poor breeding results and for juveniles that are "just not right." A complete treatment with Doxycycline/Megamix should only be administered when there is a positive response to the treatment trial. Healthy show birds being trained for the show must not be given this treatment.

Doxycycline/Megamix treatment should be continued until the birds become quiet and fluff up. This may be as short as three days (in aviaries with no Ornithosis) to 30 days (in aviaries with Ornithosis).

The food should be enriched daily with vitamins[3] and minerals during the course of treatment. These supplements may be added to the dry seed, water or into a soft food.

The surfaces of cages, aviaries and food stations must be disinfected (Protector[4]) once a week during Doxycycline/Megamix treatment.

After the Doxycycline/Megamix treatment, sugar based vitamins (NV powder[5]) should be added to the drinking water for two days, followed immediately by KD powder for one day.

The show programme should then be applied after the conclusion of this treatment.

[1] Doxycycline 10% (1 teaspoon per 2 litre of drinking water)
[2] Megamix (3mls per litre of drinking water)
[3] Turbobooster, E-Powder & F-Vite
[4] Protector
[5] NV powder (1 teaspoon into 500 ml of drinking water)

MYCOPLASMA INFECTIONS

Mycoplasma Infection is a poorly understood disease in canaries. Mycoplasma disease accompanies Ornithosis, Streptococcal and E.coli infections, Moulding Disease and Black Spot (circovirus). I believe Mycoplasma to be the result of the suppression of the immune system of young birds by these aforementioned diseases.

Young Birds & Mycoplasma

Mycoplasma Infection is a common cause of deaths in young birds soon after or during the weaning process. Infected birds fluff up, go light, don't eat and die. Other symptoms include wheezing, tail bobbing and conjunctivitis.

The administration of Tylosine tartrate (Tylan) may protect youngsters in flocks with previous experience with this disease. Preventative schedules against Ornithosis, Black Spot and Moulding Disease should also help prevent further outbreaks.

Old Birds & Mycoplasma

Mycoplasma infection appears in older hens during wet, cold winters. The symptoms of sneezing, conjunctivitis, panting, tail bob and open breathing after exercise are typical of Mycoplasma infections. Infected hens should receive a treatment with Tylosine tartrate (Tylan) as part of a pre-breeding cleansing programme in order to protect the spread of the disease to weanlings.

DIARRHEA

Possible causes include E.coli, Coccidiosis, Megabacteria, Ornithosis, Trichomoniasis (canker), mice related infections and starvation.

1. E. coli infection (food contamination)

E.coli infections may or may not produce diarrhea. Droppings, however, are always larger than normal and green/grey in color. Birds fluff-up and are obviously unwell. A chicken-like smell often accompanies the large, grey colored droppings. Some birds may show conjunctivitis and nasal discharge. Some birds, especially young in nests ("Nestling Diarrhea") may die. Stunted growth and sticky feathers are other symptoms in nestlings. Sulfa-AVS is the first choice medicine for E.coli infections.

2. Coccidiosis Infestations [Atoxoplasmosis (A. serini) & Coccidiosis (Isopspora canaria)]

"Black Spot" (an enlarged dark colored spot visible beneath the skin) a disease found in young birds at fledgling age and a cause of high mortality is caused by Atoxoplasmosis. Diarrhea often accompanies this infection that may have varied clinical symptoms including diminished appetite, "going light", and ruffled feathers. Distention of the spleen and liver (black spot) and bowel loops (bloated abdomen) may also be seen. Infection is long standing (four months duration) and recovered birds may remain carriers for life and become contagious under stress (e.g., breeding). Treatment is elimination of carriers as there is no medical cure for Atoxoplasmosis. KD powder may be used to reduce contamination in the aviary.

Coccidiosis produces a diarrhea that often smells. Canaries with Coccidiosis become fluffed up, inactive, "go light" and look very sick. The mortality rate is low. The duration of infection is short (2-3 weeks). Young birds moving into the flights are most at risk. Carlox and Sulfa AVS may be used to prevent coccidiosis.

3. Megabacteria infections

Megabacteria infections produce a dark brown/black watery diarrhea. In established aviaries, only one or two birds may exhibit the symptoms. When new birds have introduced the disease, many birds may exhibit signs of infection. Symptoms include apathy, anorexia, regurgitation and parts of or whole seeds found in the droppings.

4. Ornithosis

Ornithosis produces a green colored diarrhea in association with nostril and eye discharges. Mortality rate is usually less than 10%. Breeding failure, however, is the most noticeable sign of Ornithosis.

5. Trichomoniasis (canker)

Canker infections produce a dark green diarrhea. More common signs include death, respiratory problems, blowing bubbles and going light. Symptoms are usually seen in young birds (especially Red Factors and Glosters)

6. Mice related infections (Yersinia & Salmonella)

Both these infections cause severe diarrhea. Most Yersinia infections are seen in winter and are associated with mice. Infected birds "go light" very quickly. Mortality is high. Birds die suddenly. Respiratory symptoms may also be noticed. Salmonella infections appear mostly in outdoor aviaries and are often associated with mice. Symptoms are similar to Yersinia but deaths occur over a more prolonged period of time.

7. Starvation

Black stained droppings or diarrhea are also signs of starvation.

Squirting Diarrhea: Giardia

Norwich only. Squirting, projectile, watery diarrhea usually occurs in one or two susceptible birds. It is important to treat the entire flock or cabinet with Turbosole. These birds may develop a permanent watery dropping, where vent feathers fall out and abdomen becomes swollen. Giardia mostly afflicts hens. Affected birds do not die but fail to reach breeding condition, even though they may look normal and bright.

Dropping Changes

The dropping of a bird contains a white or clear part (urine equivalent) and a colored part (feces/dropping equivalent). The dropping of a healthy and fit canary fed a dry seed diet should be small, round, dark in color topped by a white central urate portion. Those eating soft foods may have slightly larger, more watery and pale colored droppings. Birds fed high levels of vegetables and soft food may produce more watery droppings than those birds on a seed diet alone. Changes in color, consistency, number, size or smell of droppings may indicate an illness.

A change in the character of droppings is a warning sign of an imminent health problem, because stress of any kind provokes an immediate change in the droppings of birds, especially those with a rapid metabolism such as the canary. The changing droppings reflect a bird's natural response to stress largely controlled by the body's protection and survival systems. Although signs of stress in birds are subtle, they become more obvious to the trained and observant eye. The weaker birds are the first to show signs of stress. The watery dropping is the first sign of stress but because it is very short-lived (24-48 hours) it is often missed. After a day or so sick birds fluff up to conserve heat and their droppings become larger, more watery and usually change to a khaki-grey color. These changes in dropping character are the first signs an observant fancier will notice. Treatment to restore health is best given at the first signs of dropping change. Sick canaries tend to fluff up, perch on top of feeding stations or warm spots in the aviary. These are the best places to monitor the health of the flock and to observe for dropping changes.

Changes in size, color, smell and consistency of the droppings of any one bird should be viewed with caution. Water cleansers (KD or Megamix) administered to the flock at the first sign of dropping change in an individual bird should help restore the flock's health balance within a day or two.

Dropping Size

The size of the dropping is a very good indicator of the fitness and health of canaries. The metabolism of healthy, active and fit birds purrs with efficiency and requires minimal energy to run at top capacity. Canaries in top health eat and drink less because their energy systems are highly efficient. They produce droppings that are small, tight, low in water and well formed. The fittest birds have the smallest droppings. Large droppings are produced when the birds require additional energy and eat more food.

Large Droppings

Large droppings reflect a continuing stress (food problem, cold weather, wet spells, overcrowding and so on). Bowel infections are the most likely outcome when large droppings are left unattended. The healthy cloaca prevents the dropping from contaminating the urine by a complex action of muscles that act like valves. The tone and function of the cloaca and vent muscles is weakened with continuing stress and an elevated pH. The weakened cloacal valves allow the droppings to mix with the urine, preventing the normal recycling of water back into the bowel and creates a situation where the bird defecates less often, thus producing a larger and more watery dropping. The malfunctioning cloaca then turns alkaline (increasing its pH above 7.0 and towards 7.5) and predisposes this area to Candida (Thrush) and bacterial (E.coli) infection. Megamix or KD water cleansers reduce the effects of stress and act to lower the pH. One or the other should be administered to the entire flock at the onset of large droppings in two or more birds in order to help prevent infection.

Small Droppings

Small droppings are signs of health and fitness. Healthy birds with small droppings are active and alert. Small droppings may also indicate a bird eating less because of an illness. Such birds, however, will be fluffed up, inactive and may be low in body condition.

Undigested Seed in Droppings: Megabacteria, Candida

Megabacteria, Candida (Thrush) and severe E.coli infections are common causes of large watery droppings that may also contain undigested seed. The poor absorption of nutrients weakens infected birds. They become very thin and weak. Weakness may be confused with neurological symptoms.

Megabacteria infections produce a dark brown/black watery diarrhea. In established aviaries only one or two birds may exhibit symptoms. When new birds have introduced the disease, many birds may exhibit the signs of infection. Symptoms include apathy, anorexia, regurgitation and parts or whole seeds found in the droppings.

Thrush is a likely cause of this symptom in nestlings and juveniles between the age of 10 days and 6 weeks. Nystatin (added to the drinking water) is the treatment of choice for Thrush infections.

Megabacteria and Thrush are more likely the cause of seed being found in droppings in recent fledglings or juveniles, during the juvenile moult, or after a cold or wet spell. Thrush is more likely to occur when there is concurrent Ornithosis (check fertility), overcrowding or the utilization of a poor sprouting technique. Fungilin is the first choice of treatment when the cause of seeds in droppings is either Megabacteria or Thrush.

Eating Droppings (Pica)

Pica is sign of a mineral, mineral salt or trace element deficiency. Affected birds may also pick (as if eating) at the perches, brick walls and floor. Nutritional deficiencies (vitamins or minerals) and bowel diseases (Megabacteria, E.coli, Candidiasis, Coccidiosis, fungal infections) that affect the absorption of nutrients or the wrong use of medications are common causes of pica. The use of Hi-Cal and F-Vite and the treatment of any underlying disease is necessary to stop this behavior.

Mould on Droppings

Mould on droppings may occur during prolonged wet spells (Black-topped fungus), appear on excessively wet droppings or in the droppings of birds infected with Moulding Disease (White-topped fungus, blue-green mould). The type of mould is identified by closely looking at the mould on the dropping. Black-topped (Aspergillus niger) is an environmental mould. KD water cleanser administered to the flock should protect it from the excessive moisture within the aviary that causes this mould. Fungilin

is the first choice of treatment for the serious life-threatening White-topped and Green-blue Penicillin moulds.

Dropping Color

A change in color of the droppings, together with an increase in dropping size, is often the first visible sign of a potential health problem that must be investigated.

Green colored droppings may be due to a diet change to greens, a bird eating less, diseases involving the liver and intestines (poisons, bacterial, fungal and protozoa infections), or due to the inappropriate use of medications. Sulfa-AVS should be the first choice of antibiotic for birds with green droppings. Ornithosis produces a green colored diarrhea in association with nostril and eye discharges. Mortality rate is usually less than 10%.

Mustard yellow colored droppings indicate a digestion problem. E.coli and related infections must also be considered the possible cause of mustard colored droppings in nestlings, juvenile and newly acquired canaries. An early or low grade Megabacteria infection may also produce large amounts of undigested food. Staphylococcus and Streptococcus infection of the pancreas may sometimes produce pale yellow droppings in adult birds. Moxi-T should be the first medicine chosen for adult birds because of its action against Staphylococcus and Streptococcus infections. KD powder or Sulfa-AVS should be the first of choice medicines for young nestlings with pale colored droppings.

White or creamy colored droppings indicate urine alone is being passed in the dropping. It is usually a sign of a seriously ill bird. Gizzard obstructions from gorging sand or contaminated grit and failure to eat are the most likely causes of white droppings. Birds with white droppings should receive immediate first aid treatment.

Black droppings indicate bleeding into the bowel. Starvation and Megabacteria are the most common causes of black droppings. Droppings are small, black or dark red with starvation. The droppings of birds infected with Megabacteria (AGY) and Clostridia (Bacillus) infections are soft, watery, black or dark brown in color. Birds with Megabacteria infections appear hungrier than birds with Clostridial infections. Birds with black droppings should receive immediate first aid treatment.

Yellow droppings are signs of severe liver disease. The remains of the urine part of the dropping sometimes wets and leaves a bright yellow stain on the vent feathers. Birds with yellow droppings should receive immediate first aid treatment. Sometimes the yellow stained vent feathers (from excessive bile pigments entering the circulation) reflect a liver disease or Ornithosis infection.

Bloody droppings may be due to starvation, dehydration or as a side effect of improper antibiotic administration. Birds with bloody droppings usually die but should always receive immediate first aid treatment.

Brown droppings are usually a diarrhea and relate to bacterial (Clostridial) infections associated with poor aviary or water (Pseudomonas infection) hygiene, Megabacteria infection, or sand/grit gizzard obstruction. An offensive odor may accompany Pseudomonas infections. Baytril (page 91) should be the first choice of medicine for brown watery droppings. Moxi-T is a better choice for a Clostridia infection.

Pasted (caked) vent — droppings attached to feathers around the vent. Pasted vents indicate a long-standing and potentially serious illness that is capable of infecting the entire flock. Removal of the caked dropping often reveals a sweet, chicken-like smell that indicates bacterial, usually E. coli, Clostridial, Streptococus or Candida infection. Canaries with low grade Megabacteria infections may have hard dry black droppings caked around the vent. Others with Candida infection may have dark green, greasy and sweet smelling droppings caked around the vent. Breeding hens with uterus infections (Streptococcus, Clostridial and anaerobic infections) may have moist, large, khaki green colored droppings caked around the vent that carry a particularly pungent odor when removed. Moxi-T and Nystatin are the first choice medicines for birds with pasted vents. Removal of the caked dropping from the vent feathers is necessary for recovery. KD should be administered to the remainder of the flock. Tail wagging often accompanies pasted vent, as the bird attempts to remove the caked droppings.

Smelly (malodorous) Droppings

E.coli-type, Candida, Coccidiosis, Pseudomonas and Yersinia infections cause smelly droppings in canaries. Healthy droppings carry no odor. There is a fresh, clean smell to the healthy aviary. E.coli, Coccidiosis and Thrush infections produce a sweet, "chicken-like" smell in an infected aviary. It is therefore helpful to smell the droppings of sick birds. A Sulfa-AVS/Megamix cocktail should be the first choice treatment for droppings carrying a chicken-like smell. Nystatin should be administered when there is a sweet yeast-like smell to the dropping. A pungent, necrotic (dead) smell to the dropping occurs with serious outbreaks of Salmonella, Pseudomonas and Clostridia (Bacillus) infections. Moxi-T is the first choice medicine for Clostridia infections.

Watery Droppings

Watery droppings occur in birds with excessive thirst. Hot days, protozoa parasites (Coccidiosis, Trichomonas), crop infections, Candida, Megabacteria and toxic fungal infections, fevers, sugar based vitamins or medicines can produce watery droppings because of an increase in water intake. Stress in the aviary may also produce watery droppings. Adult carriers of Trichomoniasis (canker) and Megabacteria may exhibit watery droppings as their only sign of infection.

E.COLI TYPE INFECTIONS

In this book, E.coli-type infections refers to those infections caused by members of the Enterobacte family of bacteria. They are considered the most important intestinal pathogens. Escerichia coli, Enterobacter spp, Klebsiella spp, Citrobacter, Yersinia and Salmonella are the bacteria that fall into these E.coli-type infections.

E.coli infections are common in outdoor aviaries. They may cause enteritis, septicaemia (blood poisoning) and death in canaries of all ages and both sexes.
Contaminated food, grit, water, environmental

dust, feathers and dropping residues are common causes of E.coli-type infections. Open-air aviaries with earthen floors create a perfect environment for E.coli infections to become established after rain. Soaked seed, decaying food remnants, spilled water from water displays and fountains create the moisture favored by E.coli. They may also be introduced into the aviary by a carrier bird, mice, rodents or insects such as cockroaches. E.coli infections are often associated with other concurrent diseases, notably Ornithosis, Moulding Disease and Coccidiosis. Temperature and humidity also play an important part in the onset of this disease.

E.coli is capable of rapidly killing many birds and is often the primary disease in outdoor aviaries. Sulfa AVS is the antibiotic of choice when deaths suddenly occur in the aviary but when the cause has not been determined. Sulfa AVS has a wide spectrum of application and is used as the first line of attack when birds are dying. It is effective against E.coli-type bacteria, Coccidiosis and even Ornithosis.

Canaries have no caeca and therefore do not require intestinal bacteria (flora) for microbial digestion (See "Sterile Gut Theory" in the appendix). This means canaries carry no 'friendly' intestinal bacteria and must live in dry, hygienic conditions to remain healthy. Outdoor aviaries expose canaries to E.coli infections because of environmental germs and fluctuating weather conditions. Unhygienic food preparation and contaminated grit are the most common causes of E.coli infections of canaries housed indoors

Common Causes of E. coli Infections:

- Contaminated Food
- Wet and contaminated Grit
- Unbalanced diet
- Other Diseases (e.g., Ornithosis, Moulding Disease)

Contaminated Food

Strong and healthy canaries may tolerate low levels of E.coli contamination present in their food or environment simply as a result of their natural bodily defense mechanisms. However, canaries become most susceptible to the effects of contaminated food, grit and environmental germs when breeding. At other times, they may not be affected by bad food hygiene. Strict levels of hygiene must therefore be practiced during breeding in order to avoid E.coli related infections. Weak individuals and varieties are the first to become ill from contaminated food.

E.coli infections cause serious problems in canaries, such as:

- Nestling deaths (1-3 days of age)
- Stunted growth of youngsters in nest
- Nestling diarrhea
- Sweating Disease (Wet nest)
- Sudden death of breeding hens
- Uterus infections (ascending oviduct infection)
- Illness in young birds
- Sinusitis (eye swelling)

Breeding Problems & E.coli Infections

Wet grit, contaminated sprouted seed, soft foods or an imbalanced diet are the most likely causes of E.coli infections during breeding.

An E.coli infection is a common cause of nestling deaths between 1-3 days of age. Often the interior of the nest becomes a stained yellow from the diarrhea of the nestlings. The diarrhea wets the feathers of young and their mother, giving them the appearance of "sweating." Some fanciers call this "Sweating Disease."

Wet Nest is another cause of Sweating Disease. The nest of a healthy canary should remain dry and odourless. Wet nest is due to a nutritional imbalance that increases the thirst of the feeding parent(s). Mineral electrolyte imbalances and soft foods too high in protein can cause an increased thirst in feeding parents. As a result, parents feed watery food to their young and both become weak, resulting in stunted chicks and sweating disease.

Wetness or a smell in the nest is a sign of an impending E.coli infection requiring immediate attention. F-Vite, Ioford and Megamix should be used to prevent such imbalances.

Condensation within the nest is another cause of Sweating Disease. Some fanciers place a bowl of water beneath the nest to help with the hatching process. This may produce condensation on the inside of metal or porcelain nests. Fluctuating temperatures and humidity levels in outside aviaries may also produce condensation in nests. Pasted vents (constipation) of youngsters in the nest may also result from these conditions. Pasted vents may also be the result of excessive amounts of nesting material that cause parents to become restless, weakened and unable to feed properly.

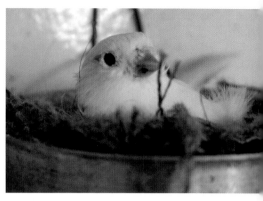

Sweating Disease is often the result of a mineral deficiency or contaminated soaked seed. Metal containers may also predispose to Sweating Disease in humid conditions.

Treatment for Sweating Disease

Stop all sprouted seed and soft food.

Remove and replace grit.

Provide Turbobooster, F-Vite & E-Powder in a tonic seed mix.

Clean nests daily to prevent re-infection.

Add Sulfa AVS/Megamix to the drinking water for 2 consecutive days.

Then add Ioford /Megamix to the drinking water for a further 3 days.

Clean pasted vents of youngsters with a moistened cotton bud.

Some fanciers use Epsom salts to unblock the vent as babies die from this constipation.

Sulfa-AVS & Megamix should be administered for three consecutive days to treat "Sweating Disease'" and save nestlings. Treatment must be restricted to individual nests unless many holes are simultaneously infected.

Some E.coli infections produce blood poisoning (toxins) that usually impact on the kidneys. This form of E.coli infection is responsible for the common condition of sudden death in breeding hens. Breeding hens are likely to die from this condition soon after the commencement of egg-laying (uterus infections and egg-related

peritonitis). An eye infection may be the only other sign of illness. Cocks remain healthy and nutritional problems (mineral, protein and energy deficiencies) remain the most likely cause of this form of E.coli infection.

Young Birds & E.coli Infections

Young birds with E. coli infections look unwell with a fluffed up and hunched appearance. They often have diarrhea. Sometimes young canaries may show respiratory symptoms (sneezing and eye signs) rather than a diarrhea.

Nutritional imbalances, parasite infestations, moist conditions and overcrowding are the most common causes of E. coli infections in young birds. Juvenile canaries weakened by disease (Ornithosis, Coccidiosis and Black Spot) are more likely to become infected with E.coli.

Individual bird treatment in an isolated cage is preferred to flock treatment unless birds are dying or many birds show symptoms of the infection.

A Sulfa AVS and Megamix cocktail is the best treatment for young birds that show symptoms because it is effective against both E. coli and Coccidiosis infections. Within 48 hours after Sulfa AVS treatment is started, droppings become well formed; birds exhibit a renewed vigour and start to flap their wings.

E. coli infections left untreated predispose young birds to more serious infections such as

Salmonella, Ornithosis and Aspergillus that are difficult to eradicate.

E.coli infections produce a typical "chicken-like" smell to the flights. A Sulfa AVS & Megamix cocktail should be used for two consecutive days when a 'chicken' smell appears. This cocktail is particularly useful when wet weather causes E. coli and Coccidiosis problems.

Prevention of E.coli Infections

1. Do not feed wet grit.

2. Use F-Vite instead of grit.

3. Use strict hygiene practices. Special attention must be taken when preparing and feeding sprouted seed.

4. Insulate the bird room to prevent fluctuations of moisture and temperature.

5. Use Megamix or KD water cleansers to help control E.coli infections.

6. Sanicheck (11/2mls per litre of drinking water) may also help control E.coli infections.

SULFA-AVS & E.COLI INFECTIONS

The combination of Sulfadiazine and Trimethoprim in Sulfa-AVS transforms it into a potent antibiotic ideally suited as a first line of attack for canaries with E.coli infections. Canaries find Sulfa AVS highly palatable, ensuring them of a very good dose. The use of tepid water rather than cold water enables it to dissolves properly and stirring before feed times is recommended. The response of sick birds moved to a hospital cage for treatment may be used to 'self-diagnose' an E.coli type infection

Sulfa AVS should be administered for five consecutive days when an E.coli infection has been diagnosed. Sulfa AVS must be administered when birds are dying from E.coli type septicaemias. Its use should be restricted to individual sick birds during the moult because it may damage growing feathers.

Sulfa-AVS /Megamix Cocktail

Many E. coli infections are associated with a high pH in the bowel that delays the natural healing process. The Sulfa AVS and Megamix cocktail lowers the pH of the bowel, thereby accelerating recovery. Megamix must be added to the drinking water first and is then followed by Sulfa AVS (Sulfa AVS will precipitate if it is added before the Megamix). Sulfa AVS is combined with Megamix when Megamix alone fails to control E.coli infections.

GOING LIGHT

Going Light is a common term to describe weight loss in a bird. When a canary is "going light" the breast muscle (the largest muscle in a canary's body) wastes away during illness to reveal a sharp edged breastbone (keelbone). Wasting of this muscle indicates an energy crisis, as this muscle provides the last source of energy for a sick canary. "Going light" is a gradual process at first but quickly progresses when the breast muscle becomes severely wasted. At this time the breast-bone becomes very sharp, the sick canary becomes lifeless and its feathers very dry and straw-like. There is little chance of recovery by this stage and the bird will usually die.

There are many causes of "going light." Going light generally presents as chronic weight loss and weakness. In canaries, Megabacteria (AGY) infection, failure to wean and Moulding Disease are common causes of this form of "going light." Poor nutrition, viruses, coccidiosis and bacterial infections are other causes of going light.

The cause of "going light" must first be determined in order for the treatment to be successful. Fungilin is the first choice medicine for treating sick individuals in the hospital cage when the cause of the illness is Moulding Disease, Megabacteria or Aspergillosis. These diseases should be considered the most likely cause when vomiting and going light occur together.

Going Light & Megabacteria

Megabacteria, known as Avian Gastric Yeast (AGY) infection is a common cause of going light in canaries.

MEGABACTERIA

The Megabacteria infection appears most often in susceptible canary families and varieties, but is an uncommon problem in the hardier varieties. It can be deduced that the disease reflects a poor genetic background and depressed level of natural resistance to the disease, rather than Megabacteria itself being a particularly nasty germ.

Megabacteria is an opportunist germ and has no harmful effect upon strong vital birds. However, it may cause illness and death in birds with a weakened immune system.

Stress precedes most Megabacteria infections in the aviary. Most birds in an aviary remain healthy during an apparent outbreak unless there is another disease present or the management is poor. The first birds to become ill during a Megabacteria outbreak in the aviary are invariably related (genetically linked). These susceptible families can be easily identified during the early stages of an outbreak and the carrier parent birds should be eliminated from further breeding. The Megabacteria infection occurs mostly after the carrier birds experience a stressful episode, such as a show. Healthy young birds may become infected under the stress of overcrowding or other diseases.

Megabacteria damages the glands and prevents digestive juices from being produced, damaging the digestive capacity of the stomach organs (proventriculus, isthmus and gizzard). In healthy canaries, these organs produce acids, enzymes, mucous and other glandular secretions, which together with the grinding action of the gizzard form essential actions for the digestion of the food. Infected canaries virtually starve to death because none of the energy or nutrients from the food eaten is digested or absorbed into the body. The result is a constantly hungry bird, which fails to gain weight, becomes very weak and may eventually die from starvation or another illness. Canaries are more susceptible to the effects of hypoglycemia (low blood glucose) and bizarre neurological signs including hypoglycaemic fits, fainting and coma because of their high metabolic rate and small size.

Increased appetite, weakness and going light thus form consistent features of the Megabacteria infection. Infected birds often sit on the feed dish or ground appearing to eat and then vomit. A variety of symptoms may be seen that reflect weakness and metabolic disturbances. Very ill birds may exhibit bizarre behavior consistent with central nervous system (brain) disturbances. Walking in circles, star gazing, vomiting, muscle twitching, incoordination during flight (backwards, upside down etc), and fainting attacks. Hens may become egg bound, lay soft-shelled eggs or become paralyzed after laying their eggs.

Birds with Megabacteria may survive for a long time. Infected birds are more likely to die during a cold spell. A low grade infection may appear as a hunched (stomach pain), fluffed up look.

Diagnosis of Megabacteria

Megabacteria is diagnosed easily by the microscopic testing of the droppings or by the examination of the organs of the dead bird. Dropping tests reveal most but not all carrier birds.

Symptoms of Megabacteria

- Weight loss and "going light" — The birds feel light in the hand, the keel is prominent and the pectoral muscles are wasted.
- Excessive hunger — Affected birds sit on the feed dish or floor looking for food.
- Fluffed up, ruffled feathers
- Regurgitation — Vomiting occurs when an excessive amount of mucous caused by the infection blocks the movement of food through the stomach.
- Soft, watery and dark green to brown/black droppings are produced. — Droppings may contain undigested grain or be blood-tinged. Birds passing this type of droppings are heavily infected with Megabacteria.
- Dark, sticky droppings pasted to the vent. — These droppings appear when secondary bacterial infections are present.
- Death. — Death results from secondary infections, exposure or starvation. There can

also be a very low mortality and birds may just linger on.

- Neurological signs — Walking in circles, star gazing, vomiting, muscle twitching, incoordination during flight (backwards, upside down etc), and fainting attacks.

Treatment of Megabacteria

For years, scientific research failed to find a medicine that actually killed this particularly large bacteria. Nowadays, the anti-fungal drug Amphotericin (Fungilin) is used to treat Megabacteria infections in individual birds. Unfortunately, this medicine can cause kidney damage and infertility in healthy birds and its use must be restricted to infected and in contact birds only.

Fungilin (Amphotericin) should not be used to treat the entire flock when Megabacteria infection has been diagnosed because it is not a highly contagious disease. The results can be short lived and repeat treatments become necessary when the underlying causes of the Megabacteria have not been identified. The end result is weak canaries, requiring constant medication to remain healthy. Such flocks become susceptible to many illnesses. On its own, the new bird with Megabacteria is not highly contagious. However, it has a harmful effect on the young birds it breeds. They are likely to also be infected with Megabacteria. The infected or "carrier" young birds then expose the healthy flock to the Megabacteria in the overcrowded young bird aviary. Every new bird entering the flock must be dropping tested prior to breeding and treated accordingly. Those birds failing to respond to the Amphotericin are best culled from the flock, because their young will remain susceptible to Megabacteria.

Infected birds must be moved to the heat of a hospital cage where Amphotericin (Fungilin) treatment may be administered. Acid water cleansers (KD) should be added to the drinking water to "clean" the remainder of the flock of Megabacteria.

Megabacteria is often a secondary disease similar in nature to and managed in the same way as Trichomoniasis (canker), Thrush and Streptococcal infections. Infected birds fail to thrive and become unwell during times of stress, notably just after weaning, during the moult and while in the breeding cabinet.

Summary of Treatment of Megabacteria

Do not treat the entire flock with Fungilin (Amphotericin)

Identify birds with signs of Megabacteria by handling every bird.

Treat these birds in isolation.

Hospitalized birds that fail to respond to Fungilin (Amphotericin) treatment within a week must be culled.

Record the ring numbers of birds showing symptoms of Megabacteria in order to identify and cull a family weakness or carrier ancestor.

The rest of the flock is "cleaned out" with a water cleanser (e.g., KD) for five days.

In order to help accelerate recovery in mildly infected birds, provide sprouted seed fortified with Turbobooster, E-Powder and F-Vite during KD treatment.

The trigger for the Megabacteria outbreak should be identified and the flock treated accordingly.

First Aid Treatment

Fungilin is administered in the drinking water for 10 days.

After ten days return the recovered birds to an empty aviary or holding cage and monitor them carefully for three weeks.

Birds failing to respond to the treatment and birds relapsing after they are returned to the aviary must be culled.

Provide additional sprouted seed, soft food or tonic seed impregnated with Turbobooster and E-Powder twice each day. They should eat this food with relish.

Prevention of Megabacteria

Good management is the best way to prevent Megabacteria. Due to the fact that most aviaries become crowded with young birds after breeding, the natural way to prevent Megabacteria relies upon the use of weekly KD water cleanser to allow the young birds to develop their own natural resistance against the disease.

Megabacteria can be eliminated by selecting genetically resistant birds as breeders and controlling for diseases that may have weakened the immune system, notably Moulding Disease and Ornithosis. It may infect weaker, young birds during the moult when poor management conditions are practiced.

Megabacteria infection has been implicated with poor breeding results in many aviaries.

Look for a "trigger" during a Megabacteria outbreak, when unrelated birds suddenly "go light." Megabacteria infections are not highly contagious from bird to bird but reflect an increased susceptibility to disease. Most birds recover spontaneously from Megabacteria after any underlying disease has been treated. Infection is also likely to recur when underlying diseases are left unattended. Look to concurrent diseases, overcrowding and weak individual families when recurrent Megabacteria infections occur.

Going Light & Moulding Disease

Moulding Disease, together with Ornithosis and overcrowding, are the most important causes of illness in canaries.

Juveniles in an overcrowded aviary, as well as genetically weakened canaries, are most susceptible to the effects of mould on feed and in the environment. This disease occurs when food or grit contaminated with bacteria, fungus or fungal toxins is fed to canaries.

Contaminated grit is a particularly common cause of "going light." Replacing grit with F-Vite should help prevent this form of going light.

Seed infected with fungus is the cause of Moulding Disease. The practice of feeding canaries sprouted seed increases the likelihood of Moulding Disease.

Fungal contamination lowers the nutritional value of seed and can irritate or infect the bowel. Its most damaging feature is its ability to produce toxins. The fungal toxins attack the immune system of birds, rendering them susceptible to many other diseases. The treatment only becomes successful when the contaminated feed has been replaced with clean seed.

Poor quality feed is old, dirty, poorly stored, fails to sprout, or has a high moisture content. Poor quality feed is especially prone to moulding. Feed must be kept free of harmful bacteria, fungus or insecticides.

The correct storage of grain is as important as the purchase of good grain and forms a vital part in the maintenance of the highest quality seed fed to the birds. Not only must it be stored correctly on the farm and in the produce store, but also after it arrives home. It must be kept dry, clean and protected from vermin and insects.

Signs of Moulding Disease

An obvious change occurs in the health of the aviary within a week of feeding contaminated feed. The signs of White Mould Disease resemble those that develop with Megabacteria and Coccidiosis.

- The birds become quiet.
- Going Light — Many birds become fluffed up, hunched and ill and sit on the floor near the seed containers. Such birds often "go light."
- Large dark green droppings — Slimy droppings with a copious quantity of green staining urate.
- Consistently poor droppings — It is impossible to get good droppings consistently, when the feed is mould affected. Look to the feed first when the droppings become green and large.
- Recurring illnesses — Most of the moulds suppress immune function and increase the

susceptibility of the birds to other infections, notably Ornithosis and E.coli infections. A flock with recurring infections may in fact have an underlying mould problem.

- Mould on droppings in the aviary — The presence of mould on the droppings on the aviary floor is the most obvious sign of moulding disease, but it is important for the fancier to look very carefully at the mould.

The Need for Clean Food

Fresh, clean food is the basis of healthy birds and successful breeding season.

Fresh, clean food is the starting point for healthy birds and a successful breeding season. The protection of the food from contamination during storage is the next important step. Spoiled seed is the most common cause of poor breeding performance and recurrent illness in canaries. It is impossible to cure illnesses and poor breeding results when bad feed is the underlying cause of such problems, and is continually used. Food cleansers are used to keep the food in storage fresh and clean by protecting it from mould, yeast and other harmful agents.

Moulding Disease and PEP Food Cleanser

PEP is a new generation, slow-release food cleanser that protects all grades of seed for three months.

The PEP Food Cleanser has been developed to protect the freshness and quality of bird-seed from mould contamination irrespective of storage conditions. It is an ideal product for the health conscious canary breeder. This palatable, controlled release food cleanser is not in any way an excuse for poor quality seed because there is no cure for seed already contaminated with fungal toxins.

It is the most advanced mould inhibitor on the market and its controlled release protects the seed for three months without affecting its palatability. Its activity is unaffected by the nature of the feed being treated and the recommended doses protect grain with extremely high moisture contents (greater than 17%) and if kept in arduous storage conditions. Pep is particularly recommended for high rainfall areas (e.g. Victoria, Northern Queensland and the eastern seaboard).

Dosage & Instructions.
Mix Pep at the rate of 5 grams (1 level tablespoon) into 25 Kilograms of seed as it is placed into the storage bins.

Mite Infestation

Red mites (Dermanyssus sp.) bite the skin and suck the blood of nestlings and their parents causing intense irritation and anemia. Heavy infestations may cause high mortality in nestling, fledgling and adult birds. Red mites do not like light. They hide in crevices of the bird room and nests during the day. They become active and attack the birds and suck their blood at night. Nighttime is the best time to confirm the existence of red mites. They can be identified in the nest or on the birds as very small red dots that move quickly away from the light of a torch.

Treatment for red mite should occur during the day when the mites are hiding in the crevices and nest away from the birds. The Northern mite (Ornithonyssus sylvarium), another blood sucking mite, spends its life entirely on the bird.

Blood sucking mites cause respiratory symptoms, general depression, anemia and in heavy infestations, can cause deaths of nestlings, fledglings and adult canaries.

Feather quill mites are usually found on the quills of the tail feathers in canaries. Quill mites are a common cause of infertility in canaries. A strong light behind the feather is used to visualize the small mites.

Depluming mites (Epidermoptic mites) cause a scaly skin irritation, leading to wing, tail and back feather loss.

Air-sac mite (Sternostoma tracheacolum) is an internal parasite that lives in airways and air-sacs. Infestation causes local irritation and secondary respiratory infections. Heavy infestations cause breathing difficulties, wheezing, open mouth breathing and death in fledglings and adult birds. Canaries are particularly susceptible to air-sac mite infestations (respiratory acariasis). Heavy infestations become obvious with a light after wetting the neck of the birds. They also appear as pinhead sized spots moving up and down the trachea (windpipe).

Red, biting and depluming mites are harmful to canaries and cause intense irritation. They are light sensitive, fast moving and difficult to find. The stamping feet and extreme agitation caused by these biting insects is often the best sign that these mites are present.

Other species of mites and lice, cause canaries to jump suddenly, anxiously preen around the base of the tail, twitch and repeatedly stretch their legs. The Quill mite is common during the warmer months. They can be seen along the quill at the base of the long tail feathers. The unrest and weakness caused by external parasites such as lice and mites often results in increased infertility (birds are too tired to breed), dead in shell (incubation failure) and illness in breeding hens.

Mite and lice infestations are an underestimated cause of decreased health and breeding performance in canaries. Blood sucking and air-sac mites can cause nestling, young bird and adult deaths and are often the underlying cause of other diseases. Always attempt to keep canaries free of mites and lice.

Treatment of Mite Infestations

Treatment for all mite infections must include an insecticide, S76 (Ivermectin: dose 200-400microgram per kilogram) for the bird administered topically (directly onto the skin) or orally (added to the drinking water). Additionally, a disinfectant (Coopex or Avian Insect Liquidator) should be used to clean and disinfect the aviary or cage of mites, lice and their eggs. These pyrethrin-based products are safe to use on canaries.

Treatment of Red Mite Infestation

Flock Treatment

S76 should be administered to the entire flock for two consecutive days.

The nests and aviary must be cleaned and disinfected with a pyrethrin spray or wipe over, on the second day of S76 treatment.

A pyrethrin must be sprayed into the crevices of the aviary.

This treatment must be repeated each week for three weeks to break the life cycle of the red mite.

Red mite is then prevented through the administration of a combined S76/pyrethrin spray/wipe treatment every three weeks (tri-weekly) during the hot months and each month during winter.

S76 is administered in the drinking water and is the best medicine available to treat lice and mites in canaries. It is given at the beginning of each season and each month during summer as routine lice and mite prevention. It is safe for breeding birds to help control red mite and air-sac mite.

Individual Bird Treatment

Individual birds covered with red mites should be removed to the hospital cage for treatment.

They should be sprayed with a pyrethrin based lice/mite spray to kill the red mites on the body. Additionally, one drop of S76 should be applied to the skin of the neck.

S76 should be administered to the drinking water for three consecutive days followed by Ioford/Megamix for two days to help reverse any anemia. Soft food enriched with Turbobooster, E-Powder and NV powder should be provided to help accelerate recovery.

Treatment of Air-sac Mite Outbreak

Flock Treatment

S76 should be administered to the entire flock for two consecutive days. The nests and aviary must be cleaned and disinfected with a pyrethrin spray or wipe over, on the second day of S76 treatment. This treatment must be repeated each week for three weeks to break the life cycle of the air-sac mite. Air-sac mite is then prevented through the administration of a combined S76/Coopex treatment every three weeks (tri-weekly) during the hot months and each month during winter.

Individual Bird Treatment

Individual birds with symptoms of air-sac mites should be removed to the hospital cage for treatment. One drop of S76 should be applied to the skin of the neck each day for 5 days.

S76 should also be administered to the drinking water for three consecutive days followed by Moxi-T for two days to help with secondary lung infections.

Air-sac mites cause the bird to stretch its neck and breathe with an open mouth.

Soft food enriched with Turbobooster, E-Powder and NV powder should be provided to help accelerate recovery.

Mite/Lice Prevention

Spring/Summer/Autumn

A pyrethrin spray and S76 should be administered every three weeks during Spring, Summer and Autumn.

A pyrethrin spray should be administered on the same day that S76 is added to the drinking water.

A KD bath given one week after S76 treatment in hot weather will help clean the feathers and remove the dead quill mites

Winter

A pyrethrin spray and S76 should be administered at the beginning of winter. A pyrethrin spray should be administered on the same day S76 is added to the drinking water.

Breeding Pairs

A pyrethrin spray and S76 should be administered every six weeks during breeding. A pyrethrin spray should be applied to the nest box prior to and after the breeding season. Pyrethrin spray should also be applied to parents with visible signs of mite or lice.

Coopex

Coopex consists of 250g/kg of Permethrin (synthetic pyrethrin). It is a safe residual insect spray for canary flights, breeding holes and nests.

Coopex can be used as a spray and is safe for eggs. However it should not be sprayed directly onto the birds, their young, live food, drinking water or seed. In ornamental aviaries with fishponds, Coopex must be wiped over rather than sprayed over surfaces and nest boxes because it is poisonous to fish. Diatomaceous earth insect powders may be preferred over Coopex for ornamental aviaries with fishponds.

Coopex powder can be added to water for spraying or wiping over the surfaces of the aviary and nests, at the dilution of 25grams into 10 liters of

Healthy birds are less likely to suffer from lice and mites, a common cause of ill health in moulting and breeding canaries. A complete health programme will ensure birds are in the best physical condition so they do not succumb to the effects of heavy infestations. During the heat of Spring and Summer, repeat lice and mites treatments are required to maintain the very best health in the breeding and young birds.

water. Apply Coopex on a dry warm day to allow for quick drying.

Coopex action lasts for 3-4 weeks. Its residual effect repels biting insects (mosquitoes, slaters, ants and other insects that are the vectors for canary pox and blood parasites) and red mite that inhabit the cage, aviary and nest.

Diatomaceous earth

Diatomaceous earth insect powders are an alternative, natural approach to insect control. The fine silicate particles kill red mites, lice, flies and ticks by destroying their waxy cuticle. This results in a loss of moisture and death of the insects. It has an entirely physical mode of action and contains no chemical pesticides.

Diatomaceous earth is non-toxic to animals and humans. It is environmentally safe and non-toxic to fish, but is inactivated by moisture. It forms a good alternative to wood shavings.

S76 for Mites, Lice and Worms

S76 consists of a combination of Ivermectin and homeopathics. It is a remarkable product because it has a multipurpose action. It may be applied topically (on the skin) or orally (added to the drinking water) for two consecutive days when an infestation appears. This treatment should be repeated each week for three weeks to break the life cycle of the mite. Tri-weekly treatments should then be used to control mite infestations during the warmer months of the year. Monthly treatments using S76 should be administered for controlling red mites, air-sac mite, blood parasites (Microfilaria), blood sucking lice, flies and hair-worms during the cooler months.

The clever combination of Ivermectin and homeopathics has made it the first choice medicine during the breeding season, moult and for young canaries. Not only does S76 kill mites, worms and lice but it also invigorates canaries. An increased vitality and activity in breeding and young birds become obvious the day after it is administered.

S76 for mites/lice and health stimulant
S76 can be added to the drinking water to kill air-sac mite, red and northern mite, depluming mite, sucking lice as well as round and hair worm. It has proven effective in treating hair worms in other species. S76 is the first choice for treating air-sac and red mites. It is safe canaries of all ages being particularly useful for young birds,

S76 is a remarkable product. It not only effectively treats lice and mites but also stimulate health in the young birds in a purely natural way.

breeding birds and during the moult. S76 should be used every three weeks during the summer months and once a month during winter. S76 has additional benefits as a health stimulant, being particularly useful for troublesome, fragile canary varieties such as Yorkshires.

S76 during the moult

S76 is especially useful during the moult. It is obviously good for mites, lice and worm control in canaries of all ages but its benefits for juveniles are especially meritorious. An obvious change occurs in the juveniles the morning after S76 is given. They become more alert and flap their wings. S76 should be administered to the drinking water as part of the Young Bird Health Programme for one day every three weeks.

S76 when birds are "just not right"

S76 is recommended when breeding pairs are showing signs of fatigue. It should be used as a first line of treatment when birds are "just not right." Often an immediate positive result is seen and breeding pairs quickly regain their breeding vitality.

S76 and Baths

S76 may be added to the bath water at a drinking water dosage rate to treat for mites and lice.

STREPTOCOCCAL INFECTIONS

Streptococcal infections are a cause of eye and respiratory problems, infertility and deaths in canaries. It often occurs together with Mycoplasma, Black Spot (Circovirus) and Ornithosis infections.

Streptococcal (Streptococcus faecalis, also known as Enterococcus faecalis) and Staphylococcal (known as Staph. infections) infections are collectively referred to in this text as Streptococcal infections.

Symptoms of Strep. Infections

The symptoms of a Strep. infection closely resemble those seen with serious outbreaks of Ornithosis. Weak families are most susceptible to Strep. infection. Infection may also appear in outdoor, overcrowded and unhygienic aviaries. Symptoms include diarrhea, skin irritation, foot infections, eye colds, tail bobbing, sneezing, beak scratching, and uterus infections in breeding hens and dead in shell. Strep. infections often occur after the introduction of other diseases (Ornithosis, Circovirus and Moulding Disease) or stressful conditions (diets low in protein, energy, minerals or vitamins, cold stress, mite infestations, during courtship and overcrowding) have weakened the immune system.

Symptoms of Strep. infections also resemble the symptoms of air-sac mite infection, Ornithosis and Mycoplasma. These signs include beak scratching and noisy respiratory sounds. Infected breeding birds may fail to go to nest and fertile eggs laid by infected birds may fail to hatch. Those that hatch may grow slowly or often die. Infected parents may suddenly die on the nest.

Symptoms of Strep infection also include coughing, wheezing, pneumonia and breeding failures, related to nutritional problems and other diseases (Staph Infections).

Strep infections are a common cause of dead-in-shell (high embryonic mortality) and lameness (swollen joints and arthritis) related to nutritional deficiencies and dusty bird rooms.

Signs of Streptococcal Infection

Strep. should be considered the cause of the following symptoms until proven otherwise:

- The sudden appearance of sickness in a cock bird during or shortly after courtship activity
- The appearance of respiratory and enteritis symptoms in breeding birds at any part of the breeding cycle
- Tail bob, labored breathing, noisy, clicking respiration, cough, sneeze and beak scratching
- Wet or pasted vents
- Dirty stained tails
- Large brown watery droppings that carry no odor

Symptoms of Sudden Onset Strep. Infection

- Always associated with a stress
- Wet or green stained vent, weight loss and often a tail bob
- Birds do not eat, become dehydrated and may die within two or three days
- Affected birds are often breeding hens (uterus infections) moulting adolescents or birds infested with mites
- Breeding birds die suddenly on the nest

Symptoms of Chronic Form Strep. Infection

- Intermittent and continuing appearance of symptoms
- Respiratory symptoms, tail bob, beak scratching (see above)
- Dull feathers, dirty stained tails
- Dead in shell/dying babies
- Rejection of babies by parents

Causes of Strep. Infection

Stress
Stress factors alter the fine balance canaries have between resistance and environmental bacteria that are ingested or inhaled. Stress-induced Strep. infections may infect inherently strong varieties housed in poor conditions (dirty, overcrowded or unsanitary ornamental aviaries). Weak birds housed in spotlessly clean indoor cages may also become infected with innocuous strains of Strep. The weaker varieties are more susceptible to the effects of cold stress, mite infestations, and dusty, unclean aviaries or overcrowding and thus are most susceptible to the disease.

Other Diseases
Streptococcal infections are associated with diseases that weaken the immune system. For example, birds 'carrying' Circovirus become susceptible to Strep. infection.

Poor Natural Resistance
Inherently weak families and varieties are susceptible to Strep. infections. These birds harbor and spread germs throughout the aviary and especially in earthen-floored overcrowded aviaries.

Environment overburdened with Strep. Germs
Very dirty, unhygienic aviaries produce large amounts of this germ capable of infecting susceptible birds, especially the young. Introduced carrier birds may also introduce the germ to an aviary resulting in breeding problems.

Strep. Infection Treatment

Moxi-T contains penicillin and tylosine antibiotics and is used to cure Streptococcus, Staphylococcus and Mycoplasma infections in canaries. Moxi-T should be administered for five to ten days.

Strep. infections may suddenly appear or persist in a more chronic form. Strep. infections that occur suddenly are always related to a stress factor and may infect previously healthy robust individuals. Breeding birds may suddenly die. The chronic form appears more frequently in the fragile varieties. Under most conditions, Megamix and KD water cleansers should provide canaries with good protection from this chronic form of Strep.

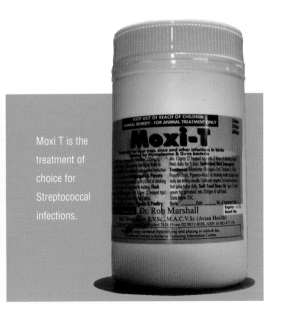

Moxi T is the treatment of choice for Streptococcal infections.

days when it has been confirmed that a Strep. infection is the cause of many deaths in the aviary. In order to prevent recurrences, the underlying causes of Strep. must be identified and eliminated.

Summary of Treatment of Strep. Infections

Flock treatment with Moxi-T for Strep. Infections when:

The aviary is crowded with young birds or very dusty.

There is a mite, lice, Ornithosis or Black Spot problem.

Moxi-T should be administered to the drinking water for five days.

Individual treatment with Moxi-T for Strep. infections when:

A sudden stress such as cold stress precipitates the infection.

Moxi-T should be administered to the drinking water for ten days (See emergency first aid treatment on page 88).

SALMONELLA-TYPE INFECTIONS & BAYTRIL

Salmonella and Yersinia infections are particularly hazardous to canaries. Baytril 2.5% (Enrofloxacin) is regarded as the antibiotic of choice for Salmonella and Yersinia, when Ornithosis is a secondary infection. It is also the first choice to treat individuals with eye colds and for entire aviaries where illness or deaths occur for unknown reasons, and while a diagnosis is being determined. It is important that Baytril be reserved for serious infections because unnecessary use of Baytril increases the opportunity for antibiotic resistance and a corresponding loss of effectiveness of this very useful medicine.

Baytril is the treatment of choice for Salmonella and Yersinia infections in canaries when rodents (mice or rats) are the cause of the infection.

Strep. infections that appear suddenly are more likely to cause high mortality rates in canary aviaries. Moxi-T must be administered to the drinking water when such outbreaks occur. It should not be administered to flocks housed outdoors when birds are sick, not dying. Instead, the aviary should be cleaned and KD added to the drinking water of the aviary.

Moxi-T should be restricted to sick individuals who have been removed from the flock into a warmed hospital cage for treatment.

Moxi-T should not be administered to the entire flock unless Strep. infection has been confirmed by veterinary analysis.

Moxi-T is the first choice medicine when an individual or group of juveniles are 'not right' "or show any of the Strep. symptoms during times of stress (winter months, moult and overcrowding).

Moxi-T should be administered to a sick individual for 5-10 days. The response to Moxi-T treatment should be noted before the entire group of juveniles receives a similar course of treatment. Birds in contact with the sick individuals should receive a five day long course of Moxi-T when infected birds respond within two days of Moxi-T treatment.

Moxi-T should only be administered to the entire flock in outdoor aviaries for seven consecutive

Together with Sulfa AVS, Baytril is a first choice option for treating seriously ill birds when the cause of illness remains unclear. Baytril causes bone defects in nestlings and should not be administered to feeding parents.

Baytril is the first choice antibiotic when:

- Adults of both sexes die suddenly.

- Smelly nests, nestling deaths and sick adults occur after rodents are seen in the aviary.

- Rodents and any type of illness appear together in the aviary.

Baytril is the best treatment for Salmonella infections.

The Salmonella infection is regarded as a serious disease of canaries housed in outdoor aviaries and it is difficult to eradicate. Even the strongest medicines are unable to cure genetically weak families susceptible to Salmonella because recovered birds remain 'carriers' for life. These 'carriers' spread the disease to other birds and future generations. Canaries housed in outdoor aviaries are usually naturally resistant against Salmonella but may be unable to resist infections introduced by rodents.

Salmonella causes a wide variety of symptoms and spreads slowly (weeks rather than days) through a flock of breeding birds. Salmonella should be assumed as the cause of sudden illness or death in breeding hens when rodents are found in the aviary or food storage area.

Symptoms of Salmonella Infection

Nest Symptoms

- Initially, a few nests show typical signs of Salmonella.

- These symptoms include pipping deaths, "sweating," smelly nests, "red" colored dehydrated nestlings and dead babies between 1-5 days of age. Variable symptoms may have a very slow or rapid onset.

Juvenile Symptoms

- Sick and dying weanlings will have watery eyes, nasal discharge, conjunctivitis, smelly pasted vents, noisy/moist respiration sounds, 'going light', neurological signs (including twisted necks and dizziness), lameness and an inability to fly. Some may develop cheesy abscesses under the skin and near joints.

Salmonella Treatment

Baytril is the first choice treatment against the Salmonella infection. It should be administered to the entire flock for ten consecutive days. The drinking water containing Baytril may be left for two days before being refreshed. Mice, rats and cockroaches must be eradicated during the treatment to prevent reinfection. The aviary must also be cleaned of rodent droppings and disinfected.

Salmonella Prevention

Salmonellosis is preventable by the use of concealed rodent baits in aviaries, especially during winter.

YERSINIA INFECTION

Baytril is also the first choice treatment against the Yersinia infection. Rodent control and decontamination of the aviary must accompany a seven day long treatment of Baytril.

Yersinia is a common cause of sudden death in canaries housed in outdoor aviaries, where rodent control is poor. Affected birds are often too sick to respond to therapy but the eradication of rodents and the administration of Baytril to the entire flock should stop deaths within one week. Yersinia is diagnosed during a post mortem by miliary pin-point (sometimes large) pale colored abscesses that cover the liver and spleen.

Baytril, rather than Doxycycline, should be administered to the flock when Yersinia or E.coli type infection (Coliforms, Salmonella, Citrobacter, Klebsiella) are associated with Ornithosis. The underlying cause of the E.coli type infection (rodents for Salmonella/Yersinia, or spoiled food/unhygienic sprouting technique for

E.coli) must also be eliminated during treatment.

Baytril or Doxycycline are common causes of Thrush (Candidiasis) in canaries and should not be used when Thrush accompanies Ornithosis or other diseases. Instead a combination of Sulfa AVS and Megamix should first be administered to control the Thrush then followed by Doxycycline/Megamix.

THRUSH INFECTIONS (CANDIDIASIS)

Thrush infections (Candidiasis) are common in canaries for a variety of reasons. Thrush is common in canaries housed in aviaries that offer little protection from changing weather conditions. Infections also appear when canaries are under stress.

Causes of Thrush

For canaries, the presence of Thrush is a reliable indication of stress. The aviary, environment, food and genetic lineage are the main areas of stress that predispose canaries to the Thrush infection. Stressful conditions that predispose canaries to Thrush include an unbalanced diet (especially vitamin A deficiency), poor hygiene, crowded conditions, excessive moisture and food spoilage, poor aviary design and the uncontrolled use of antibiotics.

The presence of Thrush in droppings of canaries also reflects an immune system under attack, and one that is not coping well. Anything that suppresses the immune system may predispose canaries to the Thrush infection. Often, other diseases damage the immune system first, allowing Thrush to invade the bowel. For example, Thrush often accompanies E.coli infections, fungal infections, Ornithosis, Black Spot and Coccidiosis. Thrush medication will give only temporary relief and will not be totally effective until the underlying disease(s) have been treated.

Symptoms of Thrush

Thrush infections produce ulcerations of the mouth, crop, stomach and bowel. These painful sores produce a 'stomach ache' stance with the head of the infected bird hunched over the crop. Infected birds eat less, lose energy, become list-

less and exhibit a typical fluffed up appearance.

The organism invades the lining of the upper digestive tract (mouth, esophagus, crop, proventiculus) and the koilin lining of the ventriculus (gizzard). The koilin lining is a hardened membrane, the cuticle of which is a strong carbohydrate protein complex used to grind and crush seeds. Thrush infections damage the koilin lining, preventing the gizzard from grinding seed, and are thus a common cause of undigested seed in the droppings. Megabacteria (AGY) infection is another cause of undigested seed found in the droppings.

Thrush should be suspected when a canary suddenly becomes ill, very quiet, still and fluffed up. At first, the droppings are wet but then turn dark green, sticky and may then stain the tail or "clag" the vent.

Severely infected birds become disinterested in their surroundings, appear tired, may vomit, swallow excessively, sneeze after drinking, become dull and dry in the feather (a sign of dehydration) and rapidly lose body condition. The droppings are dark forest green in color, sticky and often contain whole or partially digested seed. White urates may also stain the vent and tail.

KD Powder is used to treat advanced Thrush infections in canaries. Megamix used to control Thrush infections related to humid conditions.

Thrush is a common infection of breeding canaries. It is most likely to occur in weak parents during the critical stages of the breeding cycle. Hens weakened by egg laying are especially prone to Thrush. The Thrush further weakens these birds through its effect on the digestive processes. They eat less because of the discomfort caused by Thrush infections and therefore quickly lose weight and energy and become susceptible to other diseases. Listless and fluffed up looking birds infected with Thrush indicate that they are weak and are unable to keep warm.

Candida infections in nestlings and juvenile birds cause crop stasis. The failure of the crop to empty quickly promotes fermentation, visible as air in the crop. Nestlings with Thrush infections grow poorly become red with dehydration and may vomit. They often die with a 'doughy' thick walled and air filled 'bloating' crop.

Diagnosis of Thrush

Thrush is confirmed by the microscopic examination of droppings or crop contents. Thrush may also be diagnosed by the rapid (within 48 hours) response of a sick bird to the administration of Nystatin into the drinking water or soft food mix.

Thrush Treatment

Flock Treatment for Thrush

Treatment of low grade/early Thrush:

Isolate sick birds for individual treatment in a heated hospital cage (See individual treatment regime below).

Mix Turbobooster, E-Powder and F-Vite into the dry seed or a soft food mix.

Add Megamix to the drinking water for 2 days.

Check indoor temperature and lower the humidity.

Treatment for advance/heavy Thrush

Isolate sick birds for individual treatment in a heated hospital cage (See individual treatment regime below).

Assess for other diseases, especially fungus and Ornithosis .

Mix PEP Food Cleaner (antifungal) with the seed.

Add Turbobooster, E-Powder and F-Vite to the dry seed or soft food mix.

Heat the aviary and lower the humidity.

Add KD Powder to the drinking water for 4 consecutive days.

Individual Treatment for Thrush

Nystatin is the first choice medicine for treating sick individuals in the hospital cage when the cause of the illness is Thrush.

All sick canaries infected with Thrush should receive supportive emergency care. First Aid Procedures are outlined on page 88.

Immediately move sick birds to a heated hospital cage for treatment.

Administer Nystatin in the drinking water or directly by mouth for 5 days.

NV powder should also be added to the drinking water.

Add Turboboster, E-Powder, and F-Vite to the seed or soft food mix.

Observe the droppings and activity of sick bird to monitor the response to treatment.

Monitor for E.coli infections which often accompany Thrush.

Birds weakened by nutritional imbalances, poor hygiene, aviary or bad genes (Mutations) also become susceptible to E.coli infections.

Prevention of Thrush

Recurring Thrush problems occur when fungi, bacteria and fungal toxins contaminate food, particularly soft food. To avoid recurrent Thrush problems, soft foods must be removed within three hours during summer and six hours in winter.

An unbalanced diet weakens the natural ability of canaries to repel disease. This is particularly true during times of increased physical (breeding, moult, weaning) and psychological (overcrowding) demands. Additional energy (E-Powder), vitamins and protein during these stress periods should help prevent Thrush infections.

Thrush can also occur when the incorrect medicines are used or even when the appropriate medicine is administered. The Tetracycline family of antibiotics (e.g. Doxycycline) and enrofloxacin (Baytril) produce Thrush when used incorrectly or for prolonged periods. The symptoms of Thrush that appear during correct antibiotic treatment are a useful sign that the antibiotics are no longer required.

Thrush often appears together with diseases that damage the immune system (e.g., Ornithosis, fungal infections), as a result of stressful conditions (Strep. or E.coli infections) and diseases that lower the acidity of the crop (E.coli, Megabacteria, Coccidiosis and Worms). In canaries, Thrush often accompanies E.coli, Strep., Mould or Megabacteria infections.

chapter 9
Troubleshooting

Symptoms & Diagnostic Troubleshooting

It must be emphasized that it is far better to confirm a diagnosis before initiating treatment rather than to decide on a treatment based upon symptoms and probabilities. Symptomatic treatment of canary illnesses may, however, become necessary for those unable to self-diagnose by using a microscope or those without access to an avian veterinarian. This section has been written with these people in mind.

ABDOMINAL ENLARGEMENT
Possible causes are egg binding, bacterial peritonitis and Atoxoplasmosis.

ANEMIA
Most common cause is red mite (page 130) and avian malaria. Symptoms of anemia include weakness, very pale membranes when opening the beak and laboured breathing.

ASPERGILLOSIS (inhaled form)
Symptoms include gasping, open mouth breathing, clicking respiration followed by rapid death in an occasional bird. Mostly juveniles are affected. (page 99).

ASPERGILLOSIS (ingested form)
Is referred to in this book as Moulding Disease. Symptoms of 'going light' or 'wasting disease' combined with breathing difficulties or tail bob. Confined to weaker varieties or inbred families (page 100).

ATOXOPLASMOSIS (See also Black Spot)
A common disease of young birds. Symptoms include huddling and ruffling of the feathers, debilitation, diarrhea, neurologic signs (20%) and death. Mortality can be as high as 80% (page 101).

BEAK SCRATCHING
Rubbing of the beak on the perch may be a normal canary activity. Excessive beak rubbing or head shaking indicates sinus (Airsac mites, Mycoplasma or Fungus) or mouth (Candida) infections. A Vitamin A deficiency may also be involved. S76 (page 130) and vitamin A (Dufoplus on page 151) should be the first choice treatment.

BLACK SPOT
Common causes of Black Spot are Circovirus, Atoxoplasmosis, Bacterial infection and Avian Malaria (page 102). Black spot refers to the appearance of an enlarged liver or spleen pushing the liver upwards so that a black spot is seen through the transparent abdominal muscles. Black spot found in nestlings less than three days of age should be assumed to have Circovirus. Black spot in juveniles

housed indoors is more likely to be due to Atoxoplasmosis or a bacterial septicaemia (E.coli, streptococcal or staphylococcal infection). Black spot in a dead breeding hen is rarely caused by Atoxoplasmosis and more likely by a bacterial septicaemia (E.coli or staph infection). Ornithosis is often associated with many forms of Black Spot. Avian malaria should be considered a possible cause of black spot in juveniles housed outdoors.

BREATHING DIFFICULTIES

Breathing difficulties refer to any of the following respiratory symptoms, which appear as the major symptom or a part of a condition where other symptoms are more obvious.

Open Mouth Breathing with Dry Click or Wheeze (and gasping)
Airsac mite (page 130), inhaled form of Aspergillosis (page 99) or hyperkeratotic vitamin A deficiency are most likely causes of open mouth breathing, accompanying gasping and a dry click. These symptoms indicate a problem with the airsacs, windpipe (trachea) or voice box (syrinx). Gasping signals an advanced sign of illness with unlikely chances of recovery.

Open Mouth Breathing, Gasping and Death in Adults
Inhaled form of Aspergillosis is the most likely cause of these symptoms.

Open Mouth Breathing with Moist Click or Wheeze (gurgles)
Open mouth breathing (with moist click or wheeze) is an indication of a serious problem with the throat, lungs or airsacs. Possible causes include Trichomoniasis (canker), bacterial or mould (e.g. mucor spp.) infections, airsac mite infestation complicated by a secondary infection, Mycoplasma and Ornithosis or thrush (candidiasis) infections.

Breathing Difficulties and Gasping Deaths in Adult Birds
Contaminated (mouldy) "sweating" nests, egg foods, corn and other perishable foodstuffs are the most common cause of Aspergillosis in breeding cabinets. The disease is not contagious. The source of the infection (contaminated nesting material, floor covering or food) must be removed and the cabinets disinfected with KD powder or diluted bleach. Refer to page 94 for details of treatment using KD powder.

Open Mouth Breathing after Exercise
A Mycoplasma infection (page 118, 99), secondary to Ornithosis or Moulding Disease is the most likely cause of this symptom.

Laboured Breathing (at rest)
Anemia or Aspergillosis are likely causes of this symptom.

Breathing Problems where Respiratory Symptoms are Not the Main Sign
The following disease may be involved:

Avian Pox
Open mouth breathing, weight loss, scabs and pox lesions especially on eyelids, on commissure of beak and in feather follicles. Excessive mucous and tags (diptheric) lesions can be found in the mouth and larynx. Birds of all ages can be affected and the mortality rate is between 20% and 100%. The infection spreads quickly.

Toxoplasmosis
Severe respiratory signs, general illness, nervous signs and blindness after 3 months of infection.

Blood-sucking Mites (Red Mite)
Minor to severe respiratory symptoms with anemia and sometimes a high mortality. The main complaint is usually a general depression in the bird.

Sternostomosiasis (Airsac Mite)
Loss of voice, decline of physical condition, respiratory distress, wheezing, squeaking, coughing, sneezing, nasal discharge, head shaking and gasping. Few birds die from an airsac mite infestation.

Trichomoniasis
Apathy, respiratory symptoms, regurgitation, blowing bubbles and emaciation. Sometimes a green diarrhea.

Streptococcus Infections
Cough, wheezing from chronic tracheitis, pneumonia and air sac infections.

Blindness
Cataracts, eye injury and Toxoplasmosis are possible causes of blindness in canaries. Toxoplasmosis has been confirmed as a cause of retinitis and blindness in canaries. Other signs of Toxoplasmosis include crusty eyelid sores, neurological signs such as circling and head tremors. Heavy metal poisoning in canaries may also exhibit similar nervous symptoms.

BREEDING PROBLEMS

Refer to page 105 for details of Breeding Problems.

Good Fertility but Dead-in-Shell
Consider flaws in your egg collection and storage procedures, incubation failure (hens weakened by Ornithosis, poor nutrition) or thunder storm activity during early stages of incubation.

Good Fertility but Hen Fails to Feed Young Properly
This complaint appears in the more sensitive Border Fancy variety and rarely in other varieties. The cause appears to be an energy, vitamin or iodine problem. Treatment may include a pre-breeding heath programme (page 78) and providing an improved soft food/soaked seed recipe prior to hatching.

Infertility and Dead-in-Shell
These symptoms relate commonly to a bacterial or Ornithosis problem associated with a low level of nutrition in the breeding ration. Water hygiene, protein and vitamin levels in the breeding diet should be reassessed. Ornithosis and Salmonella infections commonly produce dead in shell and infertility.

Infertility and Egg Binding
Obesity, delayed breeding condition, a calcium/trace element deficiency and cold temperatures at start of breeding are likely to cause these problems.

First Round Breeding Failure
Cold, dry weather and inexperienced young hens at the beginning of their breeding life may increase the likelihood of first round breeding failure. Ornithosis and Moulding Disease are also common causes of breeding failure.

Second Round Breeding Failure
Hot, humid weather during the second round of young increases the likelihood of food contamination and Moulding Disease (page 99). Disease, inadequate energy or too much protein in the diet may weaken hens.

Stunted & Dying Babies
The death of nestlings, 1-3 days of age may occur as a result of E. coli, Black Spot, poor incubation by parents due to disease (ornithosis), cold weather or a nutritional problem.

E. coli infections produce wet smelly nests (stained yellow by diarrhea of the nestlings) and sticky wet feathers. Most deaths occur between 1-3 days of age. A chicken smell usually accompanies E.coli infections. Sulfa AVS (page 125) is the treatment of choice.

Thrush (Candida) infections produce stunted nestlings. The crop bloats with air and a thickened crop wall is relatively common.

Deaths from pin-feather age to fledging age may be related to E. coli, Thrush (Candida) infections, poor incubation by parents due to disease (Ornithosis), cold weather or a nutritional problem.

Weak Babies
Some hens become agitated and do not sit on babies at night. Babies become cold and die, often with a full crop. This complaint occurs mostly with nervous young hens. Too low or too high blood calcium levels may also cause nutritional anxiety. Brooding failure due to an inadequate energy intake may occur in larger varieties such as Norwich. Examine the brood patch to determine if the hen has lost energy and breeding condition. The brood patch should be brown not pale. Hens with a pale brood patch have lost breeding condition and are unable to brood properly.

CANARY POX (page 111)

Main signs include the rapid appearance of wart-like growths on eyelids, legs and feet. Canaries housed outdoors are highly susceptible to this virus infection when mosquito numbers increase during warm months. Up to 100% of the flock can die within a few weeks.

CATARACTS (see eye symptoms)

CANKER (page 111)

Main signs include gagging, neck stretching, regurgitation, respiratory distress, nasal discharge, green diarrhea and going light, Cheesy material may be seen in the throat of young, as well as in the crop and eosophagus.

CONJUNCTIVITIS

Mycoplasma infections cause conjunctivitis at or soon after weaning. Mycoplasma infection is a life threatening disease that responds to Tylosine. Young birds fluff up, go light, don't eat and die. Other symptoms include wheezing and tail bobbing. Ornithosis, Trichomoniasis and Streptococcal infections also cause conjunctivitis.

CITROBACTER INFECTION

Veterinary intervention is needed to confirm this infection. Symptoms are consistent with respiratory and kidney infection. The underlying cause is contaminated water.

CLOSTRIDIUM (bacillus)

Veterinary intervention is required to confirm this infection. It is the cause of sudden death, occuring after eating contaminated or spoiled egg food or sprouted seeds.

COCCIDIOSIS (page 113)

Occurs especially during and soon after weaning.

CROP INFLAMMATION

Canaries may get crop inflammation (ingluvitis) as a result of Salmonella infection. Candidiasis (Thrush) or crop worm (Capillariasis) may also cause crop inflammation .

DEATHS

Deaths occurring in adults of both sexes. Most likely causes include a bacterial infection or Ornithosis.

Deaths occurring in breeding hens. A most likely cause is egg peritonitis (E.coli or Staphylococcal).

Deaths occurring in nestlings. Most likely causes include E. Coli (page 124), Red Mite (page 130) or Black Spot (page 101).

Deaths of juveniles. Most likely causes include Coccidiosis (page 113), E.coli, Canker(page 111), Ornithosis (page 115) and Strep. infections (page 133).

DIARRHEA

Possible causes include E.coli, Coccidiosis, Megabacteria (page 119), Ornithosis, Trichomoniasis (canker), Mice related infections and starvation. See page 119 for a complete description.

DROPPING CHANGES

See page 119 for a complete description.

EGG PROBLEMS

See page 107 for a complete description.

EYE SYMPTOMS

An Eye Discharge is usually accompanied by the rubbing of the face on a perch, signaling conjunctivitis. Conjunctivitis has many causes including Ornithosis, a generalized bacterial infection (E.coli or Streptococcus), a blood parasite, a vitamin deficiency or excess or an injury/ulcer when one eye alone is infected. Sulfa AVS (page 91) should be the first choice antibiotic. Birds with Colibacillosis (E.coli infection) demonstrate a general malaise, with or without diarrhea. Some birds may show conjunctivitis or a nasal discharge (rhinitis). Some birds may die. Streptococcus infections may present as sneezing or coughing. Moxi-T is the best treatment for a Streptococcus infection.

Eye colds

The appearance of eye colds (one-eye colds, swollen eyelids, eye discharge and one or both eyes shut) in canaries should alert the fancier to a potentially fatal disease. Eye colds are a symptom of a stress induced Psittacosis infection that is often complicated by secondary bacterial (E.coli, strep. or staph.) and Mycoplasma infections. It may also be a symptom of a fungal infection associated with environmental moulds or a sign of a vitamin A deficiency. Whatever the underlying cause, one-eye colds will spread throughout the aviary via the air, infect those birds under stress (breeding hens and juveniles) and cause significant mortality. Eye colds must be considered a serious symptom in canaries.

Pinched or Triangular Eye

This is subtle sign of Psittacosis in canaries. A flock with "pinched-eye" will have poor breeding performance, characterized by infertility, dead-in-shell and dying young and breeding hen mortality. A pre-breeding season Psittacosis treatment should eradicate this disease. Birds who do not respond should be considered Psittacosis "carriers" and must be culled.

Swollen Eyes

Swelling above and below the eye ball indicates a sinus infection. Sinus infections may be chronic. Canary pox also causes eyelid swellings. The causes of sinusitis include Psittacosis, Mycoplasma, fungal bacterial infections (E.coli and strep) and a vitamin A deficiency with secondary infections.

Red Eye

Conjunctivitis and chemosis is best treated with topical enrofloxacin (see page 91). It is most likely caused by a combined Mycoplasma and Ornithosis infection.

Blue Eye

Keratitis occurs due to either the Poxvirus or the Mycoplasma infection

Cataracts

Cataracts cause blindness and are thought to be caused by a recessive gene found in certain families of Norwich and Yorkshires.

Blindness

Toxoplasmosis has been confirmed as a cause of retinitis and blindness in canaries. Symptoms may also include crusty eyelid sores and neurological signs (circling and head tremors).

FEATHER PROBLEMS

Feather Cysts

Norwich, crested breeds and dimorphic colour canaries are most frequently affected with this poorly understood hereditary condition. It occurs in heavily feathered canaries, particularly those with double buff, soft feathers. Some canary breeders add iodine (IofordNF) to the drinking water as a means to hasten the maturation of feather cysts and to allow some to desiccate and slough naturally.

Feather Loss on Head

Mites, male baldness, aggression and malnutrition are possible causes. Feather loss on the head may result due to hormonal, nutritional, behavioural and fungal or mite infestations. Breeding season baldness in hens may occur at the conclusion of the moult, just prior to breeding condition or when breeding out of season. Birds may also become hormonally confused as a result of artificial lighting and temperature control. S76 (page 131) and improved nutrition (page 152) should be the first line of treatment.

Feather Loss Around the Eye

Feather loss around the eye is a sign of sinusitis, conjunctivitis or a corneal ulcer. Causes include bacterial, fungal, blood parasite or mite infections. Moxi-T (page 91) should be the first choice medicine.

Feather Loss Around the Mouth

Feather loss around the mouth usually results from a Candida (Thrush) infection. Nystatin (page 91) and vitamin A supplements (Dufoplus on page 151) should be the first treatment used.

Feather Loss of Wing and Tail
Feather loss on the wing and tail is usually related to an abnormal moult. An abnormal body moult may occur due to a cold spell or a problem with artificial lighting. Nutritional deficiency or disease, especially Candida infections, are other causes of an abnormal moult in juvenile canaries. A soft moult is a partial moult that occurs outside the normal moult season. A sudden change in temperature, day length, food or the environment may stimulate a soft moult to occur.

Feather Picking
Self-mutilation is most often due to the presence of toxins in food. Feather picking of other birds may be the result of overcrowding, fighting, boredom or nervousness caused by a calcium deficiency or protein excess. Nesting hens may pluck out feathers from their young in preparation of her next nest. Feather plucking may become habitual and impossible to cure in some individuals.

FEET PROBLEMS

The swelling of toes or feet may be associated with mosquito bites, nesting material caught around the toe, injury or ergot poisoning. Lameness is usually related to an injury. Feet problems are extremely stressful for birds, and they should be treated in a hospital cage with nutritional supplements (Turbobooster/E-powder on page 157) and KD foot baths.

Slip Claw
This name is given to one of the most noticeable and inconvenient malformations of a young canary's foot. It is recognized by the back claw being turned forward, preventing the bird from holding onto the perch. If a hen has a slipped claw it may lead to her eggs being infertile because she is unable to hold firmly onto the perch while the cock mates with her. The treatment is to take the claw and tie it back to the leg with a piece of cotton wool for two weeks after which time the claw should grow naturally in the correct position.

GOING LIGHT (page 125)
"Going light: refers to the symptom of progressive weight loss. It means the bird is depleting its body reserves as a source of energy. Birds "go light" with Coccidiosis, E.coli, Yersinia, Salmonella and fungal infections because these diseases affect their appetite. Diseases such as Megabacteria, Giardia infections and Candida (Thrush) infections are also common causes of "going light." These diseases affect the absorption of nutrients from the bowel. Undigested seeds may also be seen in the droppings of birds with these diseases. Blood parasites and bacterial infections may also cause "going light,"

LUMPS ON HEAD
Pox or Mycoplasma infections are the most likely cause of lumps around the eyes and head. Pox produces wart-like sores. The Salmonella infection may produce cheesy abscesses beneath the skin. Feather cysts produce lumps in the feather follicles. Pox, insect bites, swelling from strangulated fibres and mites may cause lumps on the feet and toes.

MOULT PROBLEMS (see feather problems)
A double or soft moult usually results from a problem with automatic artificial lighting systems. Stress may also cause a double moult e.g., contaminated food, rat or mice worry, outside lights on all night etc.

NERVOUS SIGNS
Head twirling and star-gazing is sometimes stress-induced. Nutritional imbalances (vitamin E deficiency), poisons, starvation, Atoxoplasmosis, Toxoplasmosis or virus infections may also cause these neurological signs. Symptoms of poisoning

include an obvious salivation, breathing difficulties, diarrhea and inactivity. Symptoms of starvation include black-stained droppings or diarrhea and a weakness that is often interpreted as neurological. The sudden death of several birds and head twirling in others is a common symptom of Paramyxovirus. Mortality rate is low while symptomatic birds continue to eat. KD powder (page 92) is the treatment of choice for Paramyxovirus outbreaks. Star gazing also appears with vitamin E deficiency. Turbobooster/E-powder (page 157) is the treatment of choice for vitamin E deficiency. Atoxoplasmosis produces neurological signs (20%), fluffed-up juvenile birds, going light, diarrhea and death. Mortality can be as high as 80%. Toxoplasmosis produces neurological symptoms and temporary blindness. The diagnosis of most neurological diseases requires histopathology. Treatment should be withheld until the exact diagnosis has been reached. The Zygomycosis (Mucormycosis) fungal infection from mucor mould may cause neurological signs, respiratory symptoms and death in canaries of any age or sex. This type of infection may occur due to contaminated sprouted seed.

RESPIRATORY SYMPTOMS

Breathing difficulties with an open mouth and clicking sounds usually indicates an airsac mite infestation. Other symptoms of an airsac mite infestation include squeaking, coughing, sneezing, nasal discharge, loss of voice, head shaking and gasping. The mortality rate is low. Birds infested with Airsac mite may have bouts of normal activity. Blood-sucking Mites (Red Mite) also cause minor to severe respiratory symptoms together with anemia and at times a high mortality rate. Severe depression and inactivity is a consistent finding. S76 (page 131) and vitamin A (Dufoplus on page 151) should be the first choice treatment for both these conditions.

Coughing, sneezing and gurgling sounds may also be noticed in birds with bacterial and Thrush infections of the *throat*. These birds will be very *fluffed up and inactive*. A Sulfa-AVS/Megamix

cocktail (page 124) and vitamin A (Dufoplus on page 151) should be the first choice treatment for birds with these symptoms.

Coughing or sneezing may also indicate a fungal or bacterial *sinus* infection. Birds with this type of infection are usually *alert and active*. Coughing and wheezing are also symptoms of a Streptococcus (Enterococcus Faecalis) infection. Moxi-T (page 91) is the treatment of choice here.

Respiratory Symptoms Associated with Deaths
Yersinia infections (Pseudotuberculosis) and poisoning produce many deaths within a short period (0-3 weeks) of time. Other symptoms include diarrhea. Most Yersinia infections are seen in winter and are associated with mice. Infected birds "go light" very quickly. Mortality is high. Birds die suddenly. Salmonella infections cause symptoms similar to Yersiniosis but deaths occur over a longer period. Ornithosis elicits respiratory and eye symptoms with few deaths over a long period of time and usually after an inclement in weather. Baytril (page 91) or Sulfa AVS (page 91) should be the first medicines chosen to treat birds when deaths are associated with respiratory symptoms. Vomiting associated with respiratory symptoms may be due to Trichomoniasis, which produces respiratory symptoms as well as regurgitation, bubble blowing and emaciation. Droppings are usually slimy and dark green in colour. Turbosole (page 91) is the treatment of choice.

Ornithosis & Mycoplasma infections cause respiratory symptoms and death in young birds.

Respiratory Symptoms Failing to respond to Antibiotic Treatment
Moulding Disease is the most likely cause.

SNEEZING
The Mycoplasma infection and airsac mite infestation cause sneezing in older hens. Sneezing is often experienced at the start of a cold winter.

TOE SORES

Digit necrosis can result from strangulation with fibre or a staphylococcus infection.

VOMITING

Vomiting usually indicates crop, stomach or gizzard problems or a poison of some sort. Megabacteriosis, Trichomoniasis and blockages are also common causes of vomiting. Trichomoniasis results in depressed, inactive birds who may also show respiratory symptoms and bubble blowing but seldom develop diarrhea. Birds with Megabacteria do not show respiratory signs and may pass parts or whole seeds in soft and watery, dark green to brown/black feces. Birds with blocked gizzards become depressed and pass white droppings.

WORMS

Capillaria worms may occur in outdoor aviaries. They are spread through the ingestion of earthworms.

YERSINIA

Yersinia infections are a common cause of sudden deaths in canary rooms and outside aviaries where mice and rats are a problem. Symptoms include wheezing, diarrhea and very sick looking birds.

YOUNG BIRD PROBLEMS

Sick & Dying Juveniles

E.coli, Thrush, Black Spot (Atoxoplasmosis), Coccidiosis, Ornithosis and Megabacteria may cause illness and death in young canaries.

E. coli infections can be a cause of high mortality rates in juveniles during their moult when wet and cold weather lower their resistance to disease. A chicken smell usually accompanies E.coli infections.

Thrush (Candida) infections produce very sick and dying canaries. Infection in juveniles is often related to poor nutrition, crowded conditions, wet/cold spells, food spoilage and the uncontrolled use of antibiotics. A sweet smell accompanies watery droppings. Whole seeds may be seen in the droppings.

Trichomoniasis (Canker) commonly infects juvenile canaries. Infected juveniles become very depressed, go light, experience moult problems and may also show respiratory symptoms.

Ornithosis produces recurrent respiratory symptoms (eye and nostril signs) in juveniles.

Nutritional problems are common causes of secondary bacterial infections in juveniles.

Moulding Disease is a major cause of secondary infections in young canaries. Fluffed up, listless juveniles are signs of Moulding Disease.

Streptococcal infections are usually secondary developments to other infections.

Notes

chapter 10
Health Products
for Canaries

Vitamin Supplements

Background Information

Vitamins promote natural health and vitality. The vitamin concentrations in seeds are highly variable. Seeds do not contain vitamin A (corn provides carotenoids) or vitamin D. Vitamin E and vitamin K levels are extremely low. Among the B vitamins, riboflavin, niacin, and pantothenic acid are often low and vitamin B12 is not present at all.

The vitamins lacking in the seed must be provided to canaries in some other form. Old timers understood this vitamin need from seeing the benefits of giving endives and carrots to their birds. Most fanciers continue this practice, although the availability of fresh produce is declining. Nowadays vitamins are often added to the soft food mix or water.

There is a major increase in the vitamin requirement needed during the breeding season. There is an increased need for energy, protein and vitamins, as well as trace elements and minerals. Breeding birds tire easily and become more susceptible to illnesses when sufficient vitamins and minerals are not provided.

Canaries can survive on grain and grit alone, but they cannot reach the level of health required to withstand the pressures of breeding. Eventually their health fails. Many canary illnesses can be controlled by correct nutrition. Canaries produce their own vitamin C and inositol, but all of the other vitamins must be given to them in the feed or water.

Dufoplus

Dufoplus is the purest form of multivitamins available. It is a potent, sugar-free multi-vitamin and is the best vitamin on the market by far. It contains vitamin A, all of the B vitamins, especially Thiamine, vitamins D and E. Dufoplus is a water-soluble vitamin (A, D, E, and B Complex) free of sugar or glucose and preserved in nitrogen. Used to bring out the true colour of the "non-coloured" canaries, it improves breeding performance and relieves stress. It is commonly used in combination with Ioford NF.

Dufoplus should be given for two consecutive days each week in the drinking water, sprouted seed or soft food.

Dufoplus is one of the very few water vitamins that can be left safely in the water for two or three days without affecting its potency. This is only possible when temperatures are below 25° Celsius (77°F). Unlike the powder form vitamins, Dufoplus contains no sugar. Sugar-based vitamin powders added to drinking water provide an ideal place for germs to breed and must be changed each night.

Breeding, Fertility & Dufoplus

Dufoplus is used to improve fertility and breeding success. Breeding canaries need more vitamins and Dufoplus contains those vitamins needed for breeding success. Signs of health, such as rapid growth and pink skin colour become obvious when the vitamin, mineral and energy needs of breeding birds are catered for properly. Dufoplus plays an important role in the production of healthy, robust babies.

Calcium, Vitamin D3 & Dufoplus

Vitamin D3 is produced by natural sunlight. Vitamin D3 has an intimate relationship with the metabolism of calcium. Calcium is vital to fitness and vitality through its role in muscle and bone health. Vitamin D3 is incredibly important for egg laying, strong babies and vitality in the young birds and breeding flock but an excess of vitamin D causes kidney damage and retards growth. Vitamin D is naturally formed by the action of direct sunlight on the bird and breeding birds do better when the aviary is flooded with natural light.

Dufoplus for indoor canaries

Dufoplus is a potent source of vitamin D3, and should be added to the diet of all breeding birds kept indoors. The breeding canary is particularly susceptible to Vitamin D3 deficiency related egg binding. Vitamin D3 is needed for the bird to absorb calcium from the intestine.

Moult, Feather Quality, Vitamin A & Dufoplus

Dufoplus intensifies the yellow colour range of the feathers within three weeks of use. The yellow colour of "uncoloured" canaries is genetically determined, but the genetic potential is only realized when a pure source of vitamin is given. Within three weeks, Dufoplus reveals the true genetic intensity of the yellow range. Dufoplus produces a rich, soft, pure and even ground colour without the extreme depth and hardness seen with colour fed birds.

Vitamin A is also particularly important vitamin for the canary. Vitamin A promotes appetite and digestion. It also increases resistance to infection and to some parasites. The signs of a deficiency are subtle, but look carefully at the feather colour intensity and body condition. Feathers become pale, rough and lack lustre, and there may be an accumulation of a yellow dry scale on the sides of the mouth with a vitamin A deficiency. Look for signs of tassel foot and rough feet and legs. These signs are also associated with a vitamin A deficiency.

Illness, Health & Dufoplus

Vitamins play an integral part in the development of fitness and health. The omission or malabsorption of one vitamin can alter the metabolism and result in a deficiency disease. The signs of a vitamin deficiency in the canary are subtle. Often the vitamin deficiency relates to a bowel infection and can be confused with an illness. An important part of the recovery process after illness is the addition of vitamins to the canary's diet.

Young Birds, Stress & Dufoplus

The B vitamins in Dufoplus are used as the first line of attack against stress when the young birds enter the aviary, during the first juvenile moult and for the entire breeding season. There is a noticeable change in the noise coming from the birds the day after Dufoplus is administered. Young canaries exist under considerable stress and they need a balanced vitamin supplement to remain healthy and fit. When vitamin B12 is lacking in a bird's diet, it has little resistance against harmful bacteria. Dufoplus has high levels of the stress B vitamins, including Thiamine (vitamin B12).

B vitamins, Dufoplus & E-Powder.

The B vitamins are energy vitamins used to protect against stress. E-Powder is a very rich source of B-vitamins. The B vitamins are all involved in the energy metabolism as cofactors in enzymatic reactions. They are extremely beneficial when the energy expenditure increases nine fold during the heavy feeding of the canary chicks. They oil the energy pathways and aid in the continuing vitality of the feeding parents, thus maximising the growth of the chicks. Thiamin (vitamin B12) is an extremely important vitamin. Although seeds are a rich source of thiamin, it is destroyed in canaries with enteritis. Thiamin supplements are given to accelerate recovery from enteritis (e.g., sweating disease and nestling diarrhea).

Dufoplus and Ioford Cocktail.

Dufoplus and Ioford are compatible in water. The combination is a proven cocktail to keep young and breeding birds vital and happy. When not used as part of an ongoing health programme, Dufoplus and Ioford should be added to the drinking water at the first sign of lethargy in the flights. It is remarkable how often this cocktail brings the birds back on top of the world.

NV Powder

NV powder is a sugar-based vitamin, mineral and iodine water supplement, used after illness to promote appetite and to enhance the taste of soft food recipes for flocks not accustomed to food or water supplements.

Energy, Vitamin, Minerals & NV Powder

Its main use is for ill birds, birds recovering from serious illnesses, breeding birds returning to the aviary and youngsters entering the aviary for the first time. It provides an instant energy and vitamin source to accelerate the transition to good health under trying circumstances.

Soft Food Recipes & NV Powder

NV Powder is used in Soft Food Recipes to improve its palatability and acceptance by birds unaccustomed to soft food supplements.

NV Powder, Dufoplus and Ioford NF

It is a poor substitute for the quality provided by the products Dufoplus and Ioford, because it is sugar based and must be changed twice daily in hot weather and each day in cool weather.

Wet Nests & NV Powder

Wet nests are often caused by hormonal related mineral and electrolyte imbalances. NV powder is used with Megamix to reverse the electrolyte imbalance, thereby quickly restoring the healthy nest without the need for antibiotics.

Stunted Growth & NV Powder

Energy depletion is a common cause of weak nestlings. NV powder on a soft food mix or in the water often restores the energy levels in the feeding parents, promoting more active feeding and stronger chicks.

MINERALS AND TRACE ELEMENTS

Seeds are a very poor source of minerals and trace elements. Minerals and trace elements are the most neglected part of good nutrition for canaries.

Many believe grit provides canaries with all the minerals and trace elements required for good health. This is not so. The regular grits contain calcium but are deficient in iodine, iron and most trace elements.

Shell grit provides the canary with a source of digestive stones and contains calcium, but is a poor source of mineral salts and trace elements. Cuttlefish Bone is a source of calcium but is lacking in other minerals. Shell grit does not provide the best form of Calcium supplementation for egg laying birds.

Egg laying hens need more than twice the calcium levels of the non-laying bird. A concentrated mineral supplement (F-Vite) is the best and safest method of providing this Calcium, which is largely unavailable in shell grit.

Shell grit is the most common cause of illness in canary hens during the breeding season. Far too much shell grit must be eaten to satisfy their calcium needs and laying hens fall ill, vomit and may die from gizzard obstruction after engorging on it. Wet grit is particularly hazardous because the moisture in the grit promotes harmful bacterial growth and contamination. E.coli and related bacteria are commonly found in wet grits originating from the dead and decaying molluscs, which inhabit the grit shells. Some of the bacteria produced by these decaying marine animals are toxic. Wet and contaminated grit is a common cause of enteritis, wet nests, nestling deaths and poor breeding performance in canaries.

Canaries naturally balance their own mineral needs. They search for minerals and trace elements when the levels in the body are depleted. Depletion of minerals occurs mostly when the hens are laying eggs and when the parents are heavily feeding young. Depleted parents become agitated and pick at the feathers of their young. Cock birds are even known to kill fully feathered chicks.

F-Vite

F-Vite is a sterile grit, vitamin and mineral powder that replaces the need for any other form of grit.

F-Vite should either be provided continuously in a dish, mixed with tonic seeds or with hard seed.

It has been developed as a combination grit, protein, energy, vitamin and mineral supplement,

which is especially beneficial for breeding and during the moult. It is palatable and the birds actually look for it when feeding young, because it is rich in the essential vitamins and minerals for growing babies and is also a rich source of energy.

F-Vite provides all the necessary minerals and mineral salts and trace elements in a sterile form. There is no wastage with F-Vite as canaries consume every last portion. It contains 10% shell grit enough for canaries to digest properly. The shell grit portion of F-Vite is baked at high temperatures to ensure sterility, without damaging the potency of the minerals or grit. The end result is a concentrated mineral supplement that enhances health and vitality. The energy rich desiccated molasses and the scientifically balanced and concentrated vitamin, mineral, trace element and mineral salt mixture make this a perfect product for feeding parents.

Breeding & F-Vite

Breeding birds have extraordinarily high demands for minerals, salts and trace elements and require supplementation on a daily basis. The hens require the minerals for egg laying and the feeding adults require extra mineral salts and energy. F-Vite satisfies these needs and is ideal for egg laying hens and feeding parents.
The birds quickly accept the taste of F-Vite when it is mixed with tonic seed.

Moult & F-Vite

There is a marked increase in the requirements of the minerals Calcium and Phosphorous during the moult. These minerals are responsible for the strength of the new feathers. F-Vite provides a perfect balance of the minerals needed for a rapid moult and production of quality feathers.

Young Birds & F-Vite

The babies bred or weaned on F-Vite relish its taste in the flights. Place the powder in a small dish in the aviary preferably next to the water. For some reason, they like to eat it after drinking. Replace the F-Vite when the container is empty or when it turns brown on humid or wet days. The mineral salts attract moisture from the air on wet and humid days, turning it brown. All grits absorb moisture.

TRACE ELEMENTS

Ioford NF

Ioford NF is a health stimulant for canaries containing iodine, iron, calcium, zinc, magnesium and vitamin D. It is used in conjunction with Dufoplus to improve colour intensity, fertility and egg quality during breeding. Ioford is also used to invigorate canaries into show condition.

Ioford NF should be given for two consecutive days each week by adding it to the drinking water, sprouted seed or soft food.

Breeding & Ioford NF

Ioford NF is used to improve fertility and egg quality during the breeding season. The iodine in Ioford NF is an essential trace element beneficial for fertility, feather growth and overall health and vitality.

The calcium, vitamin D and magnesium in the Ioford NF increases breeding performance, improves feather quality and helps to prevent egg binding, soft shelled eggs, egg laying paralysis and pipping deaths. The calcium, magnesium and vitamin D are balanced scientifically to provide hens with exact proportions for the production of perfect eggs and continuing good health. The vitamin D in Ioford NF is of special relevance to the canary bred indoors.

Vitamin D3, Calcium & Ioford

Egg binding and soft shell eggs are rarely encountered in sunlit aviaries. Artificial light must produce ultraviolet B emissions between 290 and 310 nm to produce vitamin D3. In many cases vitamin D3 deficiency is indistinguishable from calcium deficiency. Bent keels, splayed legs and beak abnormalities are the most common signs of a vitamin D3 deficiency, and are almost impossible to reverse. Over supplementation of vitamin D causes kidney problems and breeding failures associated with dead in shell.

Moult & Ioford NF

Iodine is the most important trace element for a good moult and for successful breeding, but in overdose retards the thyroid gland and, therefore, depresses breeding performance and retards the moult. Many fanciers use iodine and iron but very few, if any, know the exact requirements. An overdose of iron damages the liver but given at the correct levels enhances health and accelerates the recovery from stress or illness. It also becomes necessary for young, developing birds when the nutritional requirements for the moult are complex and demanding. The iron in Ioford also enhances health and accelerates the recovery from the stress of breeding, moult and shows.

Young Birds, Moult & Ioford NF

Ioford NF accelerates the moult and development of young birds. Iodine is the most important trace element for a good moult, because it stimulates the thyroid gland to produce the hormones that control its speed. The zinc in Ioford NF is used to stimulate the immune system of the developing youngster. This promotes a strong natural resistance in the youngster during this critical developmental age.

Show Condition & Ioford NF

Ioford NF is given as part of the Show Programme to help bring the birds into show condition. Together with regular water spraying it creates perfectly tight feathers.

Hi-Cal

Hi-Cal is a potent source of calcium that is readily absorbed. It is added to the drinking water and canaries immediately accept its taste. Hi-Cal is used to prevent soft-shelled eggs and to help prevent egg binding and other related problems. Hi-Cal should be used when egg-shell problems are the result of moulding disease or bowel infections (e.g., E.coli diarrhea, sweating disease). These diseases prevent the proper absorption of minerals even though they are provided to the breeding birds. For individual birds with a history of egg-binding, Hi-Cal should be added to the drinking water a few days after the cock is introduced to the hen and continued until the fourth egg is laid.

Turbobooster

Turbobooster is a multi-purpose health product. It has been designed to provide canaries with an additional source of energy and protein for the feeding parents.

The need for Turbobooster varies from one programme to the next. Refer to each programme for the recommended frequency of administration.

Turbobooster is a concentrated form of energy, coupled with stress relieving vitamin B and the oil based breeding vitamins A, D, E and K. This multipurpose, energy rich oil is best added to soft food/sprouted seed recipes. After a short while it is relished. The birds often climb the wire in anticipation of the treat as the garlic cocktail is being prepared. E-Powder is also added to this mix for greater energy efficiency and many fanciers also add the Dufoplus, Ioford and F-Vite at the same time, giving remarkable results. It has become a simple, but highly effective feeding system.

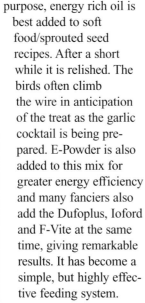

Breeding & Turbobooster

Turbobooster, being a very high source of energy and breeding amino acids, is used in combination with E-Powder to produce fast growing, robust and healthy babies. This clever combination enables the feeding parents to maintain their body condition and vitality during the entire breeding season.

It is the balance rather than the amount of protein that is critical to breeding success. The protein balance refers to the essential amino acids in the seed mix. Lysine and methionine are the most difficult amino acids to balance. These are known as the "breeding amino acids" because of their importance for breeding success. Groats, wheat and rape are the most important natural sources of lysine. Sunflower and Safflower are rich sources of lysine and methionine. Turbobooster also has high levels of lysine and methionine.

Fertility & Turbobooster

Vitamins D and E promote natural health and vitality. Turbobooster is a rich source of vitamin D and E. Vitamin E functions as a biological antioxidant that protects the membranes against damage from free radicals. This function may be important during the stress of overcrowding and breeding when the formation of free radicals is increased. Vitamin E also has a positive effect on the immune function. Vitamin E functions to improve the fertility of male canaries prior to breeding. A 30 day long course of Turbobooster, as part of the pre-breeding programme, has the same positive effect on improving fertility. Vitamin E also helps protect the health of young birds by alleviating stress.

A Vitamin E deficiency may occur when rancid oils are fed excessively to the breeding pairs. All oil preparations must be refrigerated and tightly sealed. The signs of deficiency in canaries include twisting of the neck, stiff legs and leg weakness.

The Moult & Turbobooster

Turbobooster produces feathers with a beautiful sheen and rich colour. It is the balance of amino acids and essential fatty acids in Turbobooster which is responsible for the beautiful colours and silky feather it produces within 3 weeks of use. It is also used to rejuvenate damaged tail feathers.

Turbobooster is combined with E-Powder and F-Vite to produce silky feathers with colour and life as good as they get. Turbobooster contains high levels of the essential amino acids (protein) needed for new feather formation and contains a good mix of special oils, called fatty acids, which produce an extremely silky feather. This has meant that the oil has become a favourite "secret" of the best show fanciers in Australia.

Show Condition & Turbobooster

Turbobooster should be administered as part of a show preparation programme in order to give canaries their very best possible feather quality and body condition. Turbobooster can be used together with E-Powder and F-Vite each day for three weeks prior to the show in order to produce a silky sheen, porcelain like tightness and a deep rich colour to the plumage.

Young Birds & Turbobooster

The time between weaning and the completion of the moult is an extremely difficult period for young canaries, and they must receive special care with every effort being made to boost their immune system. Turbobooster is an ideal product to help young develop a natural strength. Weaning youngsters accept the taste of Turbobooster immediately and become lifelong lovers of this treat, providing them with immediate health protection.

Turbobooster stimulates fitness and health in the young birds. This product contains high levels of the essential amino acids (protein) needed for fledgling muscle development. The result is vigorous flight that soon produces the heightened health characteristics of top fitness. The special mix of omega 3 essential oils stimulates the immune system to repel illness and together with garlic oil offers strong protection against the stress-induced illnesses of the overcrowded young bird flight.

Turbobooster is a necessary part of the recovery process following illness of any type.

E-Powder

E-Powder is an excellent source of Thiamin and B vitamins and is recommended for all breeding canaries on a daily basis. E-Powder contains the by-products of cultured yeast and can be mixed into tonic seed, soft food/sprouted seed recipes or kept on its own in finger drawers. It is highly palatable, but some birds need a few days to totally accept the new taste on the food.

The need for E-Powder varies from one programme to the next. Refer to each programme for recommended frequency of administration.

More than anything else, a constant supply of energy is needed for good breeding results and continuing health in young birds. It is a rich source of energy and is used to promote good health and protect the flock from stress.

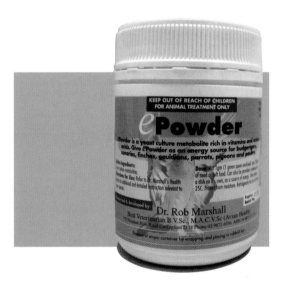

Breeding & E-Powder

The rate of growth of a chick is determined by the energy content of the food, its genetic make-up and the ability of the parents to feed it to its full capacity. The full potential for growth is achieved by protecting the feeding parents from fatigue and ensuring the baby utilizes the available energy fully. The faster the baby converts energy for growth, the quicker the crop empties and the more food the adult can feed. E-Powder accelerates the conversion of energy into growth and prevents fatigue in the feeding parents. The result is a parent that feeds more, a chick that grows faster and a show bird that fulfils its genetic potential.

Moult & E-Powder

The moult is an energy sapping process for canaries and is accelerated through the use of E-Powder.

Young Birds & E-Powder

E-Powder is a rich source of vitamin B energy enzymes, breeding proteins and immune modulating minerals. E-Powder protects young birds from the stress of overcrowding. It is especially useful in helping control enteritis caused by bacteria, Megabacteria, Coccidiosis or worms. Mixing E-Powder with F-Vite into a tonic seed mix provides the ideal method for providing these important supplements to young birds.

KD Powder

KD contains organic acids that protect the health of seed eating birds by acidifying the water they drink and thus also the contents of the crop. The blend of organic acids, hydrogen ions and surfactants also helps to keep the water containers clear of sludge and germs. See page 92 for further details.

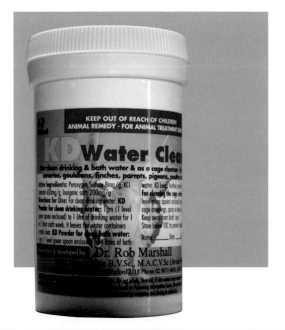

RECIPES & APPLICATION OPTIONS

Drinking Water: Dufoplus & Ioford

Dufoplus and Ioford can be added to the drinking water.

Tonic Seed: F-Vite & E-Powder

Young Birds

Tonic seed is a convenient and effective way of providing E-Powder & F-Vite to young birds during the moult and provides an easy method for providing these two most important supplements. Tonic seeds play an important part in the weaning process. The addition of E-Powder and F-Vite to tonic seed is recommended for weaning and young birds. E-Powder keeps youngsters healthy by maintaining their energy needs and also prevents stress. F-Vite helps strengthen bones and stimulates the growth of new feathers.

Show Birds

F-Vite & E-Powder mixed into a tonic seed helps bring show birds into show condition.

Hard Seed: Turbobooster, F-Vite & E-Powder

Turbobooster, F-Vite & E-Powder may be added to a hard seed mix. E-Powder and F-Vite should be mixed well into Turbobooster impregnated seed. This combination is recommended during wet weather, when medicating, and for young or breeding birds returned to the flights. The prepared seed may be placed in a hopper and refreshed each three days in summer or weekly in winter.

Soft Food: Turbobooster, E-Powder, NV Powder & F-Vite

Weaning & Young Birds

Young birds and weanlings reared on Turbobooster, F-Vite and E-Powder, readily accept this soft food mix. The older birds need much longer but soon accept it as they watch the new youngsters devouring this treat.

Breeding Birds

A soft food recipe should provide everything breeding birds need to rear their young successfully. E-Powder provides additional energy, Turbobooster provides a good protein balance and F-Vite provides minerals required for egg laying and feeding young. Hi-Cal may also be added to a soft food recipe.

Soft Food Recipe

Ingredients

One freshly boiled egg, Polenta, Turbobooster, E-Powder, NV powder, Hi-Cal & F-Vite.

Preparation

Blend one boiled egg (shell and all).

Then mix 200 grams of polenta, 1 teaspoon of E-Powder and 1 teaspoon NV powder thoroughly into the egg mixture. 2ml of Turbobooster is then mixed into the combined dry mix.

Hygiene

Uneaten remnants must be removed within 6 hours.

Sprouted Seed: Turbobooster, Dufoplus, Ioford NF, E-Powder.

Sprouted seed is a convenient and useful vehicle for providing the supplements to canaries. Canaries should be fed sprouted seeds in preparation for breeding, during breeding, weaning and as young birds.

Breeding Birds

Sprouted seed must be free of bacterial or fungal contamination. The supplements should be mixed through the sprouted seeds after their final rinse.

Ingredients

Supplements: Equal parts rape, sunflower and millet, Turbobooster, Dufoplus, IofordNF, E-Powder & F-Vite. E-Powder and F-Vite may also be provided in finger drawers at all times.

To each kilogram of soaked seed, after the final rinse, add and mix thoroughly :

Dufoplus	.2.5ml (1/2 teaspoon)
Ioford	.5ml (1 teaspoon)
Turbobooster	.5 ml (1 teaspoon)
E-Powder	.10 gram (2 teaspoon)

Weanlings and Young Birds

Dufoplus and Ioford are preferred and accepted by most weanlings. NV Powder is an alternative to the Dufoplus/Ioford Combo. It is a sweet tasting glucose based vitamin and mineral water that is added to the soaked seed, enticing fussy weanlings to accept the new soft food. They quickly learn to love this delicious meal.

Ingredients

Sprouted millet and plain canary seed, Turbobooster, Dufoplus, Ioford NF (or NV powder).

Preparation

10 drops of Turbobooster, 5 drops of Dufoplus and 10 drops Ioford (or NV powder) are added to 100gms of soaked seed after the final rinse and allowed to soak into the seed for a few minutes. E-Powder and F-Vite are sprinkled onto the soaked seed after it is placed in the nursery

PEP Food Cleanser

PEP is a new generation, slow-release food cleanser that protects all grades of seed for three months.

PEP Food Cleanser has been developed to protect the freshness and quality of seed from mould contamination irrespective of the storage conditions and is an ideal product for the health conscious canary breeder. This palatable, controlled release food cleanser does not provide an excuse for poor quality seed, because there is no cure for seed already contaminated with fungal toxins. It is the most advanced mould inhibitor on the market and its controlled release protects the seed for three months without affecting its palatability. Its activity is unaffected by the nature of the feed being treated and the recommended doses protect grain with extremely high moisture contents (greater than 17%) and during arduous storage conditions. PEP is particularly recommended for high rainfall areas (e.g. Victoria, Northern Queensland and the eastern seaboard).

Dosage & Instructions

Mix PEP at the rate of 5 grams (1 level tablespoon) into 25 Kilograms of seed as it is placed into the storage bins.

Protector

Protector is a pleasant smelling cabinet, flight and show cage cleanser.

The common outstanding feature of every successful canary bird room is the time and attention that the fancier takes to keep the cages clean. Cleanliness is the first and most important step in protecting the healthy flock from illness. The underlying aim is to keep the germ count in the aviary, water and food low, because even the most vital and naturally resistant bird succumbs to illness when it is exposed to a foreign germ or an overwhelming number of germs.

Protector is a Quaternary ammonium compound used to kill Ornithosis germs in the aviary and show cage.

It is used each week during an Ornithosis treatment plan, prior to breeding, and is continued once a month during the breeding season. Used in rotation with KD, these two cleansers play an important role in the control of the three most important diseases of the breeding season — Ornithosis, E.coli and Moulding Disease.

Used before and after to clean the show cage, these two cleansers prevent the spread of Ornithosis and other germs from the show cages into your bird room.

Wear gloves when using all cleansers. Avoid contact with eyes. Avoid prolonged contact with skin.

appendix
Appendix

The following article outlines Dr. Marshall's Sterile Bowel Theory for canaries.

Sterile Bowel Theory

At an Association of Avian Veterinarian International Conference held in 1989 I was surprised to hear that both Dr. Gerry Dorrestein and Dr. Helga Gerlach believed that the bowel of healthy finches and canaries is sterile. At Veterinary school I had been taught that bacteria played a vital role in the continuing health of the animals we studied (dogs, cats, cows, and horses, as well as poultry). I instantly accepted the opinions of these two eminent bird pathologists and used this new found knowledge to help me understand the special nature of Passerines in general and canaries in particular.

The Sterile Bowel Theory is supported by the following facts:

1. Canaries belong to the most advanced order of birds: Oscine passerines.

2. Oscine passerines have developed specialized adaptive anatomical and physiological systems that are different from the more primitive bird orders (e.g., Galliformes)

3. The high metabolic rate of Oscine Passerines (e.g., canaries) requires a higher degree of energy. In passerines, more advanced and improved chemical digestion and intestinal absorption provide this additional energy.

4. Bacterial fermentation is an inefficient source of energy. Birds with caeca utilise bacteria to help digest fibrous matter. Canaries have no caeca.

5. Canaries have no resident bowel or so-called "friendly bacteria." "Friendly Bacteria" is a concept that explains the theory of probiotics.

Knowledge of the special position Passerines hold in the bird world should help you understand the notion of a sterile bowel in these birds.

Passerines are the most recent and advanced order of bird species. They account for approximately three fifths of all living birds, or some 5,739 of the 9,702 species of 1,168 genera. Other birds such as poultry (Galliformes) belong to much older and more primitive orders of birds.

Passerines broke away from the normal avian (more primitive bird orders) mould to become the most successful group of birds. They appeared in force through adaptive radiation, after the Paleogene time period moving them into unexploited and unrestricted ecological zones, largely because their complex nest building behaviour released them from the limited resource of cavity nesting. Passerines were so successful during the late Tertiary period that lines of demarcation among families and higher groups are poorly defined. Differences among many passerine families are therefore not as great as those among non-passerine genera. Almost all recent workers have considered the order Passeriniformes to be monophyletic, sharing many anatomical and physiological similarities (a special type of palate and syringeal anatomy, bundled spermatozoa, the distinctive passerine foot and an elevated metabolic rate).

The elevated basal metabolic rates of Passerines compared to other birds provide an indication of the uniqueness of this group of birds. This finding also supports a view that their bowel is sterile. The basal (at rest) metabolic rates of Passerines average some 50-60% higher than non-passerines of an equivalent size. This feature found in Passerines, reflects a significant move away from the physiology found in more primitive bird forms such as Galliformes (poultry).

Passerines can be divided into two broad groups: Suboscines and Oscines. The Oscines constitute about four fifths of the Passerine birds and are extremely uniform in their morphology. They are referred to as the "songbirds" that largely inhabit temperate zones of the world. Canaries and finches are a part of the Oscine group of Passerines. The suboscines are slightly less morphologically uniform and are prominent in neo tropical regions. The Australian Lyrebird and scrub birds do not fit into the classical definition of suboscines or Oscines.

Our interest lies in the Oscines that occupy the temperate zones of the world. The Oscines represent an absolute extreme among birds and perhaps all living vertebrates in their morphological uniformity. Most are small land birds primarily adapted for feeding on insects, small fruits and seeds and therefore, many of the differences we do see among them are in the feeding mechanism and bill structures that are often convergent rather than indicative of any evolutionary link. Similarly, the digestive tract of the seed-eating finches should be viewed as an adaptive change

with no evolutionary link to more primitive orders of birds.

The lack of major gaps among many Oscine families suggest that the adaptive radiation of modern, advanced Oscines is probably quite recent, perhaps dating to the Medial to late Tertiary period of time. For this reason we should not assume any evolutionary link between the digestive physiology of primitive birds forms such as Galliformes (poultry) and the most advanced and recent birds; the Passerine Oscines.

Current knowledge concerning the digestion of food in birds is the result of scientific studies performed on poultry. Poultry belong to the Galliformes, a most primitive form of birds. In these birds, the crop, proventriculus, gizzard, small intestine and caeca are all involved in the digestive process. The gastric apparatus includes the proventriculus (secretes acid gastric juice and pepsin) and gizzard action (grinding action and acid proteolysis). The principal organ for chemical digestion and absorption is the small intestine. Here the chyme from the gizzard is neutralised by the highly buffered bile, pancreas juice and succus entricus. The pH, especially in the ileum, is between 6 and 8. The chemical digestion of starch is effected largely in the small intestine through activities of pancreatic amylase and of intestinal and pancreatic maltase. Lactose and sucrose are hydrolysed by lactase and maltase respectively in the succus entricus.

In birds that must digest fibrous plant foods the caeca (birds have paired caeca) are well developed and the combined length of the caeca may equal the length of the small intestine. The caeca harbour bacteria that help break down plant cellulose into simple digestible carbohydrates. Food reaches the caeca by anti-peristaltic movements of the rectum. Recent research has shown that bacterial fermentation in the caeca supplies only a small fraction of the total energy requirements of birds, so the real importance of the caeca in the domestic fowl remains in question. Canaries have no caeca.

Although microbiological digestion and fermentation of cellulose occur in the caeca of some Galliform species, the frequently repeated suggestions that these processes also occur in granivore species such as parrots, pigeons, finches and canaries which have no functional caeca has not been experimentally substantiated.

Passerines have no caeca and therefore no intestinal flora for microbiological digestion.

Food eaten by canaries is digested chemically and then absorbed in the small intestine without the presence of symbiotic bacteria. Passerines are not considered to have a permanent gut flora. The microscopic examination of faecal smears from healthy canaries does not reveal bacteria or other organisms. Routine aerobic microbiological cultures taken from droppings of passerine birds do not produce any bacterial growth.

Discussion

It is commonly accepted that Oscine Passerines are the most modern and advanced of birds. Their small size and high metabolic rate (65% greater than for non-passerine birds) which have allowed them to occupy their dominant numerical position in the bird world has meant that further physiological adaptations have become necessary. The Oscines require an increased source of energy to maintain their high body temperature (2 degrees Celsius higher than other birds). They must eat (up to 30% of their body weight daily) and drink (25-30mls per 100grams body weight daily) relatively enormous amounts to maintain their energy levels. The food must also be digested and absorbed as quickly as possible. Death from haemorrhagic diathesis that occurs in finch species (e.g., canaries) that have not eaten within 48 hours is testament to the vascularity and highly efficient absorption mechanism of the small intestines of finches.

Bacteria present in the bowel of the more primitive bird forms (e.g., Galliformes) that help with digestion and also produce vitamins and other metabolites are not required in Passerines. The extremely high-energy requirements of these small birds are covered by an increased activity of the enzymes lipase and amylase. Refined chemical (enzymes) digestion and enhanced absorption capabilities present in canaries is a far more efficient method of energy production.

The environmental niches occupied by the more mobile oscines are also more likely to provide the required dietary vitamins and other metabolites.

Resident bacteria exist in many bird species. They help repel potentially harmful environmental bacteria. These "friendly bacteria" vary from one bird species to another and relate to their natural environment. For example, my studies on the wild Budgerigar have revealed the presence of Streptococcus faecalis as a normal inhabitant of the bowel. Under adverse conditions this normal bacteria may produce disease. Poultry have a wide range of normal gut bacteria as they have adapted to an environment rich in these bacteria and germs. Probiotics have been produced mainly for poultry species in order to counteract the potential harmful effects of normally encountered bacteria. In order to work properly, probiotics must colonise the bowel and to do so they must form part of the normal gut microflora.

Consequently, probiotics designed for poultry will not be effective for parrots or canaries. The acidifying effect of Lactobacillus acidophilus, a common ingredient of probiotics, is responsible for a beneficial effect experienced with "generic" probiotic use. Probiotics do not apply to Oscine Passerines (finches) because it is commonly agreed that temperate zoned finches (canaries) have no resident gut bacteria. This may not be the case with tropical zoned finches (e.g., coloured canaries).

The notion that finches have a sterile gut is important but often misunderstood. Autolysis that occurs after death does not require the presence of bacteria in the bowel. The proteolytic tissue damage that results following death allows anaerobic bacteria to colonise these tissues from the outside to the body. Resident bacteria found in the more primitive bird species play a part in preventing bowel infections but the more conventional immune modulators remain the main barriers to infection from environmental germs in these species. The role of the very high body temperature of finches should not be underestimated as an important supporting role in preventing colonisation of the bowel with harmful bacteria.

Canaries fall into two main groups that have been developed by man essentially for their singing ability. Coloured canaries originate from the Red Hooded Siskin (a tropical zone finch). Non-coloured varieties are derived from a Seran finch found in the Canary Islands (a temperate zone finch). The different origins of each may explain in part an increased susceptibility of coloured varieties to diseases that rarely affect non-coloured varieties such as Trichomoniasis and Mycoplasma infections.

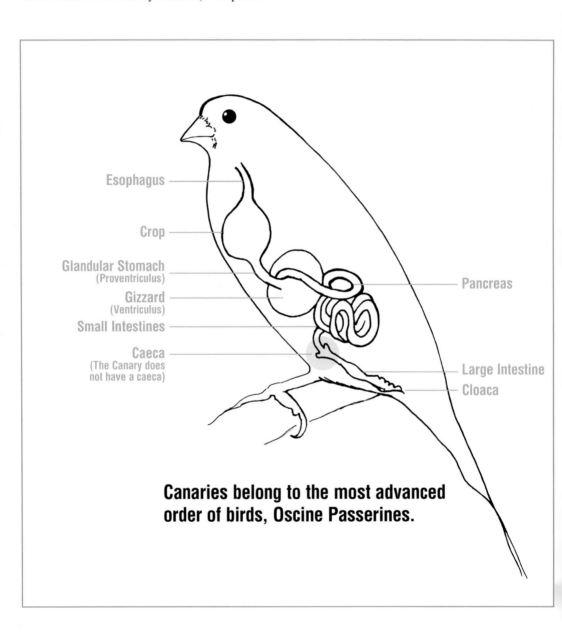

Esophagus

Crop

Glandular Stomach
(Proventriculus)

Gizzard
(Ventriculus)

Small Intestines

Caeca
(The Canary does
not have a caeca)

Pancreas

Large Intestine

Cloaca

Canaries belong to the most advanced order of birds, Oscine Passerines.

O

Open mouth breathing, 112, 130, 142
Ornithosis, 71, 75-77, 108-109, 115-118, 148
  Signs, 76, 115 119, 144
  Prevention, 116-117
  Treatment, 115-118
  Doxycycline/Megamix, 75, 116-118
  Baytril, 135

P

Pet Canaries, 17-28
  Health Signs, 22-23
  Moulting Programme, 29
  Ongoing Care, 23-26
  Preparing your home, 19-22
  Selecting a Pet Canary, 18-19
  Singing Health Programme, 26-28
  Training, 25-26
Pep Food Cleaner, 110, 129, 138 160
Protector, 49, 77, 161
Protein for breeding, 6, 9, 59, 61, 156
Psittacosis: See Ornithosis, 115-118

R

Red mite, 129-133, 142
  Signs, 130
  Prevention, 131
  Treatment, 130
Rodents, 119, 136
Running Eggs, 52

S

Salmonella infection, 110, 135-136
  Symptoms, 110, 136
  Prevention, 136
  Treatment, 135-136
Sprouted seed recipes, 159
Sprouted seed technique, 61-64
Soft foods, 62, 79, 81, 83
Soft food recipes, 64, 153, 156, 159
Shell grit, 12, 39, 89, 112, 123, 154-155
Soft-shelled eggs, 110
S76, 25, 91, 130-133
  During breeding, 131
  During moult, 74, 133
  First choice medicine, 91
  For Young Birds, 67
  *S76/Coopex combo*67, 130-131

Sterile Bowel Theory, 163
Stress, 15, 68-69, 71, 112, 120, 126, 134, 137, 152
Streptococcal infection, 110, 133-135, 148
  Control, 110, 133
  Symptoms, 110-134
  Streptococcus faecalis, 133
  Strep/Staph infections, 133-135
  Treatment with Moxi-T, 134-135
Sulfa AVS, 90-91, 114, 124-125, 147
  First Aid Medicine, 90
  First Choice Medicine, 91, 121, 147
  For coccidiosis, 114
  For E.coli, 124-125, 143
  For Juveniles, 124
  For Sweating Disease, 124
  Sulfa AVS/Megamix, 97, 124-125
Sweating Disease, 6, 96, 123-124, 136
Symptoms
  Air sac disease, 131
  Atoxoxplasmosis, 102, 109, 113-115
  Avian Gastric Yeast Infection, 119, 126-128, 137
  Black Spot, 101-104
  Breathing Problems, 100, 111, 142, 147
  Breeding Problems, 105-107, 143
  Canker, 111, 144
  Circovirus (also see Black Spot), 99, 103
  Coccidiosis, 113
  Diarrhea, 119
  Droppings, 120-122
  Early signs of illness, 120, 122
  Egg problems, 105-110
  Eyes, 111, 144-145
  Feather Plucking, 145-146
  Guestimating diagnosis, 90
  Going Light, 111, 125, 128, 146
  Mite infestation, 129-133
  Moulding Disease, 99-101
  Nervous signs, 146
  Ornithosis, 76, 115-118
  Respiratory signs, 147
  Salmonella Infection, 135-136
  Self diagnosis, 71, 76-77
  Strep. Infection, 134
  Thrush Infection, 137-139
  Vomiting, 77, 101, 111, 112, 137, 148, 187

T

Temperature, 19-20, 34, 71, 95, 123
  Control, 34
  Fluctuations, 20, 95
  Heating, 50

Rob Marshall

BVSc MACVSc (Avian Health)
Carlingford Animal Hospital, Carlingford, Sydney

Rob Marshall graduated from the University of Sydney in 1975. He established the Carlingford Animal Hospital, a bird, cat and dog practice, four years later and still practices from there.

Rob has had a lifelong interest in birds, particularly pigeons, which he races as a hobby. He has been fortunate in being able to study overseas on several occasions, in the USA, Germany and the Netherlands, to further advance his knowledge. He received his Membership of the Australian College in 1988.

Rob has been a prolific avicultural author over the years, writing several books, book chapters and magazine columns. He is the author of "A Guide to Pigeon Health," "Health Programmes for Racing and Show Pigeons","Pigeon Medicine", "Budgerigar Medicine", "Squab Pigeon Production and Health," "Gouldian & Finch Health," and will be publishing "Pigeon Health" later this year. He has been a co-author for several ABK "A Guide to" books, including Grass Parrots & Neophemas, Rosellas, Gouldian Finches, and Eclectus Parrot (first edition and now the revised edition). He is a regular columnist in the Pet Industry News and a regular nature writer of bird stories for the popular press "Northern Beaches Journal." Rob has also produced two videos on pigeon health: "The Health Management of Racing Pigeons" and "Super Health in Racing Pigeons."

He has lectured at several veterinary conferences, both in Australia and in the United States. In 1991 he won the national Beecham Prize for most interesting original clinical case presentation entitled "Pyometron in a Sulfur Crested Cockatoo." He had a paper on "Anthelmintics and Antiprotozoals for Birds" published in the international scientific journal "Seminars in Avian and Exotic Pet Medicine."

Rob also conducts seminars for clients on pigeon, budgerigar and canary health and disease. He has also assisted in the production of a code of practice for keeping racing pigeons in South Australia and Western Australia. He is a member of the Animal Ethics Committee at Macquarie University, Sydney.

In 1995 he was the veterinary consultant for the Northern Territory Nature and Conservation Commission for a scientific study of the disease status in wild population of the endangered Gouldian Finches as it related to a "Recovery plan." This entailed field work on the endangered Gouldian Finch in the Kimberley, Western Australia and Keep River National Park Northern Territory, funded by the Nature and Conservation Commission of the Northern Territory.

Rob's current veterinary interests are focusing on wild bird biology and ecology as it relates to captive birds, especially pigeons, exhibition budgerigars, Gouldians, and the Eclectus. To this end, he has conducted field research into the biology of the wild budgerigar and the Gouldian Finch. These trips have taken him to western NSW and the Northern Territory, where he collected samples to analyse the diet of wild birds and their normal bacterial flora. Other research projects have included microscopic assessment of budgerigar feathers to examine the structure and colour theory of exhibition budgerigars, and causes of breeding failure of the Australian Eclectus (E.r.macgillivray).

Away from work his interests include his family, Aboriginal affairs, creative writing, painting, photography, sculpture, and running. He is married with 3 children (8 yrs, 13 yrs, 15 yrs).